# The History of
# Mirabeau B. Lamar High School
## Houston, Texas
## 1937–2012

### by Anne Sloan

COPYRIGHT © 2013 BY THE LAMAR HIGH SCHOOL ALUMNI ASSOCIATION

All rights reserved, including the right to reproduce this work in any form whatsoever without permission in writing from the publisher, except for brief passages in connection with a review. For information, please write:

The Donning Company Publishers
184 Business Park Drive, Suite 206
Virginia Beach, VA 23462

Steve Mull, General Manager
Barbara Buchanan, Office Manager
Heather L. Floyd, Editor
Amanda Dawn Guilmain, Graphic Designer
Kathy Snowden, Project Research Coordinator
Tonya Washam, Marketing Specialist
Pamela Engelhard, Marketing Advisor

James H. Railey, Project Director

**CATALOGING-IN-PUBLICATION DATA**
Sloan, Anne.
 The history of Mirabeau B. Lamar High School, Houston, Texas, 1937-2012 / by Anne Sloan.
    pages cm
 Includes bibliographical references and index.
 ISBN 978-1-57864-831-3 (hardcover : alk. paper)
 1. Mirabeau B. Lamar High School (Houston, Tex.)--History. 2. Education, Secondary--Texas--Houston--History. 3. Preparatory schools--Texas--Houston--History. I. Title.
 LD7501.H833S65 2013
 373.764'1411--dc23
                    2013020657

Printed in the United States of America at Walsworth Publishing Company

## DEDICATION

The Lamar High School Alumni Association expresses its deep appreciation to J. Doug Pitcock, Jr. and the other donors whose generosity made this book possible.

# TABLE OF CONTENTS

| | |
|---|---|
| 5 | FOREWORD |
| 6 | PREFACE |
| 8 | CHAPTER ONE—Architecture and Built Environment |
| 22 | CHAPTER TWO—The Beginning, 1937 to 1939 |
| 42 | CHAPTER THREE—The 1940s |
| 68 | CHAPTER FOUR—The 1950s |
| 110 | CHAPTER FIVE—The 1960s |
| 140 | CHAPTER SIX—The 1970s |
| 154 | CHAPTER SEVEN—The 1980s and 1990s |
| 178 | CHAPTER EIGHT—The Years 2000 to 2012 |
| 196 | APPENDICES |
| | Lamar High School Principals |
| | Lamar High School Class Officers |
| | Lamar High School International Baccalaureate Graduates |
| | Lamar High School Cheerleaders |
| | Lamar High School PTA and PTO Presidents |
| | Lamar High School Alumni Association Distinguished Alumni |
| | Lamar High School Alumni Association Board Members |
| | Lamar High School Alumni Association Presidents |
| 214 | ENDNOTES |
| 218 | SELECTED BIBLIOGRAPHY |
| 220 | INDEX |

# FOREWORD

In 1937, in the midst of the Great Depression, Houston civic and community leaders, along with a forward-thinking school board, dedicated a new school at the intersection of River Oaks Boulevard and a rutted, two-lane Westheimer Road… Lamar High School. The first school day began with 1,310 students, and, with their eyes on the stars, these students and their progeny have established a standard of excellence and a record of achievement unsurpassed in our state's history.

When World War II occurred in 1941, Lamar graduates served with courage and pride, defending our nation from those who threatened our freedom. In every conflict since, Lamar alums have answered our country's call.

Lamar's graduates have held numerous elected offices, including school board member, City Council member, mayor, state representative, state senator, lieutenant governor, governor, and U.S. congressman. Surely, among current graduates or those to come, there will be a Lamar alum who will become a U.S. senator, or yes, even president of the United States.

Getting elected to office may be the easy part. Who could imagine that among Lamar grads there would be one who would become a prima ballerina, physicist and winner of the Nobel Prize, Broadway musical star, Grand Master at chess, or a multi-starred general in the U.S. Army? Lamar grads include racecar drivers, musicians, educators, business leaders, authors, TV anchors, professional athletes in almost every sport, and actors on the stage as well as the big and small screen. That takes real talent!

These achievements didn't come by accident. Every success story is coupled with the inspiring leadership of a teacher, counselor, administrator, or coach, educators who gave their time and intellect to ensure that each of us had the foundation for meeting the challenges of the future.

It is this heritage of excellence and accomplishment that binds Lamar alums not only to our school, but also to each other. This pride isn't confined to each graduating class, but exists for all those who call themselves "Redskins."

Many thanks to the Lamar High School Alumni Association, which funded the research and production of this book. Now, all Lamar alumni and friends will have available to them the history of the school and the story of those who helped make it what it is today.

This book is dedicated to those students, teachers, and administrators who began the tradition of excellence in 1937, graduates over the intervening seventy-six years, and to those future alums, who like their predecessors, will continue to "REACH FOR THE STARS."

Mark White
Texas Governor 1983–1987
Lamar High School Class of 1958

# PREFACE

When I accepted the commission to write the seventy-five-year history of Mirabeau B. Lamar High School, I naïvely forecast a four-month, one-hundred-hour job. I still can remember the half-smile Fran Callahan gave me when I told her this. This indefatigable leader who has her finger on the pulse of Lamar knew what I was undertaking, but she quietly let me find that out for myself. I have spent over a year and hundreds of hours chronicling the fascinating and complex history of this school. When Chapter One yielded so many surprising and previously unknown facts about Lamar's construction, I should have known that every decade of the school's history would be similarly revealing and time-consuming. No single volume can do justice to the magnitude of illustrious Lamar graduates who have shaped our city, our nation, and even impacted world history. This commemorative history presents only a sampling of the outstanding Lamar graduates who have successfully "reached for the stars."

Writing this history enabled me to recognize the potential triumphs of a public high school. Thinking like many that a first-class education requires matriculation in a private school—preferably an East Coast boarding school—I was amazed to discover the level of academic excellence that has always existed at Lamar. Studying the school decade by decade, I tried to figure out, "What factors make this school so special?" I never answered the question satisfactorily, but I have described school events and allowed the students and faculty members to explain how they feel about Lamar's illustrious graduates, always placing the school's history in the context of that of the city with which it is so inextricably intertwined.

Highlights of my journey through Lamar's history include talking with stonemason Tommy Schlitzberger, who put me in touch with the Lenarduzzi family. Roland Lenarduzzi, the youngest son of the sculptor who created the map of Texas, and his son Dr. Roland Lenarduzzi provided important details about Eraclito's life and career. I visited with graduates of the Classes of 1938 and 1939, who still remember the thrill of first entering the new school. The Class of 1947, especially Bertha Gray Jamison, Grace Griersen, and Patty Peckinpaw Hubbard, helped me realize the indelible connection that exists between Lamar graduates. Nancy Brock (Class of 1957) introduced me to the 1950s and provided invaluable assistance in contacting the graduates from this decade. Ken DeLorenzo (Class of 1962) not only arranged meetings with graduates from the 1960s, but also read the manuscript, offering invaluable suggestions. John Adkins (Class of 1970) provided important information about the 1970s. My thanks go to all of the graduates who were willing to tell me their stories and to Sherry Evans (Class of 1957), who pounded away at my sentence structure and checked my sources, doing all of this from Boise, Idaho. Former faculty member Florine Carr was especially helpful regarding the Science Department's important contributions to the students. The Lamar archives were an inexhaustible resource for photographs and other material used in this book to illustrate Lamar's amazing seventy-five-year history. Photographer Will LeBlanc took these archival photos and magically transformed them into indelible memories, and his contributions to this book were monumental. Unless otherwise noted, the images used throughout the book are from the Lamar Archives.

With the opening of various magnet schools, especially HSPVA, the list of Lamar's "stars" has shrunk, but as you will find, there are still outstanding graduates from the 1980s and 1990s. Many of the post-millennium graduates are still in college, except for outstanding Lamar athletes, who are already making a name for themselves in professional sports.

The story of the contributions of Lamar graduates to city, country, and even world history needed to be told. My greatest concern is for those illustrious graduates of whom I am unaware. I apologize for omissions and errors, but the organization of seventy-five years of material was a formidable task.

The 2012 bond election provided for the total renovation of the school, and Lamar's principal expects to go "paperless" into the new facility. Will writing the next history of the school be easier? Possibly, but electronic records seem somewhat sterile, and one wonders about the tenure of information from Facebook, Twitter, and blogs. Future generations of Lamar alums may consider my account of their school's history quaint and irrelevant, but those who have lived through these decades will hopefully enjoy reading about classmates, teachers, events, and the memories of these bygone days.

# CHAPTER ONE
## Architecture and Built Environment

On March 13, 1936, Dr. Ray K. Daily, the only female member of the Houston Independent School District school board, pushed a spade into the dirt at 3325 Westheimer Road, breaking ground for Southwest High School, the first new high school in Houston in nearly a decade. The site was a swampy, twenty-three-acre prairie outside the Houston city limits. In the ensuing seventy-five years, the school, later named Mirabeau Bonaparte Lamar High School after the early Texas politician, birthed and continued to produce distinguished alumni who have made a name for themselves in the city, the state, and the nation in numbers unparalleled in Houston and perhaps nationwide.

What set this high school apart from its rivals? How did this happen? Was it as early graduate Camille Dockery (Simpson) (Class of 1943) suggested, that "the stars in the sky just came together"?

Or was it, as another Lamar alumna suggested, that Dr. Daily, a woman who dedicated her life to medicine and public school education, performed some sort of alchemy, transforming the excavated dirt on this two-lane, shell-topped road into a school that would become an incubator for scholars, politicians, and athletes; for stars of Broadway, Hollywood, and television; for prima ballerinas, writers, and musicians? Dr. Daily, a native of Lithuania who graduated at the head of her class in 1913 from the University of Texas Medical Branch at Galveston, practiced ophthalmology in Houston for sixty-one years. An outspoken woman who served on the HISD school board for twenty-four years, this brilliant physician became known in Houston as a "courageous warrior on behalf of Houston's children."[1]

The answer to Lamar's success is not as simple as an astrological alignment or a magical act of alchemy. Part of the answer is the trusted real estate adage: location, location, location. HISD chose a site adjacent to the new, exclusive, 1,300-acre River Oaks subdivision. That choice became an important factor in the shaping of Lamar's history.

*Above: This early photo of the new Southwest High School indicates the isolated and barren site that was twice as large as that of any other HISD high school.*

*Left: In September 1937, River Oaks Magazine described the newly opened Mirabeau B. Lamar High School as "our new pride and joy" that "stands in beauty at the very gates of our community." (Courtesy of River Oaks Property Owners Association)*

Another factor that cannot be overestimated in the long-term success of Lamar is demographics. While it is true that River Oaks youth attended Lamar, demographics of the student body in the fall of 1937 included primarily the Montrose area west of Shepherd and south of Washington Avenue, Southampton, Southgate, West University Place, and Bellaire. Census records for 1930 indicate that residents of these largely white-collar neighborhoods were not wealthy by River Oaks standards, but were educated and middle- to upper-middle class.

There were 1,310 students that first semester. According to the 1938 Lamar Directory, River Oaks youth constituted less than 10 percent of that number. Twenty-eight students came from twenty-six different high schools in thirteen different states, a confirmation of the rapid growth taking place in southwest Houston. Eleven orphans came from the Mary Burnett School in Bellaire. Forty students gave downtown addresses. Two lived in hotels. Twenty-eight came in pickup trucks from "the country." Despite the variety of backgrounds represented, the aura of River Oaks permeated Lamar throughout the coming years.

By 1936, in spite of depression and recession, Houston had grown rapidly from its 1930 population of 292,352. Several of the five high schools were now badly overcrowded. Houstonian Jesse H. Jones, who chaired the Reconstruction Finance Corporation (RFC), was able to direct funds to Texas from President Franklin D. Roosevelt's Public Works Administration (PWA), a New Deal agency established to provide employment in civic-oriented job programs. Texas benefitted greatly from the PWA, with projects totaling $224,551,492. The city's growth, coupled with the PWA's offer of funds to help with construction, precipitated HISD's decision to begin planning two new high schools, East End High School and Southwest High School.

*Houston City Hall, designed by Joseph Finger, is shown under construction. Right of City Hall is Sam Houston Coliseum and Music Hall. The city's first PWA project, Alfred C. Finn, Jesse Jones' architect, designed the two latter buildings which were later demolished. (Courtesy of Story Sloane Gallery)*

*Sam Houston Elementary is Lamar Cato's modified version of Lamar High School. The two schools not only had the same architect, but opened one month apart and were built by the same contractor. Located at 601 W. Lewis, Conroe, Texas, this school is now a resource center for the Conroe Independent School District. (Courtesy of Will LeBlanc)*

### THE DESIGN AND CONSTRUCTION OF LAMAR HIGH SCHOOL

"The Assignment of Architects" was the subject of the December 12, 1935 HISD board meeting. Board member Mrs. B. F. (Eletha) Coop made the motion that the Reagan High School plans be used for the interior of the new Southwest High School and recommended Harry Payne, Lamar Q. Cato, and Louis Glover be assigned to design the exterior. Some members believed that, since John Staub had designed Reagan, he would be most familiar with the plans; in addition, it was pointed out that excluding Staub from the team might raise legal issues, since the team would be using his design. After much discussion, a motion passed that John Staub would be the corresponding architect, and Louis Glover, Lamar Q. Cato, and Harry Payne would be his associates. Lamar Q. Cato had already designed the first two Moderne-style buildings at the University of Houston, together with Sam Houston Elementary School in Conroe, called by architectural historian Stephen Fox a miniature Lamar High School. The Conroe school was built concurrently with Lamar by the same contractor and subcontractors even though it was not an HISD school. Sam Houston Elementary opened in August 1937. Kenneth Franzeim is listed as a partner of John Staub on the Dedication Plaque, but no mention is made of him in the HISD board minutes.[2]

The HISD board had obviously decided the new Southwest High School was not to be Tudor, Jacobean, or Romanesque. It would be Moderne: Greek urns, Classical friezes, and swags were eschewed in favor of a streamlined, unadorned façade that relied for its effectiveness on imposing stone curves, horizontal lines, and horizontal metal banding.

Lamar benefitted from both its stellar location and the fact that its architects created an innovative building in sharp contrast to Houston's five other high schools. Four of these earlier buildings still exist, and an examination of their architecture underlines the contrast between Lamar and its sister schools. San Jacinto High School (1914), which serves today as the Houston Community Center Learning Resource Center, is a Classical-style building with Doric columns and stone figures. Houston Heights' John H. Reagan High School (1926), designed by John Staub, is a Tudor Gothic building that incoming seniors described as a "fortress-like stockade." Jefferson Davis High School (1927), designed by Birdsall Briscoe and Maurice J. Sullivan, is another Classical-style high school, with cast stone Georgian details. The Charles H. Milby High School (1928) is a substantial buff-and-brown brick Romanesque structure with four imposing Ionic columns. These four handsome buildings are all very traditional in style. According to the Greater Houston Preservation Alliance, "Lamar was designed to be Houston's showcase school."

*The Moderne letters used for the name of the school are spotlighted. Eraclito Lenarduzzi cut the two-foot-tall, 2.25-inch-deep letters out of twelve-inch-thick limestone slabs.*

The school board's choice for Lamar High School was an architectural style that was definitely the "soup du jour" in Houston and across the nation. Three important civic buildings—Houston's City Hall (1939), the Sam Houston Coliseum and Music Hall (1937), and Jeff Davis Hospital (1937)—along with both Southwest High School and East End High School—were built in the Moderne style, an overlapping of the uniquely American Art Moderne with the Parisian-born Art Deco style. Houston's examples of the Moderne style tended to combine elements of both.[3]

As pointed out by Jim Parsons, who has written about Houston's Art Deco structures,[4] "Art Deco was never the prominent architectural style in Houston, but its popularity is evident in the number of Deco structures built around the city between 1929 and 1950." Structures built in the same area and during the same time period as Lamar High School included The Temple of Rest, Beth Israel Cemetery, 1207 W. Dallas Avenue (1935); the L. D. Allen residence, 2337 Blue Bonnet Boulevard (1936); the Tower Theater, 1201 Westheimer Road (1936); Clarke & Courts Printing & Lithography Company, 1210 W. Clay Avenue (1936); the Virgil Childress residence, 3239 Locke Lane (1937); and the River Oaks Community Center, 2017-2048 W. Gray Avenue (1937). These buildings serve to place the design of Lamar into context.[5]

Typically, Art Deco buildings used Texas shell limestone and bas-relief stone sculpture. The design for Lamar High School used these features, along with the rounded corners and horizontal lines characteristic of Art Moderne.

Moderne embodied a sleeker, more streamlined design than Art Deco. "Streamlined," a late nineteenth-century word, described the use of curving lines to shape objects, such as locomotives, in order to cut down wind resistance and make them move more efficiently. Lamar High School, a three-story high school building, perfectly embodied Moderne features with its "extreme horizonality" and the "layering of vertical or horizontal wall planes."[6] The precision of its lines, the duplication of its functional features, and its swelling curves are all characteristics of this style of architecture. The name of the school is carved over the entrance in 2.25-inch relief cutback Moderne-style limestone letters. Parsons points out that the "modernistic style" promoted "Houston's image as a progressive city." A new, bigger, and bolder architectural style, Moderne suited Houston to a "T."

On January 18, 1936, the HISD board unanimously awarded the contract for building Lamar, subject to PWA approval, to Dallas/Ft. Worth's Nathan Wolfeld Company. Wolfeld, the low bidder at $679,554, agreed to complete the building in 300 working days by August 15, 1937.[7] The board accepted the project as complete on September 13, 1937, and authorized payment that exceeded the original bid by $3,554.76.[8] The board already knew that the high school would need sidewalks, a shell parking area, and 25,000 cubic feet of fill dirt for the athletic field. Objections that Lamar High School was given an additional $20,000 for improvement of the site prompted Dr. Dailey to say, "Those on a higher economical level demand more and get more."[9] Lamar also received an additional PWA grant for $12,286 for improvement of the grounds.[10]

## An Interview with Harry D. Payne

Shortly after Lamar opened, architect Harry D. Payne, in an interview with Pauline Mills (Delaney) (Class of 1939), the editor of the school newspaper, *The Lamar Lancer*, explained the architectural team's design concept.[11] Payne stated that the first objective was "to design a building that exemplified the spirit of today." Editor Mills wrote that the architects "translated the modern trend toward rhythm and simplicity into a limestone building that has been termed the most beautiful in South Texas."

Payne pointed out that one of their greatest exterior changes was the windows, "which instead of the ordinary two-pane [wooden] kind, are an ultra-modern three tier metal type of commercial project-out windows, designed especially for schools." In *Houston Architectural Survey* (Vol. II), these windows were described as "awning-type windows, trimmed in light green… arranged in horizontal strips across the length of each floor level." Two important interior features Payne noted were their use of "an acoustical [tile] treatment on all classroom ceilings that reduces echo and thus makes it easier to hear," and their design of a corrugated folding wall to divide the girls' and boys' gymnasiums, a wall that could be pushed back to allow greater flexibility for use of the space.

Believing that "color has much to do with one's attitude," Payne said the architects chose to cover Lamar's walls with six feet of glossy "calm yellow tile," and decorated the auditorium in a combination of "gay warm red and a cool gray." According to Payne, the architects were given only six weeks to draw up the plans. As has been pointed out, they used the John H. Reagan High School interior floor plan for Lamar. This reuse of school plans was a common architectural practice that saved time and money. Maurice J. Sullivan used the interior floor plan of Jeff Davis High

School as a basis for Stephen F. Austin High School. The *Lancer*'s editor applauded the designers' genius, as illustrated by their ability to use John H. Reagan's fourteen-year-old plans, and, in a limited amount of time, to design a building that "symbolizes all that is modern."

### THE ARCHITECTURAL DESIGN OF STEPHEN F. AUSTIN HIGH SCHOOL

Birdsall P. Briscoe, Maurice J. Sullivan, Sam H. Dixon, Jr., and Joseph Finger, the architecture team that designed East End High School, were just as highly regarded as those who designed Lamar High School, but their design was a far more conservative example of the Moderne style. The architects' use of traditional red brick for both the exterior of East End High School and Romanesque arches fronting the entrance created a weak Moderne style that was no match for the sleek new Southwest High School that opened that same fall. The school board, in answering critics of East End High School, said they never saw the brick until it was on the building.[12] The somewhat lackluster design of the East End school was especially odd, since the East End is home to the largest number of important Modernistic buildings in Houston, several of which were erected concurrently.

How did East End High School and Southwest High School get their new names? Various patriotic organizations in Houston urged that the two new schools be named for Texas heroes. The HISD board renamed East End High School for Stephen F. Austin, the "Father of Texas," and Southwest High School for Mirabeau B. Lamar, "The Father of Education in Texas." The choice of a lesser Texas hero for the Southwest school and a major hero for the East End school was an unintentional stroke of diplomacy, given the East Enders' ensuing jealousy and envy of their sister school.

*The four shades of terrazzo—black, dark gray, gray, and light gray—used in the auditorium's foyer provide additional examples of the architectural planning given to Lamar's design. (Courtesy of Will LeBlanc)*

### REACTION TO THE ARCHITECTURAL DESIGN OF LAMAR HIGH SCHOOL

*River Oaks Magazine* (November 1937) was ecstatic about the interior of the new school. The article called the architects' use of color "a case of imagination and carefully applied cosmetics" and said, "it takes an artist to use aquamarine tile for the swimming pool and pale aquamarine paint for the ceiling." The magazine praised the "noble proportions of the auditorium" and the architects' use of a sound-deadening "painted burlap covered panel that progresses from a rich white to an almost pure white as it reaches the ceiling," and continued, "It also takes an artist to use deep red linoleum dado on auditorium walls and in the foyer," trimming it all with "bands of stainless steel." The auditorium's lights were concealed in the "ocean wave ceiling." Accolades from the *Lamar Lancer*'s editor and this neighborhood publication were echoed throughout the city and the nation.

In an article entitled "Secondary Schools," New York City's *Architectural Forum* for May 1939 called Lamar "an imposing building." The article discussed the nationwide curriculum changes during the past three years in secondary schools and the resulting effects of these changes on school architecture. Three photographs of Lamar High School were used to illustrate the journal's approval of Lamar's "functional" design. The building contained, "in a single well-knit unit, all of the facilities of the modern secondary school, with swimming pool, gymnasium, vocational shop and auditorium properly located at its extremities."

The November 1939 issue of *The Architectural Record*, also a New York journal, contained an article entitled "Houston's Citizens Vote on Recent Buildings," featuring a photograph of Lamar High School and five other local buildings. In this nationwide survey, citizen committees from each major city were invited to choose their architectural favorite. Houston City Hall received the most nominations with fifteen votes; the Houston Fire Alarm Building and the Continental Oil Company's Oil and Gas Building each received eight votes. Lamar High School received seven votes. The San Jacinto Monument and the Gulf Building each received only two votes. The committee, composed of "lay" citizens, included among others Houston Mayor Oscar Holcombe, Episcopal Bishop of Texas Clinton S. Quin, and geologist Michel T. Halbouty, who voted as to their architectural preferences for these newly constructed Houston buildings. Lamar High School's inclusion on this list and its creditable showing were further indications of the national attention and accolades accorded its architecture.

## THE EXTERIOR SCULPTURED MAP OF TEXAS

Many who drive by Lamar High School notice the large bas-relief map of Texas above the auditorium's entrance. Few high schools in the nation have an exterior sculpture of this magnitude. The map, constructed of Texas cream-colored limestone, is approximately twenty-four feet high, twenty feet wide, and twelve inches thick, with bull-nosed curved edges. It was sculpted by Italian immigrant Eraclito G. Lenarduzzi, who left his native country for Mexico in 1908, but immigrated to Houston in 1910 because of his concern over Pancho Villa's activities. Lenarduzzi had seven children and lived on a twenty-acre farm that he gradually expanded to 300 acres in Manvel, Texas. His Lamar High School map of Texas, his sculpture at the Monkey House in the Houston Zoo, the Baptistry at Trinity Episcopal Church at Main and Holman, the various sculptures he produced at Rice Institute, and his wonderful large cemetery monuments, as well as his later restoration work at the San Jose Mission in San Antonio, attest to his experience and skill. According to Lenarduzzi's grandson, Dr. Roland Lenarduzzi, his grandfather received no commissions for his work, did not sign his work, and was paid six dollars a day—stone sculptors in the 1930s were considered artisans, not artists. The sculptor's youngest son, also named Roland, vividly remembers their modest farmhouse with its kerosene lanterns and outdoor plumbing. It was 1949 before they had electricity.

*The* Orenda *called the iconic bas-relief map of Texas that fronts the school's auditorium "an indelible memory for every student." Constructed of Texas limestone, it is approximately twenty-four feet high, twenty feet wide, and twelve inches thick.*

Eraclito Lenarduzzi may have received the Lamar High School commission from the H. B. Cearly Marble and Granite Company, where his son Nino was working. Cearly would have been given the plans by the architects and would have offered the job to Nino's father. Having no shop of his own, the fifty-three-year-old sculptor probably used Cearly's facility to create this map of Texas, with its distinctive topological details and identification of major cities. He sculpted the six sections separately, chiseling the cutback letters into the stone. The sections were then erected over the main entrance to the auditorium, and caulking was used in between each one to make the seams less noticeable. Lenarduzzi's son Nino, then twenty-six years old, undoubtedly helped with the map, but contrary to previously published information, the father was in charge of the project, called by *Houston Architectural Survey* a "remarkable architectural element."

*The February 14, 1937* Houston Post *printed this photo of the map's sculptor Eraclito G. Lenarduzzi on a scaffold, probably smoothing the caulk used to seal the seams of the six sections. (Courtesy of Houston Metropolitan Research Center, or HMRC)*

Sculpture was an important part of many PWA buildings, but the architects' choice of a map of Texas and the "1936" numerals in the lower left corner of Lenarduzzi's map offer an additional answer for this carving. In 1936, the State of Texas celebrated its centennial, the one-hundredth anniversary of the state's independence from Mexico. Houston businessman Jesse H. Jones had proposed building permanent shrines to educate people about Texas history and culture. The erection of the San Jacinto Monument was one such shrine, built to memorialize this yearlong celebration. The architects of Lamar High School undoubtedly had the Centennial in mind when they drew a plan creating for the school's exterior a sculpture of the map of the State of Texas and the five-pointed Texas star. The map has remained a familiar landmark in Houston and is yet another indication of the serious attention given by the architects to this school building's details.

### An Unexpected Storm of Protest

Considering the splendid building, its location adjacent to a well-planned, affluent subdivision, and the twenty-three-acre site, it is surprising that Lamar High School engendered a storm of protest that has seldom, if ever, greeted the construction of any other HISD school. Opponents fell into two categories: residents of the East End, who felt their new school, Stephen F. Austin, looked like a "penal institution" in comparison to Lamar High School, and Southwest neighborhood residents, who voiced strenuous objections to the chosen site.

*Lamar High School opened the same day as Stephen F. Austin High School, located at 1700 Dumble Street. (Courtesy of Will LeBlanc)*

Many East End residents objected to Lamar High School's imposing exterior and felt the difference between the two schools was blatant discrimination. In an attempt to refute the East Enders' criticism, HISD Business Manager H. L. Mills stated flatly, "I am an East Ender and there is no discrimination against East End." That Mills regarded himself as an East Ender is misleading. The September 1937 issue of *River Oaks Magazine* spotlighted H. L. Mills and noted, "We are proud to have among us, the new resident of 2145 Brentwood." Mills, a confirmed bachelor, did not purchase a home in River Oaks. He moved into his sister's house. Mrs. Annie Lee Mills Worsham, widow of Jesse L. Worsham, provided her brother with a home, and he in turn helped rear her children.

East Enders objected to what they saw as unattractive, dark gray, painted wainscoting in the halls of Stephen F. Austin High School that was already cracking. They disliked the small cafeteria windows that did not provide adequate ventilation, the unattractive auditorium, and the size and number of the classrooms. In comparison to Lamar, they saw their high school as plain and not very decorative. Birdsall Briscoe and Maurice Sullivan were asked by the school board to come to a meeting of protesters. Briscoe said to the group of unhappy East Enders, "Architects are like children. They should not be heard. This building needs no defense. It stands for itself." Unlike Lamar, Stephen F. Austin High School received no accolades for its architecture. East Enders resented this fact and attributed their school's conservative design to the fact that Lamar was built for what they called "rich kids."

Regarding the East Enders' complaint that Lamar was fancier because it was built for wealthy people in River Oaks, H. L. Mills claimed, "Not a person in River Oaks showed the slightest interest in that school. They don't particularly want it. We didn't build it for River Oaks. We placed it there for the vast territory surrounding River Oaks."[13] The East Enders' objections to size were also not considered of any merit, since the neighborhoods around Stephen F. Austin could not have filled the sixty-three classrooms constructed for Lamar. In an editorial in its June 21, 1935 edition, the *Houston Post* pointed out that more than one quarter of Houston's population lived in the section south of Buffalo Bayou.

Lamar High School cost $162,023 more than Stephen F. Austin High School, but it accommodated 550 more students. Austin's location on Dumble Street was already owned by HISD. The site for Lamar had to be purchased.

The school board had estimated they would be paying $150,000 for the twenty-three acres for Lamar. Owners of the property, which ranged from a thirteen-plus-acre plot to a 65-by-150-foot lot, were the Fidelity Development Corporation, the Citizens State Bank and Trust, Goose Creek, Texas, the Irvin tract, the E. C. Crawford addition, and Ewing Werlin. Wade Hampton Irvin, the property owner who sold the largest amount of land to HISD, owned Citizens State Bank and was a resident of River Oaks. It is not known if the actual cost exceeded the school board's projected figure, nor is it clear whether the cost of the land was added to the reported construction cost figure.

West End residents whose children who were zoned to go to the new Southwest High School had complained about the location of Lamar High School ever since the newspapers announced the site, and with good cause. The site was outside of the city limits and not served adequately by any major thoroughfares. Protestors urged the school board to use property at Richmond Avenue and Dunlavy

*An early aerial view of River Oaks Boulevard portrays the door-to-door connection between Mirabeau B. Lamar High School and the River Oaks Country Club, lending credence to the oft-repeated adage that this is the only street in America with a country club at both ends. (Courtesy of River Oaks Property Owners Association)*

*A modern-day view of the same site indicates the development along River Oaks Boulevard, as well as the renovations to the school. (Courtesy of Will LeBlanc)*

Street that the district already owned. They also suggested vacant property at Westheimer and Kirby, or the acreage at Kirby and Bissonnet. They believed that the proposed site was too far west, and it was inaccessible because it was in the "swamps."[14]

On January 17, 1936, the school board stated that it would not change the site despite its knowledge that the streets leading to the school were often impassible or inadequate. Houston's annual rainfall of forty inches greatly hampered automobile travel on the unpaved and shell-topped roads in the area. Westheimer Road, the street that fronts Lamar, was a narrow, two-lane, shell-topped road with ditches on both sides. The nearest major thoroughfare, Kirby Drive, was considered a "dry weather route," West Alabama was a dirt road, and Buffalo Speedway stopped a mile or so short of Westheimer Road. Frank Sterling owned the two acres of land that were finally condemned by the city to obtain the right of way to extend Buffalo Speedway to Westheimer. When interviewed about his opposition to allowing his property to be used for the extension, Sterling justified his recalcitrance by pointing out that "the location of Lamar High School is very unpopular anyway."[15]

R. J. Depenbrock, spokesman for the West University Place Civic Club, objected that, while they had been told that Lamar High School was being erected for West University Place, "Everyone calls that new school the River Oaks School, and that will be hard to live down." He also complained that "River Oaks doesn't want us in their school," arguing that, if they were wanted at Lamar, "why don't they [HISD officials] give us some roads to get to the school."[16] Students from West University,

Southside Place, Bellaire, and Southgate were required to travel eight miles to get to Lamar because there was no direct route.[17]

Contrary to popular belief, Lamar High School was not built to provide a secondary school for River Oaks residents' offspring. More than likely it was built to provide a buffer for the exclusive new subdivision. Developers were concerned about the large tract of unimproved acreage that lay at the foot of River Oaks Boulevard. Memorial Park had been created to serve as a buffer for the north end of the subdivision. A splendid new country club with a golf course sat at the north end of the boulevard, but there was no end cap for the south. Hugh Potter, in one of many brochures printed to promote the subdivision, set forth "The River Oaks Aims and Ideals," which were "to intelligently locate shopping centers, schools, churches, parks and playgrounds, so as to protect the homeowners from the accidents of neighborhood."[18] Presumably, Potter and others in the neighborhood believed that occupancy of the vacant twenty-three-acre property across Westheimer from River Oaks Boulevard could not be left to chance. The HISD school board's somewhat obdurate decision to ignore the groups of twenty or more protestors who regularly came to every school board meeting to voice their objection to the site, to disregard the fact that the property was not even in the city limits, and to ignore the lack of adequate routes to the property, seems to indicate that the board's motives may have been influenced by the developers of River Oaks.

### A Traffic Nightmare

The school board finally acknowledged the mess they had created with their choice of the Westheimer site and voted to request City Council take immediate action to open Buffalo Speedway and surface Kirby Drive to make Lamar High School accessible.[19] Because the school was outside the city limits, however, the City of Houston lacked authority to make traffic decisions.

Lamar was soon scheduled to open. In August, HISD officials asked Harris County Judge Roy Hofheinz to take immediate action to improve street access to Lamar. Hofheinz asked, "Did you request street improvement before building the Lamar School?" H. L. Mills answered, "No, we put it where we thought best."[20] There is no record of Hofheinz's response, but the tone of his question suggested that he, along with many others, may have wondered, "What were you thinking?"

Anticipated problems had already become reality. Bus service was spotty—an eastbound bus and a westbound bus could barely pass each other on Westheimer. HISD Superintendent Dr. Edison E. Oberholtzer sent out an SOS to the city and the county asking that Westheimer be reserved exclusively for Lamar students. Hugh Potter, president of the River Oaks Development Corporation, stated that under no circumstances would traffic be rerouted through River Oaks. City of Houston motorcycle policemen were on duty to make sure a hastily imposed (and illegal) fifteen-miles-per-hour speed limit was observed. The city and the county continued to discuss the problem, batting the ball back and forth. Meanwhile, the fall semester of 1937 was about to begin.

# CHAPTER TWO
## The Beginning, 1937 to 1939

The Houston Independent School District opened the school year on September 20, 1937. *The Houston Press*, dramatically underscoring the difficulties of getting to the "magnificent" new school, referred to Lamar as "The Island School," and described it as being on an "isolated island."[21] School board members and architects who came to admire the new building "stumbled across a block or more of muddy plowed campus before reaching the temporary board walk constructed for their first visit."[22] Lamar officials had expected 1,300 to 1,500 students, and actual enrollment was 1,316, the low-spectrum figure attributed to the inaccessibility of the location. Three days after the school's opening, the *Houston Post* reported that HISD's site selection had become a "boomerang," and that Lamar High School was a "no man's land."[23] The bus company suggested that school hours be changed and classes start at 9:30 a.m., so that those who worked downtown would be out of the way. HISD refused.[24]

### Birth of the Redskins

Before Lamar High School opened, important decisions had to be made. During the summer of 1937, the school board selected as principal William J. Moyes, a University of Texas graduate described by former students as a quiet gentleman who habitually wore three-piece suits with his Phi Beta Kappa key on a chain stretched across his vest.

Moyes was a fortunate choice for Lamar High School. He was a scholarly man who taught Latin and Greek at a prep school in San Antonio and actually purchased the prep school where he taught, but the school went under when the young men left school to go overseas to fight in World War I. Looking for a new job, Moyes came to Houston and began his outstanding career as a Houston educator. His first job as principal was at the downtown Sam Houston High School, formerly Central High, where he served for fourteen years. When Moyes left to become Mirabeau B. Lamar's first principal, he brought with him from Sam Houston twenty-one teachers who formed the nucleus of Lamar's faculty and many remained there for the rest of their careers.

In addition to appointing an administration, a new school must select a mascot and school colors. Contrary to a *River Oaks Magazine* report that the River Oaks neighborhood as a body was responsible for choosing the school colors and mascot as well as naming the newspaper, these decisions were actually made by the student yearbook staff in consultation with faculty members. Seven of the

*Lamar's first principal, William J. Moyes, is standing in an unidentified garden setting, a lovely backdrop for the scholarly gentleman whose leadership created the foundation for the school's superiority.*

*Lamar's 1950 cheerleaders, left to right: Glenna McCarthy (Shamrock Hotel owner Glen McCarthy's daughter), Ed Grubbs, Shari Collins, Ben Kostial, Barbara Brown, and Pat Whitworth are pictured on the auditorium stage, barefooted, wearing Indian costumes and war paint. (Courtesy of Barbara Lee Brown)*

yearbook staff were River Oaks residents; the remaining fourteen were not. How and why were these decisions made? The 1938 *Orenda* staff explained: "Lamarites are known as Redskins by their own choice. We felt the Indian background of Texas was sufficient basis for our choice." They chose the Cherokee red rose as their school flower because these roses grew wild on the property surrounding Lamar. The summer before school opened, Major George Brunson, director of athletics of HISD, arbitrarily chose scarlet and royal blue for Lamar's colors.[25] The Indian motif was used for all of the school's activities, clubs, publications, and athletics. The students named their school newspaper the *Lancer* for the lances carried by the Plains Indians and for the name of the cavalry corps which Mirabeau B. Lamar commanded at the Battle of San Jacinto. The yearbook was titled *Orenda* after the Iroquois name for the "Great Spirit."

Almost certainly, no one in that first class foresaw the controversy that would arise in later years over the use of American Indian mascots. The National Congress of American Indians, on its website, makes the complaint that "Indian mascots and stereotypes present a misleading image of Indian people and feed the historic myths that have been used to whitewash a history of oppression. Despite decades of work to eliminate the use of discrimination and derogatory images in American sports, the practice has not gone away." A poll taken in 2004 by the Annenberg Public Policy Center, however, found that 91 percent of American Indians surveyed found the name "Redskins" acceptable.[26] From time to time the political correctness of Lamar's mascot is still called into question, but no change is anticipated.

## Mirabeau Bonaparte Lamar

The yearbook staff hoped that everyone would be satisfied with their choice of an Indian motif. One person who probably would not have been satisfied was the man for whom the school was named. Mirabeau Bonaparte Lamar had always made clear his aversion to American Indians. Twenty-six years after Lamar opened, *Lancer* reporter Lyn Bracewell, in an article entitled "Funniest Thing About M. B. Lamar: He Hated Injuns!" informed the student body that this was the case. Bracewell believed that if "President Lamar" had come "face to face with the grinning hulk of Big Red, the mascot of the school," he would have demanded that changes be made.[27]

*Mirabeau B. Lamar, small in stature compared to his nemesis Sam Houston, fancied himself an impresario and is described by historians as a dapper intellectual president whose enduring legacy is his provision for the education of Texas schoolchildren. (Courtesy of Will LeBlanc)*

As the second president of the Republic of Texas, Mirabeau B. Lamar opposed U.S. statehood and felt that Texas would one day be a nation stretching all the way to the Pacific Ocean. Upon taking office, he immediately reversed Sam Houston's benevolent Indian policy and replaced it with one of "sternness and force," drove the Cherokee to Arkansas, and waged an unsuccessful campaign against the Comanche. It is doubtful that Mirabeau B. Lamar would have been happy with the school's decision to incorporate Indian names and traditions into the high school that bears his name. He did, however, convince the Texas Republic's legislators to establish an educational system that would be endowed by public lands, thus earning him the title "Father of Texas Education."

## A Traditional Framework

A traditional school framework includes the establishment of publications, a student council, an honor society, and a PTA. In the first issue of the newly organized Lamar newspaper, *The Lamar Lancer*, Principal Moyes urged his students to build traditions and to preserve the beauty of what he considered one of the most attractive schools in America.

*The first issue of* The Lamar Lancer, *the school's biweekly newspaper, was issued a mere seventeen days after the opening of the school, an amazing journalistic feat. (Courtesy of Will LeBlanc)*

In the first *Orenda*, the school yearbook published annually since 1938, Moyes wrote a letter reminding students that it was their privilege to establish the traditions "that will live long after you yourselves will have passed on" and expressing hope that they recognized their part in this historic first year at Lamar High School.

The Lamar Student Council was formed to "uphold the honor of Lamar, and to promote school spirit." It was composed of representatives from each homeroom and was responsible for helping to form the policies of the new school and promoting school spirit. It was also responsible for raising money for the new library. Activities in the second year, as documented by the 1938 *Orenda*, included a "Book Week" program, a style show put on by home economics classes, and the purchase of the first Lamar High School banner.

Most high schools in the United States have just one honor society. Lamar has two. The Arrowhead Club, formed in the fall of 1937 before the National Honor Society chapter, is the "official honor society of Lamar." Nominations for Arrowhead membership originated in the first semester of the students' senior year. Members were to be senior boys and girls who had a 4.6 or better GPA (on a five-point system) and were outstanding in leadership, loyalty, and willingness to serve Lamar.[28] Throughout the school's history, membership in Arrowhead has remained Lamar's highest honor. Lamar High School's chapter of the National Honor Society was not formed until the spring of 1939. The NHS inducts both juniors and seniors.

Lamar was initially denied secondary school accreditation because there were too few volumes in the library.[29] Immediately after the school's opening in 1937, the Parent Teacher Association was organized, and by November 5th, members had launched a drive to fill the shelves. C. S. Simmons, father of student Frank Simmons and a Southgate resident, was the first president of the PTA. Simmons was a teacher, coach, principal, oilfield worker, soldier, and salesman. The 720 PTA members were divided into many departments: Membership, Hospitality and Room Representatives, Finance and Budget, Public Welfare, Safety, Legislation, Citizenship, Health and Student Aid, Study, Publicity, and Faculty Representation. These departments, listed in the 1938 Lamar Directory, surely included every conceivable aspect of student life, and each was presided over by a director. Today, the PTA is the Parent Teacher Organization (PTO) and continues its enthusiastic support of Lamar's students and faculty.

*This photograph of Lamar PTA officers indicates the strong support given to this organization by prominent community leaders. Back row: Mmes. McCall, Fonville, Tellepsen, and Hoover. Front row: Mrs. Moore and William Dickey.*

The Senior Cabinet of Lamar High School held its first meeting on February 10, 1938, to nominate class officers and select a class motto. Principal Moyes attended every Senior Cabinet meeting until his retirement in 1953. He worked with Cabinet members on their budget, made suggestions, and quietly acquiesced if his suggestions were not adopted. He gave the Cabinet the dates for graduation activities: commencement exercise, Class Night (forerunner of the senior prom), and baccalaureate service. The Cabinet then planned the activities and decided where they would be held and how much would be spent on each event. The Senior Cabinet planned to elect class officers as soon as possible, nominating candidates and conducting the election in each of the homerooms.[30] The first election was held on February 18, 1938, and ballots were counted by the Senior Cabinet the same day. Senior class dues, used to fund class activities, were set at $1.50 per person. Senior rings could be ordered with the following options:

| All Metal | | With a Stone | |
|---|---|---|---|
| Heavy (weight) | $9.80 | Heavy (weight) | $10.90 |
| Medium (weight) | $9.45 | Medium (weight) | $10.55 |
| Light (weight) | $8.80 | Light (weight) | $9.90[31] |

The Senior Cabinet considered several class mottos:

"Too low they build who build beneath the stars."
"Fearless minds climb soonest into crowns."
"A man must carry knowledge with him if he would bring home knowledge."

In the end, it chose "Va-T'en Aux Etoiles," loosely translated as "Reach for the Stars." Initially chosen for only the senior class, "Reach for the Stars" was subsequently adopted as the motto as was the seal shown below for Lamar High School. This motto and seal of Mirabeau B. Lamar's family had been located by the students in November 1937, and they obtained permission from the family to use both. The motto and seal were those of the French branch of the Lamar family, according to Justice Lucius Q. C. Lamar (1825–1893), Mirabeau B. Lamar's nephew.

The seal was blazoned in color on the frontispiece of the 1938 *Orenda*. Students were delighted that the red rose pictured in the lower left quadrant was the one they had chosen as their school flower.[32] For seventy-five years, the motto has been alluded to in publications and class poems and has provided a lifelong goal for Lamar students.

The first graduating class presented to the school a leatherbound book with the signatures of all the seniors of the Class of 1938. Among the signatures is that of James H. Fields, who joined the Army in 1942, went into combat, and was awarded the Medal of Honor (later known as the Congressional Medal of Honor) in the field by General George S. Patton, Jr. Fields, the first man in Texas to be awarded the Medal of Honor, was also awarded the Silver Star, the Bronze Star, the Purple Heart, and the Croix de Guerre.

*The Mirabeau B. Lamar family's coat of arms is the emblem of Lamar High School along with the family's motto "Va-T'en Aux Etoiles," loosely translated as "Reach for the Stars."*

The humble commencement address given by 1938 Senior Class President Fenwick White summarized the students' recognition of what their brand new school had given them:

> Lamar has certainly lived up to the expectations which we have placed on the school. We only hope that we have given enough of ourselves so that following classes will look up to the ideals which we have fostered and not have to ridicule them as being too small and too ignoble.

White's words would become especially poignant, since he was killed in an automobile crash the summer after his graduation. The grief-stricken student body organized library memorials to keep his name alive.[33]

## Lamar's First Luminaries

Even in Lamar's earliest graduating classes, there were outstanding graduates who made notable contributions to society. Elizabeth Dennis (Rockwell) (Class of 1938) graduated from River Oaks Elementary and Lanier Junior High, and then attended San Jacinto High School for two years. She transferred to Lamar when it opened in 1937, and was a member of the first graduating class. After graduation from the University of Houston (UH) with a business degree, she tried to get a job on the East Coast, but returned to Houston, a city she said was more progressive about hiring women. Rockwell began at Heights Savings and Loan, later entering the brokerage business, where she became a successful financial planner. Rockwell was a devoted supporter of UH and her generosity is indicated by the number of campus buildings that bear her name. She also endowed chairs for deans of the library, the College of Education,

*The flag in front of the school flies at half-staff in memory of David Fenwick White, Lamar's first senior class president. His death in the summer of 1938 seriously impacted his classmates and the whole student body.*

and the Cullen College of Engineering. In 1992, she received the College of Business Administration Alumni Award, and in 1996, the University of Houston Distinguished Alumni Award. In 2000, she was honored as a Distinguished Lamar Alumna.

Jack M. Ilfrey (Class of 1938) became a World War II hero. He left Texas A&M before graduating in order to join the U.S. Army Corps in April 1941. Flying his P-38, or "Happy Jack's Go-Buggy" as it was called, he served two combat tours and flew 142 missions. In 1944, Ilfrey was promoted to captain and served as commander of the 79th Fighter Squadron Group based in England. His medals included the Silver Star, the Distinguished Flying Cross, and the Air Medals. His wartime adventures and the name of his plane have appeared in many books, magazines, and newspapers.

*Betty Ruth Robbins Tomfohrde, a concert pianist, performed as a soloist for the Houston Symphony, the Seattle Symphony, and the St. Louis Philharmonic.*

Betty Ruth Robbins (Tomfohrde) (Class of 1939) spent her life making music at Lamar and around the world. She performed her first piano concert at the Los Angeles Conservatory of Music when she was four and a half years old and moved from California to Houston as a teenager. At Lamar, Robbins wrote the first Lamar fight song:

"Our High School"

What's the school that's far above the rest?
It's Lamar, that we all love the best;
For we Redskins are a loyal tribe.
To our colors we point with pride.

We will fight, fight, fight for the red and blue.
To their standards we will all be true.
We are out to win, but win or lose,
We'll always choose Lamar as our high school.

After graduation, she was awarded a six-year scholarship to New York City's Julliard Conservatory, studies which she interrupted during World War II when she was chosen to play with the USO Concert Division, performing 161 European concerts. She resumed her studies at Julliard after the war, then came back to Houston and taught piano before marrying John Tomfohrde. Her husband's job as a traveling Shell engineer provided her with overseas opportunities to perform in London and other European cities. International record companies Albany and Koch handled her BBC recordings. After returning to Houston, she taught for thirty-two years at Moore's School of Music at the University of Houston, and her pupils have won national and international competitions. Betty Ruth Robbins Tomfohrde was the first of Lamar High School's celebrated musicians.

The school's first internationally known scholar was Jess B. Bessinger (Class of 1939). While a student at Lamar, Bessinger distinguished himself by winning Best Actor in the twelfth state UIL One-Act Play Championship.[34] He served as president of Arrowhead and appeared at the Houston Little Theater. Graduating from Rice Institute in 1943, Bessinger served in the Army from 1943 to 1946, received his MA and PhD in English from Harvard University, and taught at New York University until his retirement.[35]

An expert on Beowulf, Bessinger's six books total forty-nine editions. Perhaps reflecting his early acting success, his recordings of Chaucer and Beowulf have gone through forty-one editions. His works are held by over 1,000 libraries worldwide.[36]

Ralph Anderson (Class of 1939) made a name for himself as an artist and an architect. He was the son of Andy Anderson, sports editor of the *Houston Post* and later the *Houston Press*. Ralph Anderson served as assistant editor of the *Orenda* for two years. The unsigned artwork in the 1939 *Orenda* has been identified by artist Henri Gadbois (Class of 1948) as an early example of Anderson's artistic talent. Ralph Anderson, like many Lamar students, lived in West University Place.

The cover of the 1939 *Orenda* represents the two landmark structures of central significance to the 1939 New York World's Fair: an enormous ball called a Perisphere, and a 700-foot-tall obelisk called a Trylon. These adjacent structures were stark modern buildings that supported the theme of the fair, the first world exposition based on the future. Members of the New York Yankees baseball team, to promote the fair, wore on the sleeves of their jerseys fabric patches displaying the Trylon and the Perisphere.

The fair's opening slogan, "Dawn of a New Day," beckoned 44 million visitors to look at the "world of tomorrow." The 1939 *Orenda* borrowed this theme, entitling its essay preceding the beginning of class photos "World of Tomorrow." Ralph Anderson, assistant editor of the *Orenda*, is thought to have been the creator of the cover, the unsigned Art Deco and Modernistic illustrations that fill the book, and perhaps the editorial comments.

*The 1939* Orenda *used the 1939 New York World's Fair as its theme, the only time a national event was incorporated into the cover and theme of Lamar's yearbook. The embossed cover (above) pictures the Trylon and the Perisphere, two buildings familiar to those who attended the fair or read about it. (Courtesy of Will LeBlanc)*

*This 1939 three-cent U.S. stamp features the same images indicating the national recognition of the fair and its theme. (Courtesy of Will LeBlanc)*

*Within the covers of the 1939* Orenda, *Ralph Anderson created stunning drawings (right) used to mark the yearbook's divisions. Note that each of his images incorporates the Trylon and the Perisphere.*

A graduate of Rice Institute, Anderson served in the United States infantry during World War II. His career included creation of a "stripped down modernist style" for the Houston World Trade Center (1962), the Astrodome (1965), and the Austin American-Statesman Building in Austin. He also designed event centers at the University of Texas and other universities in Texas and other states, as well as noteworthy residential dwellings.[37]

## ATHLETICS

Texas high schools always began by organizing an athletic department. Lamar was no different. Football was coached by Ed Duggan, who had played football for Knute Rockne at Notre Dame. The 1938 *Orenda* commended the team's efforts despite the Redskins' dismal season. The only game the twenty-member Redskins team won was the first one, against the Humble Wild Cats. In the remaining eight games, Lamar scored a total of twenty-one points. As the yearbook noted, the Redskins had not even one experienced player, "so a championship team was not to be hoped for."[38]

Lamar's second venture into district football wars was a decided improvement. The 1938 "Rampaging Redskins," as they were called by sportswriters,[39] finished three places higher than the 1937 team. Co-captains were Donald Puntch and Billy Thompson. Tom Hardy was, as the *Orenda* pointed out, the "hustling halfback," judged "the most outstanding player Lamar will have for a long time." The *Orenda* noted that it wasn't about winning—it was about Coach Duggan having "the respect and friendship of all the boys who play under him." The juniors and sophomores looked promising.

The night before Lamar's first game with Austin High School, a midnight event occurred at 3325 Westheimer Road that set the scene for many future raids by Austin and other HISD students. When Lamar students came to school Thursday morning, they saw green paint smeared on the sidewalks and flagpole. Since green and gold were Austin's school colors, it wasn't too difficult to pinpoint the culprits. In case there was any doubt as to the perpetrator, the rivals spelled out "Mustang," Austin's mascot, on the flagpole and erected a crudely painted flag atop Lamar's sixty-foot pole. The entire surface of the flagpole had been greased and the rope used to hoist flags had been cut. The rival also left their prediction for the upcoming game in large green letters on the front sidewalk: Austin 50, Lamar 0. Adding to the insult was the bucket of green paint left on Lamar's steps.

*Arrowhead club members had the football used in Lamar's first winning game painted bronze and mounted for display in the trophy case. Principal Moyes said it was his favorite trophy. (Courtesy of Will LeBlanc)*

*School Life, an HISD publication, used Lamar football player Tom Hardy (Class of 1939) on as its cover. He was also a fine basketball player and an outstanding student at Lamar.*

Principal Moyes' response was, "I wish I had a football team that could whip them." George A. Loescher, Austin's principal, decried his students' poor sportsmanship as he watched his crew scrubbing off the paint.[40] Thus began a football rivalry that was perhaps natural, given that the two new schools opened on the same day, but the rivalry was really spurred on by the East Enders' resentment of the architectural splendor of Lamar in contrast to that of Austin.

Donald Longcope accepted the job of coaching the basketball team and said he would consider their first year "a successful season if the team broke even." The team did just that: they won six and lost six. Six lettermen on Longcope's thirty-one-member team returned for the next season. One team member, Lloyd Gregory, known as "the Judge" and described as having an "unorthodox style" and "lots of hustle," undoubtedly made his father proud when Lamar won city and district championships his junior and senior years. Lloyd Gregory, Sr. wrote a daily sports column, "Looking 'Em Over," and conducted a popular sports quiz show, *Sportfolio*, on KPRC-TV. Later he became managing editor of the *Houston Post* and was one of the founders of the Bluebonnet Bowl.

*Coach Longcope is pictured with seven of the star players who helped win Lamar's first city and district basketball championship: Dudley Wright, Clifton Wilson, Buck Crate, Donald Puntch, Tom Hardy, Bill Thompson, and Weldon Mallette.*

After his second season at Lamar, Coach Donald Longcope was called the happiest of all the coaches. His team, laughingly referred to as the Lamar "Jitterbugs," had a very fine season, winning the city championship and the district championship. In addition to Gregory, lauded football player Tom Hardy was also a valuable basketball player, called by the *Orenda* "an inspiration to the fighting spirit of the team."[41] Speedy Clifton "Buster Keaton" Wilson was a consistent offense player.

The track team, coached by Harold E. "Mr. Mike" Mickelson, fared somewhat better their first year. The team took the blue ribbon in its first meet against the Jeff Davis Panthers, and after that continued to do well. The eighteen team members practiced despite the lack of a track or any other facilities. Coach Mickelson, described as a likeable man for whom nobody had a harsh word, created a "makeshift track and a pit where all jumping was provided for."[42]

Lamar girls' athletics were lumped together under an umbrella organization known as the Cherokee Club. Open to all Lamar girls, the club existed to promote their interest in athletics and to coordinate their intramural sports. Active members had to participate in at least one intramural team sport. Eight sports were represented: basketball, archery, riflery, softball, volleyball, swimming, tennis, and badminton. Eight girls were elected as student directors, one for each sport. In 1940, HISD's seven high schools gathered for "Sports Day," an all-day event where teams of girls exhibited sportsmanship, "winning gracefully or losing graciously, all in a spirit of friendly rivalry."[43] By 1943, the Cherokee Club had over 900 active members and continued to grow for many years. It also organized and sponsored the Lamar May Fete.

*Some people believe that the "first tier" of social life at any high school is the cheerleading squad. Lamar's first cheerleaders wore school sweaters instead of uniforms. Top row: Betty Jo Tomfohrde, Hester Stewart, and Mary Ann Anderson. Bottom row: "Stoop" Settlemyre, Joe Gilmore, and James Whitehurst. The* Orenda *praised head cheerleader "Stoop's" natural ability to lead the students in "whoops."*

### NO GIRLS' MILITARY DRILL SQUAD FOR LAMAR

Lamar High School broke with the local high schools' drill squad tradition in order to get away from "the militarism" and to do "something original and different." Instead they formed the Pep Club, which was most emphatically not to be confused with the drum and bugle drill squads that were an important unit of Houston high schools and 150 other high schools across the state. The Pep Club welcomed 100 percent of "Lamar's feminine enrollment," differing from the "military organization of a picked few," as with other schools' drill teams.[44]

Wearing "royal blue tailored dresses with red accents for carrying out the school colors," Pep Club members represented the school as guides for school visitors and ushers for school functions. According to plans for the fall of 1938, they were to have "a more definite function at the football games to represent the student body spirit."[45] In November, the *Lancer* announced that half-time activities at football games would be "built around peace pipes, war dances, and Indian lore in general—a welcome departure from the precision of the drill."⁴⁶ Lamar's Pep Club folded after one year. No evidence indicates the reason. Perhaps faculty believed that the Pep Club's presence at football games made it appear too similar to a drill squad.

Not having a drill squad brought Lamar a great deal of criticism from other HISD high schools, all of which had drill teams. The San Jacinto Gauchos, the Reagan Red Coats, and the new Scottish Brigade at Austin were among groups recognized citywide and received significant press coverage from Houston newspapers. Lamar's decision served to widen the gap between them and students in other HISD schools—not that anyone at Lamar cared.

*When Lamar's faculty and students chose social clubs over a drill team, they may have been objecting to the military uniforms worn by the latter. Pictured is a member of Sam Houston High School's group, known as the Black Battalion. (Courtesy of HMRC)*

In May 1939, *Lancer* editor Nell Joan Ransom addressed the criticism by quoting from a piece of anonymous advice placed in the *Lancer*'s suggestion box, advice that made clear Lamar's derision of Houston drill teams. The anonymous author claimed to have attempted planning for a Lamar drill squad, but after "wracking his brains," could not think of any organization that would be appropriate for Lamar. He expressed regret that Lamar's not having a drill squad indicated to the other Houston high schools that Lamar was "indulging" in a "great originality" that made the students mentally deficient "outcasts."⁴⁷ Faculty or students' decision not to have a drill squad was a choice they made and defended, a decision that announced to Houston that Lamar was not interested in "following the pack."

## The Lamar Social Clubs

Instead of a drill squad, Lamar students elected to have social clubs. These clubs had their roots in the national Greek sororities and fraternities which had a total of 650 members in various HISD high schools. In the summer of 1937, however, the HISD board banned membership in these sororities and fraternities, despite the efforts of national representatives who came to Houston that summer to present a plea for the continuation of their organizations. For some years, the school board had been trying, without success, to put an end to "secret societies." Shortly after the 1937 fall semester began, board member Holger Jeppesen stated, "It shall be the duty of all principals to suspend and recommend for expulsion any student who belongs to a high school fraternity or sorority. We intend that no compromise be worked out by club officials."⁴⁸

Greek fraternities and sororities had been an integral part of the students' social lives. Their friendships and parties stemmed from the clubs to which they belonged. Those students transferring to Lamar High School, or LHS, had intended to take their "secret society" memberships with them, but when the school board handed down its decision, all of the Greek societies were forced to disband and send their charters back to the national headquarters.

*Because so many questioned the social clubs' method of selecting their members, by the 1950s the drawing of names was held in Principal Moyes' office.*

*The pins worn by members of the Lamar social clubs resembled those of the college sororities and fraternities. Shown above are club pins from Ramal Mirabeau and Irari. (Courtesy of Larry Hitt, Carol Holmes, and Dick Gregg)*

Students at Lamar High School, therefore, formed "charitable and literary organizations," the replacements recommended by HISD officials.[49] These male and female clubs became an important part of Lamar social life for the next forty-five years. What constitutes a "secret society?" The membership is not a secret, but the method of selection is. At Lamar High School, membership was selected by the drawing of lots. Some raised doubts whether the membership was ever a random choice. The clubs, both male and female, preserved the sorority and fraternity "legacy" tradition for younger siblings, as well as the pledge period and initiations for new members.

The Belles and the Chums were two social clubs formed by transferring members of sororities from San Jacinto. The Thirty Club consisted of former San Jacinto fraternity members. Conrad Bering (Class of 1939) organized the club in 1939 and served as its president. Bering was a "Big Man on Campus" because he had a car, his grandfather's 1927 Model A Ford.[50]

*The Thirty Club social club expected thirty members. Its purpose was "the development of poise in speech, and the promotion of social functions." Back row: George Dow, Mr. Wilbern, David Ball, John Rugel, John Lindsey, Harry Hudson, and Mahlon Johnson. Front row: Sam Moss, Clifton Wilson, Ford Albritton, Conrad Bering, George Albritton, and Tom Powell.*

After graduation, Bering enrolled in Texas A&M, but left in 1943 to join the U.S. Army, where he served honorably and earned two battle stars. When he returned to Houston, he fulfilled his lifelong dream and became a radio disc jockey in Beaumont. In 1957, he returned to Houston and joined the family real estate business where he remained for sixty years. In 1972, he was recognized as Houston's Realtor of the Year, and in 2007 he received the John E. Wolf Citizenship Cup. Bering actively supported his profession, his neighborhood, his church, and the arts. A devoted graduate of Lamar High School, in 2011 he was chosen as a Distinguished Alumnus.[51]

Among the fifteen charter members of the Thirty Club was Bering's lifelong friend, Ford Albritton, who graduated from Texas A&M, Class of 1943, with an economics degree, became a World War II artillery pilot, flew 108 combat missions in the Pacific, and was awarded a Purple Heart.

Following the war, Albritton started a business constructing jalousies for windows. His factory, located outside of College Station, expanded into the production of aluminum windows and sliding patio doors. After selling the business, Albritton moved to Dallas and concentrated on banking, oil, and real estate. A successful businessman and investor, Albritton has been a staunch supporter of A&M, serving as a member of the Board of Regents (1968–1975) and in many other positions. Albritton's generosity to his alma mater includes the Albritton Tower and Carillon; "Space Flight," a metal sculpture at the entrance of Teague Research Center; and a President's Endowed Scholarship.

### OTHER EARLY ORGANIZATIONS

Besides the social clubs, the 1938 Lamar Directory listed more than twenty additional clubs, an indication that the first students were an energetic group. In the school newspaper's third issue, editor Pauline Mills announced, "NO MATTER what your hobby is, or what your secret ambition may be, there is a club in Lamar devoted to the study of that very thing." A study of the club offerings indicates the truth of her claim. From the popular Kampus Kamera Klub to the Safety Patrol Club, the Hiking Club, and the Typing Club, there was assuredly an activity for everyone.

The Reserve Officers Training Corps (ROTC) program was quickly formed at Lamar, but some of the first one hundred boys who signed up may have mistaken it for a social club. ROTC sponsor Sergeant Stanley Byrd complained that "only 73 can be accounted for."[52] Apparently the boys did not understand that this was not a club and resignation was not allowed. The members went on encampments in Memorial Park and were issued rifles that had a "bloody history."[53] According to the article, these Army surplus weapons had been used by World War I soldiers during the battles of Argonne Forest, Marne, and Chateau-Thierry, a possibility not easily substantiated. Surprisingly, by 1939, Lamar High School's ROTC would be the largest in the city, with an enrollment of 230 boys.[54]

---

**LAMAR TRIVIA**

Lamar was the first high school in HISD to have a public address system. Nearly two miles of wire were required to install the public address system. There were sixty-four loudspeakers capable of two-way communication. The main control board was arranged so that one program could be sent to one room, while a different program could be sent to another room!

*The 1939 cheerleaders were called an "untiring bunch of pep booster-uppers." Pictured in front of the school are Betty Jo Tomfohrde, Hester Stewart, Grace Picton, Laverne Pass, Maurice "Greasy" Thompson, and Bob Shepherd. As indicated, the grass planting was proceeding faster than the work on Westheimer Road.*

## EAGERLY AWAITED CAMPUS IMPROVEMENTS

The school was off to a great start, but getting there was still a problem. *The Lamar Lancer* (November 5, 1937) reported that in sixty days, work would begin on opening Buffalo Speedway and widening Westheimer Road. Harris County and the City of Houston would fund the project, "each participating jointly in the project." Unfortunately, the actual paving had to wait until sewer pipes had been laid. In January 1939, the *Lancer* reported that an official from Brown and Root, the street contractors, said the paving would begin in about three or four months. Westheimer would be paved only from Shepherd to River Oaks Boulevard, indicating the absence of development west of the school. The $76,954.30 cost would be paid by the city, the federal government, and Westheimer property owners.

The student body's frustration was expressed by the *Lancer*'s headline on April 18, 1939: "Fix It Or Close It!" Lamar High School's major thoroughfare was described as a "high narrow structure" with "deep ditches" unsafe for one-way traffic, much less traffic passing in both directions. Pointing to the common sights of a car and even a school bus in the ditch, bicyclists weaving in and out, and pedestrians "clinging to the edge of the pavement," the editor suggested that the City Council fill the "excavation-like holes" or close the street completely.

Work on the campus, however, was progressing. The *Lancer* reported that in December 1937, Horace W. Elrod of the PWA addressed the Lamar PTA and outlined plans for six tennis courts, three of cement and three of clay, which were already nearing completion. It is not known if any other HISD high schools had clay courts. Elrod promised over 100,000 square feet of cement would be poured to provide sidewalks and tennis courts, and described the landscape architect's blueprints as calling for planting St. Augustine or some sort of evergreen grass and "twenty-four live oak trees" to line the front of the campus.

Adjacent to the flagpole, a rose garden was planned for "350 rose bushes of assorted variety." Additionally, a football stadium and athletic track were to be built, along with two softball fields and one regulation baseball field. An ROTC parade ground was planned to be located between the football and baseball fields. The rifle range would be at the "extreme end of the grounds near West Alabama."[55]

*The rosebushes were planted on the front lawn to soften the severe architectural lines of the new high school. (Courtesy of River Oaks Property Owners Association)*

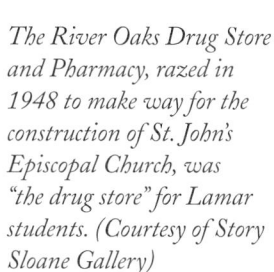

*The River Oaks Drug Store and Pharmacy, razed in 1948 to make way for the construction of St. John's Episcopal Church, was "the drug store" for Lamar students. (Courtesy of Story Sloane Gallery)*

## Students' Diversions and Concerns

The River Oaks Drug Store was the Lamar students' hangout both before and after school. Jimmy Brill (Class of 1951) referred to the establishment as "the drug store."[56] This was the place to be seen, a hub of social activity for everyone and an impressive stone building that also housed the offices of Hugh Potter, president of the River Oaks Corporation. As a response to the increase in customers from the opening of the new high school, the River Oaks Drug Store owner announced "installation of a new and larger soda fountain." Until the River Oaks Drug Store was demolished to make way for the new St. John's Episcopal Church building, local paperboys customarily sat on the right side of the drug store and folded their newspapers before loading them into their bicycle side bags. Since many of the young men with paper routes weren't terribly hefty, they had to counterbalance their own eighty or ninety pounds carefully against the weight of the load they were carrying. *The Houston Press* was a popular choice for route carriers because it was a lighter-weight newspaper, easier to fold, easier to carry, and easier to throw. A River Oaks route was not considered a plum assignment since the lots were so large that throwing the route took a longer time for fewer customers.

*This lovely drug store interior was located in either the River Oaks Drug Store or in the original Avalon Drug Store. Both claim it, but students cannot recall seeing it at either location. (Courtesy of River Oaks Property Owners Association)*

The first Lamar May Fete, the beginning of a favorite Lamar tradition, was held on Mary 29, 1938. It was held in the auditorium because of "unsettled weather and the incomplete condition of the school grounds."[57] Fenwick White and Betty Knapp reigned as king and queen with a court of fifty dukes, duchesses, princesses, and other royalty. The event was sponsored by Arrowhead for the first few years, but by 1946 had become a Cherokee project. Selling ads for the program and seventy-five-cent tickets was a major fundraiser for the girls' sports club and some years netted as much as $400.

*Pictured are Fenwick White, king of Lamar's first May Fete, and Betty Knapp, first winner of the Arrowhead Cup.*

*The "Rockettes" from Lamar's annual variety show The Frolics in 1948 are, left to right: Paula Meredith, Betty Gossey, Ruth Ann Ryba, Mary Nell Swartz, Ann Coe, Jeanette Grogan, Betty Pennington, and Beverly Smyth. Gloria Ross and Shirley Edwards are not pictured.*

Lamar students held senior banquets and staged drama productions, including The Frolics in 1939, which became an annual event. Picnics, dances, style shows, athletic events, and interscholastic contests all provided harmless entertainment and educational stimulation.

The *Lancer* listed fifteen "Do's and Don'ts" for "Dames on Dates." Included were these: "Don't eat too much; your date wants to be able to afford college… Do your education justice by keeping the conversation interesting… Don't be a walking cosmetic counter."[58] A poll conducted by the *Lancer* showed that *LIFE* was the students' favorite magazine.

Articles in the *Lancer* indicate that by the fall of 1939, Lamar students were apprehensive about what was being called the "European conflict." A series of articles entitled "Boxing the Compass," written by *Lancer* journalist Betty Sue Young, discussed worldwide problems and readers' responses. President Roosevelt had called a special session of Congress to revise the 1935 Neutrality Act passed to prohibit arms sales and loans to nations at war. Young's article, entitled "Neutrality Act Change Favored by Students," reported students' opinions about this Congressional debate. Some students favored giving Roosevelt the power "to do anything he wanted"; others favored only those provisions that would allow building factories to produce war-related equipment so that unemployed citizens could go to work and "build up the U.S. Treasury." All Lamar students agreed with the American public's unanimous desire to "keep the war over there."[59] The next two years would demonstrate the impossibility of their wish, and result in the intrusion of World War II into their lives.

*When Betty Finnegan was queen of the May Fete, the* Orenda *photographers spliced the masthead of* LIFE *Magazine onto her picture.*

*The school's first commencement program, or "Class Night Exercises," as it was called, was held on June 2, 1938, at 8:00 p.m. (Courtesy of Will LeBlanc)*

# CHAPTER THREE
## THE 1940s

### THREATS OF WAR CONTINUE

Though Lamar students were fully aware of the threat of world war, their optimism, in contrast with the concerns of their parents, was unmistakable. In "Youth Advances," a one-page essay in the 1940 *Orenda*, staff member Peggy Bentz wrote, "Lacking the pessimism of their plodding elders, they [Lamar's students] have faith in their future, hope for its security, and love of life." No mention exists of the students' reaction to the Houston Independent School District's board meeting on March 11, 1940. Board members voted unanimously to add a year to its school program: six years of grammar school, three years of junior high school, and three years of senior high school.[60]

Teenagers' goals were to balance the war with having fun, and fun in the 1940s included dancing. Yearbook photos showed a breakfast dance that included entertainment by an organ grinder and his monkey. Formally dressed couples did the "Put Your Little Foot" dance step and students enjoyed sock hops in the gym. According to the *Lancer*, "The Big Apple" dance craze had already hit Lamar. The Big Apple was a combination of the latest dance fads, such as "Truckin'" and the "Susie Q," with a little barn dance thrown in.

The Plantation on Main Street was a favorite Lamar hangout. "The Plant," as it was called, was a supper club that brought the best dance bands to Houston. Those who could afford it feasted on thirty-five-cent shrimp cocktails and twenty-five-cent bacon and tomato sandwiches, sipped ten-cent Cokes, and danced to big band music.

### THE OPEN FORUM

In sharp contrast with this fun and frivolity, a scholarly organization at Lamar called the Open Forum focused attention on world events and political issues. Lamar's club was probably inspired by the Houston Open Forum, an adult lecture platform that existed from 1926 to 1938. Organized by Rice professor Curtis H. Walker and modeled after a similar Dallas organization, Houston's club was part of the Progressive era's "intellectual awakening" that occurred nationwide during the 1920s. Public lectures began at Rice Institute, the Museum of Fine Arts was built, and the League of Women Voters was created.[61] The Houston Open Forum brought well-known but often controversial speakers to

*Ed Duggan's city and district championship football team is shown after its splendid defeat of the Milby Buffs in November 1944. First row: Warren Settegast, Jack Hughes, Bobby Ricks, Coach Ed Duggan, Frank Champion, ___ Pasche, Preston Locher, and Don Wilhelm. Second row: Paul Koomey, Jack Gwin, John Champion, Jack Hoeffler, Bobby Norris, and ___ McDonald.*

town. Lectures were free until 1936, when a twenty-five-cent admission fee was introduced. Audiences both rich and poor sometimes numbered in the thousands. Audiences heard lectures by speakers like famed "birth-controller" Margaret Sanger, socialist Lincoln Steffens, and philosopher and social critic Bertrand Russell. Lectures often sparked creative debate and aroused storms of protest in Houston newspapers.[62] The city's Forum membership read like a "Who's Who" list of Houston: Ima Hogg, Bishop Clinton S. Quin, Will Clayton, Oveta Culp Hobby, Dr. Edison Oberholtzer, library director Julia Ideson, and perennial school board member Dr. Ray K. Daily to name a few.

In 1937, Hawthorne Elementary School Principal Edith H. Wright asked the Houston Open Forum to help create similar organizations in the public schools. Though the Houston Open Forum ceased in 1938, a few members perpetuated the spirit of their organization in Houston high schools.

### THE LAMAR OPEN FORUM

Why was an Open Forum organized at Lamar? San Jacinto and Sam Houston high schools had similar organizations, but they were merely social clubs for debaters. At Lamar there was a conscious effort to emulate the city's adult lecture and debate format.

The Houston Open Forum's membership had strong connections with Lamar High School. Among its forty members was Blanche Higginbotham, principal of Lanier Junior High, a school many Lamar students had attended. Other active members included Higginbotham's friend Drew Black Staggs, a Lamar English teacher, and attorney Selden Leavell, whose wife Ruth was Lamar's dean of women. Forum member Hugh Potter, president of the River Oaks Corporation, was the parent of two Lamar students and annually donated a $50 watch to the outstanding debate student.

*The Lamar Open Forum was formed by Lamar students to debate current events. Club members were members of the National Forensic League, Arrowhead, and the National Honor Society.*

Lamar's Open Forum, sponsored by Lamar history teacher and Rice graduate Louis Kestenberg, began in 1939. It dealt with topics of current public interest, and students gave speeches in a round-table format. Topics included "The Value of Standardized Medicine," "The Halt Hitler Movement," "Peace After the Present War," and "Should the United States Recognize Franco's Government in Spain?"[63] The Forum folded briefly when Kestenberg left to pursue graduate studies but reemerged as the "Lamar Open Forum."[64]

The Lamar Open Forum underscored the atmosphere at Lamar, where students set a pattern for thinking seriously and debating current events. A total of 261 Lamar students graduated from Rice Institute during the 1940s, four times that of other Houston public high schools combined. Lamar's Class of 1945 alone produced forty Rice graduates. The Class of 1948, which Principal Moyes considered the finest class he had seen, produced forty-one.[65]

Thomas Barrow was a 1941 Lamar honor graduate who gained national recognition. Two geology degrees from the University of Texas and a PhD from Stanford University in 1953 prepared Barrow for a career in the oil business. Rising to senior vice president and director of Exxon Corporation, he served on many boards. His honors include Distinguished Graduate in Engineering and Distinguished Alumnus from the University of Texas, and Fellow of the New York Academy of Sciences and the American Association for the Advancement of Sciences. He served as vice-chairman of the Board of Trustees of the Baylor College of Medicine and trustee for the Houston Grand Opera and the Texas Medical Center. Barrow was honored as a Distinguished Alumnus of Lamar High School in 2003.[66]

General Carroll "Curley" Lewis, also a 1941 Lamar graduate who entered Rice but graduated from the University of Houston, was one of the most interesting students in his class. Lewis, a native Houstonian, attended Edgar Allen Poe Elementary and was chosen poet laureate. At Lanier Junior High, he won a scholarship to the Museum of Fine Arts. At Lamar, he formed his own twelve-piece band. He continued his musical studies by playing in the Rice Band and the Knight Owl Orchestra. When World War II interrupted his college work, he joined the Air Force and flew twenty-five missions as a B-17 bomber pilot.

Lewis returned to Rice after the war and founded the Rice Veterans Association. He became president of the Rice Owl Band, and his "outrageous innovations created a spirit that was thereafter adopted by the MOB (Marching Owl Band)."[67] The 1947 Rice Institute yearbook shows a photo of his secret flight over Kyle Field one Friday afternoon before a Rice-A&M football game, when he dropped a stink bomb and one hundred pounds of rice on an A&M pep rally.

Lewis' business ventures included building and operating the Post Oak Twin Drive-in Movie, Giant Slide, and Movieland Golf, a miniature golf course where each hole represented a famous movie. In 1969, he persuaded Governor Preston Smith to reactivate the Texas Army and was appointed and served for forty years as the commanding general. He wrote the definitive history of Fort Anahuac, which went through five printings. Lewis met monthly with friends from his Lamar Class of 1941 and hosted an annual fish fry for them at his Kemah home. His funeral service was held at the San Jacinto Monument, where the United States Air Force fired a salute and performed the flag presentation ceremony.[68]

## Lamar Joins the War Effort

Nena Conn (Dahlstrom Stowers) (Class of 1939) remembers attending a crowded Sunday matinee at the Tower Theater on December 7, 1941. The film was suddenly stopped, the curtains were closed, and the manager came onstage to announce that the Japanese had attacked Pearl Harbor. The film was restarted for naught. The audience stood and left the theater. With the United States declaration of war, every aspect of American life changed. Lamar High School was no exception.

No copies of the school newspaper recording Lamar students' response to Pearl Harbor have survived, but in February 1942, the *Lancer* editor urged his fellow students to accept their challenge, "the most difficult and important task any country ever faced—that of winning a war." He warned, "We students know nothing yet of the grim, relentless reality of war," and he implored students across the nation to recognize the "great unity that binds us together."[69] In 1943, publication of the *Lancer* was actually suspended for several years because of the paper shortage.

The 1942 *Orenda* yearbook, published only four months after Pearl Harbor, provided a powerful example of the war's impact on Lamar's students, faculty, and activities. William Fox, *Orenda* editor, began on page two by calling Lamar students the "future defenders of our flag." The ROTC had advanced in importance and was now placed at the front of the yearbook, rather than in its usual placement in the section with clubs.

Four pages of the *Orenda* were devoted to the "Lamar Battalion," which had increased to 400 cadets divided into five companies, the largest unit in the city. According to ROTC major Micky Carmichael (Class of 1943), the ROTC units combined from all of the other high schools in Houston barely equaled this number. The yearbook applauded the membership of Lamar's ROTC and suggested "it may soon be given a junior college rating," so that students who completed the rigorous training could receive some college credit. An "Officers' Club," composed of the Lamar Battalion officers who had been "democratically elected," also included the "highest ranking non-commissioned officers." By 1945, the Lamar ROTC had split the NCOs off into a separate Sergeants' Club.

*Melanie Levy's artwork in the 1942* Orenda *was all about the war.*

Not only the organization of the *Orenda* but also its artwork reflected the students' preoccupation with the war. Patriotic graphics were used as the background for the favorites pictures. Two pages of photographs were devoted to "Defense Doings," providing an interesting look at Lamar students' war efforts.

During the fall preceding student Micky Carmichael's scheduled June graduation, he was called to Principal Moyes' office and offered a plan. Carmichael had enough credits to graduate in January 1943, and if he immediately enrolled in college he would meet the requirements to join the Naval ROTC or the V-1, as it was known. Despite having to miss commencement celebrations with his class, Carmichael jumped at the chance. Following his mid-term graduation, he officially matriculated at UH. He successfully enrolled in the V-1 program and then, three days later, withdrew from college as planned. It was wartime, and he was ready for action.

A Lamar chapter of the Junior Red Cross was formed, membership requiring a minimum of fifteen hours of first aid instruction. Lamar's first air raid drill was held and brought "immediate and well ordered action," and the PTA eagerly listened to a representative from the Office of Civilian Defense speaking on the "Homemaker's Place in Civilian Defense."

*Jimmy Bayless was elected Most Popular Boy. All of the class favorite photos in the 1942* Orenda *reinforced the military theme.*

And then there was the war effort of history teacher Miss Mabel Clapp. Gum-chewing offenders in her classroom were given three options: stay fifteen minutes after school, receive a *P* (Probationary grade) in conduct, or pay five cents. The five cents was used to buy defense stamps, and the *Lancer* announced that $1.50 worth had been purchased since Pearl Harbor, a total of thirty offenders.

Charles Boyd (Class of 1950) says that Lamar held a scrap drive in 1943 for the war effort. Similar campaigns were being held all over Houston and the entire country. The metal was collected and converted into weapons and war materials. Even Houston Lighting and Power participated by cutting off the tops of 175 streetlamp posts, netting 80,000 pounds of metal.[70]

*Lamar students supported the war effort in different ways.*

# ATTENTION! LAMAR PASSES IN REVIEW

|      |                                   | Page |
|------|-----------------------------------|------|
| I.   | Reserve Officers Training Corps   | 5    |
| II.  | General Staff                     | 9    |
| III. | Infantry                          | 21   |
| IV.  | Regiments                         | 71   |
| V.   | Regimental Favorites              | 107  |
| VI.  | Panzer Divisions                  | 117  |
| VII. | Camp Life                         | 137  |
| VIII.| Official Communiques              | 147  |

*The 1942* Orenda *chose a military motif. "Lamar Passes in Review" substituted General Staff, Infantry, Regiments, Regimental Favorites, Panzer Divisions, and Camp Life for the usual divisions of faculty, students, and clubs.*

## Students of Lamar?

You are the future defenders of our flag. From each of you should go up a fervent prayer for the preservation of those principles—liberty, justice, humanity—which have made your nation greater than any other nation in the world. With profound reverence you should repeat with sincerity:

"I pledge allegiance to the Flag of the United States of America and to the Republic for which it stands; one nation, indivisible, with liberty and justice for all."

WILLIAM FOX, *Editor*

*Ewell Clarke's political cartoon from the* Lancer *reflected how the war impacted Lamar students. Mr. Rogers was a popular math teacher who left Lamar to go to Annapolis.*

Lamar students and Lanier Junior High Boy Scouts went up and down the streets asking people for donations of scrap. Their efforts produced a huge store of scrap metal consisting of bicycles, wheelbarrows, pipes, and similar items, which were piled in front of Lamar. The stack was two stories high when, according to Charles Boyd, a student brought a Model T Ford and built a ramp to try to drive the automobile to the top.

Lamar's V-Girl patriotic contest, which netted $6,000 for the war effort, was won by Betty Baker, who received a photograph taken by Paul Gittings as her prize. The contest was called the most successful in the history of the school. Ballots were cast by buying defense stamps, the purchase of a ten-cent stamp entitling one to cast ten votes for a candidate.

Charles W. Duncan, Jr. graduated with the Class of 1943. He was a native Houstonian who went to Rice and graduated with a degree in chemical engineering. After serving in the United States Army Air Force during World War II, he returned to Houston and joined the family business, Duncan Foods, which he led until 1964, when Duncan Foods merged with The Coca-Cola Company. Duncan became president of Coca-Cola in 1971. From 1977 to 1979, he was deputy secretary of the United States Department of Defense, and from 1979 to 1981, secretary of the Department of Energy.

During Duncan's public service career, he also served as past chairman of the Board of Governors at Rice University and trustee emeritus of the Brookings Institute. He also served a four-year term on the Texas State Board of Education. An outstanding Lamar graduate, Duncan was honored as a Distinguished Lamar Alum in 2006.[71]

### School As Usual with a Few Adjustments

The Class of 1942 totaled 575 graduates and held its commencement in Jeppeson Stadium, the new $1-million football field built across the street from the UH campus. At this time all HISD seniors graduated together in a joint commencement. The Senior Cabinet announced a fee of one dollar for general dues to help pay for end-of-school festivities. The fee entitled the graduate to attend the picnic and dance for three hours at Sylvan Beach, but the barbecue lunch cost forty cents extra.

In 1943, the Lamar Senior Cabinet decided not to hold the traditional picnic. Gas rationing made destination events difficult, and as Principal Moyes pointed out, because of meat rationing a barbecue couldn't be held as in previous years. It was

*Pictured are the 2006 Distinguished Alumni: Charles W. Duncan (Class of 1943), Dr. Louise Connally Strong (Class of 1962), and Harry Glauser (Class of 1963), president of the Lamar Alumni Association.*

decided that each student would bring their own lunch. This subject was revisited at the next meeting, and, accepting Mr. Moyes' suggestion, the Cabinet decided to have a "Class Morning," with a play, cold drinks, and dancing in the gymnasium. The budget for the event was as follows: a ten-dollar royalty fee for the play they staged, twenty dollars for drinks and ice, and ten dollars for miscellaneous. The Class of 1943 spent $255 for the senior prom, fifty dollars for Class Morning, twenty-five dollars for Class Night, twenty-five dollars for miscellaneous, and fifty dollars for the Fenwick White Library Memorial.[72]

Extracurricular activities were developing their own traditions. Sequoyah, the writing club, referred to as the "Scribblers Club," was a "group of self-styled literary geniuses who delightedly argued over the slaying of a sentence, the torturing of a participle, or the resurrecting of an iambic foot." Sequoyah undoubtedly contributed to Lamar's winning the State University Interscholastic League (UIL) Championship in Ready Writing five times during this decade. (The University Interscholastic League, established in 1910 and governed by the University of Texas in Austin, administers almost all public school athletic, fine arts, and academic contests in the State of Texas.)

*The 1948 Ready Writing Trophy won by an unnamed Lamar student. In 1947, Walter Clemons won the Ready Writing Trophy. (Courtesy of Will LeBlanc)*

The Junior Academy of Science, formed at Lamar in 1937, was a member of the state organization called the Texas Junior Academy of Science. The Lamar students attended two annual state conferences. The club's purpose was to discuss scientific matters and plan outings to study "unusual biological and mineralogical specimens." At the 1945 state conference in Austin, the Lamar club's president, Bob Albertson, was chosen the most representative science club student in Texas.

Lamar High School, because of its reputation and location, benefited from the involvement and support of many local corporations. Some of the larger companies contributed to the enrichment of all

Houston high school students. A contest was sponsored every year by the Humble Oil Company for Junior Achievement chapters, promoting student ingenuity and teamwork. Students were to invent a new product and create a marketable prototype of their invention. Lamar's entry in 1945 was a "Plastic Weiner Electrocuter." An article in the *River Oaks Times* magazine (Vol. 1, No. 2) does not attempt to describe this hot-dog-making invention, but lists the tools required for its production: a band saw, a sander, and plastic to form a mold. The use of an electric oven would be necessary. How they were going to put a plastic mold in the oven was not explained.

The male and female students met one night a week to work on their invention. Unfortunately, no photograph exists of their invention, but the team members were listed as John White, Doug Nelson, Marilyn Howell, Val Werner, Ralph Bowen, Betty Claire Criner, Jane Hogue, Clay Umbach, and Crete Freud. The Lamar team won a seventy-five-dollar prize.

Palamar, Chums, and the newer club Niwauna were thriving, along with Belles, Seminar, and Tawasi. These clubs fostered a sisterhood similar to the spirit of the Greek sororities that had been banned. Once you joined a social club, you never switched your membership to another club. Their camaraderie was indicated by a remark overheard at the Class of 1947's sixty-five-year reunion, "all Chums are joined at the hip." The six clubs spent much of their time on charitable projects, ranging from selling Christmas seals to knitting and sewing for the American Red Cross.

Ramal (Lamar spelled backwards), a "young man's social club," was formed in 1942 by a group of students to "provide social functions for the entire school and promote good fellowship and school spirit."[73] Annual events included an athletic contest with the worthy goal of helping coaches discover new talent. Ramal gave a trophy to the Most Outstanding Junior Girl and held an annual formal dinner dance said to be one of the year's outstanding social events. Ramal also contributed to charitable enterprises and beautification projects for the campus. Membership required an *H* in conduct and a *B* average.

Pow Wow was founded by a group of boys in 1943 as a "medium for their common interests: athletic, social, and recreational." The club's stated objective was to "gain a better grasp of current activities." Members pledged to make regular donations to the library. The club's membership did not rely on academic excellence, requiring only a *C* average and an *S* in conduct.

Lest some think the Indian names of the Lamar Social Clubs were peculiar, an interesting comparison can be made by looking at some clubs listed in Stephen F. Austin High School's 1940 yearbook, the *Corral*: Ginty's Goofy Ginks, the Swingin' Socialities (male and female), the Sub-Deb Club, Ruthie's Reckless Rinkydinks, Carleton's Corny Crumbs, Whim Wham Whackies, and the Dumble Street Dummies. Unlike the Lamar clubs, Austin's social clubs did not indicate any charitable work.

A "congregation of thrushes," Haienonis was the all-girl choir that "promoted interest in music on campus and off." Each year, the Most Outstanding Member was presented with a bracelet. Lee S. Keding, their sponsor, chose "Be Happy with Harmony" as their motto. The Choralettes club is perhaps a direct descendent.

In addition to the girls' chorus, Keding directed the Lamar Marching Band and The Frolics, while also sponsoring Ramal, the largest social club for boys.

During the war, Keding explained to his band members that they would not be able to march in all of the customary activities because football games and parades required cars, and traveling was seriously hampered by gas rationing and rubber shortages. The band practiced by marching up and down River Oaks Boulevard, its music heard by residents several blocks away. In 1945, Keding wrote the current alma mater, "Hail to Lamar," and he later went on to write the rest of Lamar's school songs.

In 1943, the *Orenda* published a slim, twenty-four-page paperback yearbook, the *Papoose*. Despite its unprepossessing appearance, this yearbook had terrific cartoons drawn by Burdette Keeland, who became an important Houston architect and a University of Houston professor who taught for forty years. Among Keeland's impressive works were his "1954 Parade of Homes" house in Bellaire, the Kipling Street townhouses, and the Winchell Photography Studio. An obituary written by Joe Mashburn for *Cite* magazine stated, "He loved his city" and he "helped shape Houston through his service as President of the Park People and serving on the city's Planning Commission." Phillip Johnson, an internationally known architect who designed Transco Tower and other landmark Houston structures, said Keeland was the Houston architect he most admired. When Keeland's class held its fiftieth reunion, Keeland contributed a new cartoon in honor of the occasion.

## A Teenage Night Club

*The Houston Press*' August 21, 1943 headline read, "NEW HOUSTON TEEN AGE NIGHT SPOT IS KNOCKING 'EM COLD." The opening of this club filled a need of students to enjoy affordable entertainment while the owner and many of his patrons were "waiting for their call to the Army," a poignant reminder of the ongoing war which put so many teenagers' lives on hold.

*Lee Keding came to Lamar in 1942 and achieved iconic status during his forty-six years on the faculty. For many years, Keding was the Music Department at Lamar.*

*Keding wore his military uniform when leading the ROTC Regimental Band. The band practiced by marching up and down River Oaks Boulevard and its music could be heard by residents several blocks away.*

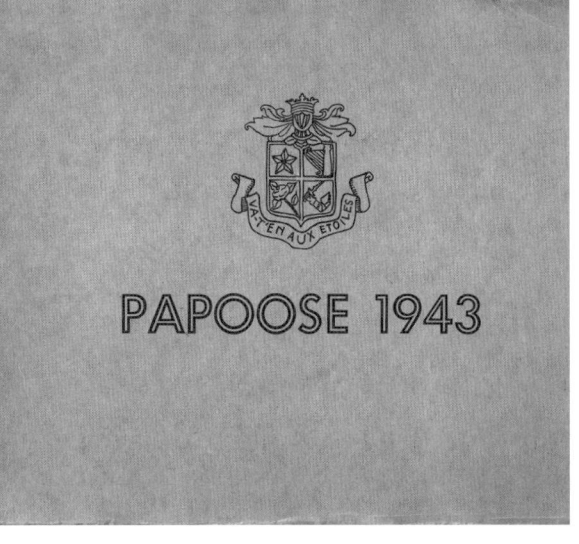

*Critical shortages during World War II necessitated HISD high schools cutting back expenses involved with their yearbooks. The 1943* Papoose *was a paperback edition. (Courtesy of Will LeBlanc)*

*Despite its unprepossessing appearance, the* Papoose *had terrific cartoons drawn by senior Burdette Keeland and is a treasured collectible today.*

The nightclub, Tune in for Teens, on Post Oak Road, was started by seventeen-year-old Rudy Hagelman, a Lamar High School graduate. For thirty-five cents, teenage couples between the ages of thirteen and nineteen could dance to the jukebox vocals of Bing Crosby and Frank Sinatra and big band orchestra music.

The club gave teenagers a chance to jitterbug and sip sodas where no adults could bother them and there were few rules: no stags allowed, no bottles taken outside, and no shirttails hanging out. Rudy's mother, Mrs. W. C. Hagelman, acted as chaperone and assured the reporter that they had no "rough stuff."

### Athletics

Despite the war, athletic competition continued. In May 1942, the *Lancer* announced that this had been the most eventful year in the history of the school. Of course, "eventful" usually meant sports' victories. The Redskins football team won its first city and district championship in 1944 in a season called by the 1944 *Orenda* "the greatest a Lamar football team has ever had."

In 1947, Coach Duggan's Redskins continued to the state semi-finals before losing to the Temple Tigers. The co-captains, center Richard Stubbs and halfback Raymond Borneman, made All-State. Borneman continued on to play for the University of Texas, where he was named All-Southwest Conference. After graduation in 1948, he was drafted by the Los Angeles Rams.

The basketball team tied with Milby for the city championship, and the track team won victories in various events. Both the girls' and boys' tennis teams swept the city tournament.[74] Cheerleaders Lawrence Blieden, Joe Moss, Pat Dougherty, Lois Holmes, Trebie Perry, and Marjorie Lawry kept spirits high.

*In 1941, Mary Jo Clark and Lois Clement won this archery trophy.*

*The 1940 archery team seems to be aiming for a different target than the pictured bull's eye.*

### OUTSTANDING LAMAR GRADUATES

One fifteen-year-old graduate of the Class of 1942 became an internationally known model whose face is familiar to thousands of Houstonians. Elsa "Elsie" Roberts (Rosborough), who describes herself as a shy tomboy in high school, was surprised when she won "Most Beautiful" at Lamar, unaware that her history teacher, Mrs. Ellana Ball, had sent in a photograph of her. She began her modeling career at Sakowitz Brothers as a high school senior when asked by their head model to try on a garment. As journalist Linda Gillan Griffin said, this event set in motion a six-decade career.[75]

*Elsa Rosborough, a Houston icon who helped women believe that getting older did not mean becoming unattractive, told a* Chronicle *reporter that she would retire only when she got to the point of not being able to apply her false eyelashes. (Courtesy of Elsa Rosborough)*

After graduating from the University of Houston, Rosborough was asked to create a revolutionary course to teach women how to be competitive.[76] She continued teaching at UH for thirty-five years. The position for which she is best known, however, began in 1960, when she became "Miss Maryland Club." Elegantly poised with her coffee cup, the now gray-haired Elsa Rosborough was shown on national TV saying, "The coffee you would drink if you owned all the coffee in the world." Over the years, she combined her career with the birth of four children, while continuing to work for most of the major fashion magazines as well as Bill Blass, who called her "the lady with the gray flannel hair."[77] She was named a Distinguished Alumna of UH in 1971 and Lamar High School in 2001.[78]

Another successful graduate, J. Doug Pitcock, Jr. (Class of 1945), enrolled in summer school after his junior year in order to graduate early, and is not sure of which class he is actually a member! Elected cheerleader as a junior, Pitcock says he enjoyed the social activities of Lamar very much, but also received an excellent preparation for college. After he arrived at Texas A&M, his first semester was a "breeze." He was prepared to coast but was rudely awakened the second semester, when he had to buckle down and study. He graduated with a degree in civil engineering, served in the Army, and partnered with the Williams Brothers to start a highway and heavy construction company. Pitcock bought the brothers out in 1955, but did not change the name. Pitcock's success includes building bridges and freeways in Houston and all over the United States. He has also worked tirelessly as an industry advocate and a political activist for the construction industry and has served on many state and national boards. His generosity to Lamar High School and to A&M includes many scholarship programs for deserving students.[79]

## THE BEGINNING OF LAMAR HIGH SCHOOL'S PROMINENCE IN THE FINE ARTS

Despite popular opinion, Lamar's reputation as an incubator for successful contributors to the fine arts preceded by eleven years the remarkable tenure of Ruth Denney. Kachina was the club that provided encouragement for Lamar's outstanding drama students in the early 1940s. Their member Andy Duggan (Class of 1941), Coach Duggan's son, won first in the citywide One-Act Play championship three times and went on to have a successful film and television career. One source cited the number of his television series, saying with reruns, Duggan could be seen on TV as many as three times in one day.

Jeanette Clift (Class of 1942) is an outstanding actress who first achieved fame as a member of the Alley Theater before going to New York City, where she performed in Off-Broadway theaters, the New York Shakespeare Company, Philadelphia's Playhouse in the Park, and Washington, D.C.'s Arena Stage.

Clift has been nominated for a Golden Globe Award and the Golden Apple Award for her film work. She founded the respected and beloved A.D. Players Theater, a Houston-based Christian theater company that performs plays worldwide. Her many community awards include the Matrix Award for playwriting, the Alpha Delta Fraternity Shield Award, and Rotary International's Jean Harris Award. She holds honorary doctoral degrees from Dallas Baptist University and Houston Baptist University.[80]

*Jeanette Clift says her theatrical career was launched at Lamar when she went with her cast to Indiana to present their One-Act Play.*

Lawrence Blieden (Class of 1942) was a Kachina member who contributed behind the scenes more often than onstage. He was a member of Houston's Radio Guild while a student at Lamar and hoped to become a radio announcer. His career greatly surpassed his high school dreams. After serving in the Marines, Blieden graduated from UH and left for New York City, where he would achieve "marquee value" on Broadway, winning a Tony for his performance in *A Funny Thing Happened On the Way to the Forum*. In Hollywood, he played supporting roles in such films as *Bachelor Party* and *On a Clear Day You Can See Forever*, and later became a popular panelist and host of television game shows. Blieden, who changed his name to Larry Blyden, was named a Distinguished UH Alumnus in 1972.

Vassar Miller (Class of 1943) was elected the class poet. During a meeting of the Senior Cabinet, Principal Moyes remarked that Miller was "the only student to be nominated and elected by unanimous vote for a class office."[81] Miller, a descendant of poet Sidney Lanier (1842–1881), used the school's motto for her class poem, creating a moving tribute to youth's optimism and courage in the wake of a world conflict beyond anyone's imagining.

"Va-T'en Aux Etoiles"
June 1943
Vassar Miller

The sky overhead is darkly spread
With human defeat and fears,
For the planet Mars has eclipsed the stars
As he sheds his bloody tears.

Is the heav'n that God has giv'n—
This gaping horror of night?
Is this the truth that is given youth—
That darkness has stolen light?

But Youth has eyes in which there lies
The power to see afar.
Beyond the rim of its vision dim
Youth dreams of the fartherest star.

Youth sees a way to the stars of day
With the eyes of a strong, young soul;
Sees through the mist of a land light-kissed
That marks man's final goal.

With reverent hearts Youth onward starts
To capture that land of charms;
And up and on to the of stars of dawn
Youth carries the world in its arms.

A gifted student, Miller suffered from cerebral palsy, which affected her speech and her ability to get around the school. A classmate remembered that Miller's heavy book bag often impeded her progress when she climbed the steps between floors. Classmates made a habit of following behind her to assist if she faltered. One of her classmates recalled that the president of the senior class escorted her to the senior prom.

Miller's first book of poems, *Adam's Footprint*, was published in 1956. Her poetry is currently included in hundreds of anthologies and earned her a Pulitzer Prize nomination in 1961. When Lamar celebrated its fiftieth birthday, Miller wrote a letter apologizing for her inability to come to the celebration and praising her teacher, Miss Nina Covington, who had taught her, not English as would be expected, but history and civics. This woman remained her "truest friend for over forty years." In the letter, Miller bestowed three "gifts" upon the 1987 graduating class, "a continuing love of learning, a deep, although never a naïve faith, and a friend like Miss Nina Covington."[82] Miller was an advocate for the rights of the handicapped and in 1994 was named an Outstanding Woman of Houston by the YWCA.[83] In 1997, Miller was posthumously chosen for the Texas Women's Hall of Fame by the Governor's Commission for Women. The *New York Times* obituary quotes Larry McMurtry as lamenting the lack of attention paid to Miller's poetry.

Wordsmith Walter Clemons (Class of 1947) was senior class president. His commencement address acknowledged what his Lamar diploma meant to him: "I think that instead of being sad at leaving school, we ought to be happy that we're graduating from such a fine one… We've never known what it must be to come into an old, dark building every morning. We've had a clean, new school, good books and fine teachers. And above all—this class came to Lamar during the war, and we've seen it end victoriously. The boys in this class can make their own plans, instead of knowing that they will spend next year on a ship or a battlefield."

*Walter Clemons became a nationally known writer. He credited longtime Lamar English teacher Margaret Buchanan with fostering his professional writing career.*

Orenda *editor Walter Clemons chose cartoonist Milton Caniff to select Lamar's Most Beautiful Girl. The creator of the comic strip* Steve Canyon, *Caniff picked sophomore Jane Putney as Lamar's Most Beautiful Girl and drew a cartoon of his female protagonist Copper Calhoun for his "friends at Lamar."*

His words echo the sentiments of members of these early graduating classes. Clemons made significant contributions to Lamar, winning many high school writing awards. Clemons chose cartoonist Milton Caniff, the creator of *Steve Canyon*, to select the beauties for 1947. Caniff chose sophomore Jane Putney as Lamar's Most Beautiful Girl and drew a cartoon "for my friends at Lamar High School."

Following graduation, Clemons earned his AB degree in English with highest honors at Princeton University, and a graduate degree from Oxford University, where he was a Rhodes Scholar. He returned to Houston and worked as a seaman in the Gulf of Mexico, then as a pianist in London and Rome, letting his education gel while he worked on a book of short stories that was published in 1959. During his career, Clemons was an editor for McGraw-Hill, contributor and book editor at *Vanity Fair* magazine, and book critic and writer for *Newsweek* and *The New York Times*. He died at age sixty-four of complications from diabetes. Obituaries praised him as an author and a critic who, because of his knowledge of traditional literature, appreciated and brought sensitive insights to contemporary literature. Clemons, in many ways, embodied the finest of Lamar's students. While excelling in academics and the arts, he still found time to serve as class president and as president of his social club.

Another wordsmith who graduated with the Class of 1947 was Madge Thornall (Roberts). She worked on the *Lancer* staff and still feels very close to her fellow classmates with whom she worked on war bond drives, scrap metal collections, and "goody bags" for the American Red Cross. She describes the dedication of their teachers who seldom took time off from school. When Roberts' math teacher at Lamar was notified that her husband had been killed in action, she missed only one day of school. Students were never disrespectful to their teachers. Following graduation from Southwestern University and Trinity, Roberts taught school for thirty-eight years before achieving her dream of being a writer. North Texas Press has published five of her books. *Star of Destiny: The Private Life of Sam and Margaret Houston* won the 1993 Best Book Award from the East Texas Historical Association. Her four-volume *The Personal Correspondence of Sam Houston* won the 1996 Best Book Award from the Texas Historical Commission, and all four volumes were chosen by the *Austin American-Statesman* as one of the twenty best Texas history books of the last decade of the twentieth century. Roberts has written articles for newspapers and magazines and chaired the committee which designed the permanent outdoor exhibit at the Alamo.

Nationally known and respected author Gene Wolfe (Class of 1949) is a short story writer and novelist who has won six Locus Awards, two Nebula Awards, and four World Fantasy Awards for his science fiction novels, including a Life Achievement Award. After graduation from Lamar High School, he attended Texas A&M University but was drafted to fight in the Korean War. He returned to Houston and graduated from UH with a BS in Mechanical Engineering. While working for Proctor and Gamble, he designed the machine that makes Pringles potato chips. Because of his interest in writing, he left this company for a job as editor of an industry publication, writing fiction on the side. After some success, he was able to quit and write science fiction full time. Wolfe does not follow genre conventions and writes in a "tongue that has not achieved existence into English," said to be confusing for the new reader. Among the books written about Wolfe by others, there are several lexicons designed to help readers understand the archaic words used in his various works. His books are not bestsellers, but critics consider him to be one of the greatest living science fiction authors. Celebrated science fiction author Michael Swanwick has said nobody can even approach Gene Wolfe for "brilliance of prose, clarity of thought, and depth in meaning." Wolfe is a member of the Science Fiction Hall of Fame.

His classmate Donald Barthelme (Class of 1949), who moved to Houston in 1933 so his father could take a position as professor of architecture at UH, became a well-known short story writer. In college, Barthelme studied journalism and wrote articles for the *Houston Post* but was drafted into the U.S. Army to serve in Korea. When he returned to Houston, he resumed his studies at UH and

**LAMAR TRIVIA**
"What won't they think of next?" This question was asked in 1944 by an amazed English class that has just listened to a Shakespearean play which "came forth on the Victrola."

writing for the *Post*. In 1961, he became the director of Houston's Contemporary Art Museum and that same year published his first short story in the *New Yorker*. The magazine published many of his stories, and his compact fiction, sometimes called flash fiction, "defined the next several decades of short fiction." Barthelme was one of the founders of the UH Creative Writing Program. His former graduate student Thomas Cobb says his character Bad Blake, hero of the recent movie *Crazy Heart*, was modeled in part on Barthelme.[84]

Ty Hardin (Class of 1949) was Orison Whipple Hungerford when he graduated from Lamar, but "Ty" was already his nickname. After serving in Korea, he went to Texas A&M on a football scholarship. He left and moved to California, where he was working as an aircraft technician when Paramount Pictures discovered him. They offered him a contract and changed his name.[85]

*Ty Hardin's acting career soared when Clint Walker walked out on the television series* Cheyenne *and the studio chose Hardin to replace him. Other roles followed and after his contract ended he went overseas, where he appeared in everything from spaghetti westerns to an Australian television series.*

Any discussion of Lamar's contributions to the fine arts during this decade must include mention of the artists who were mentored by Norma Henderson, a proponent of contemporary art who made her studio available to her students. This Lamar teacher had a tremendous influence on her students, and though she produced little art herself, she had an extraordinary apartment on Mid Lane Street that Leila Gadbois calls "her canvas." Not only did Henderson inspire her art students, she also masterminded the sets and stage decorations for the various performances at the school.

James "Jack" Boynton (Class of 1945) was one of Henderson's many students who gained national recognition. A UH alum, Boynton taught there as well as at the San Francisco Art Institute, but the bulk of his time was spent painting. Worldwide art exhibitions and major collections at museums from New York City to Texas confirm this Lamar graduate's reputation. Boynton's work, which consisted of Modernist abstract paintings, made him an important person in the post-World War II Houston art world. In 2008, Boynton listed Houston artists who were active in the 1950s, 1960s, and 1970s, including his colleagues Henri Gadbois (Class of 1948) and Dick Wray (Class of 1952).

*Fine arts teacher Norma Henderson inspired two generations of Lamar artists.*

Henri Gadbois married Leila McConnell (Class of 1943), who is also an artist, and has spent six decades as a Houston artist. His work has been exhibited in such places as New York City, New Orleans, and Germany. He was honored in 1998 and 1999 as one of the Top 200 American Craftsmen by *Early American Life* magazine and *Early American Homes* magazine for the creation of artificial food safe for public display, and designed the pineapple ornament for the White House Christmas Tree. He says he still owns his classmate Jack Boynton's canvas that he spent a whole month's salary to purchase. Henri and Leila Gadbois were honored as Distinguished Alumni of Lamar High School in 2009.[86]

Another illustrious alum is noted physicist R. Norris Keeler (Class of 1947). He earned his BS in Chemical Engineering from Rice, MS from the University of Colorado, and PhD from the University of California, Berkeley. During his distinguished career Keeler has served as head of physics at the Lawrence Livermore National Laboratory and founding director of the Office of Naval Technology. He has received a "multitude of professional awards," including the Gold Medal of the American Society of Naval Engineers, which stated that Keeler had enhanced "the strength of the Nation's maritime power through innovative thinking, research acumen, and engineering expertise." In 1990, Keeler was appointed a member of the Technical Committee of the Armed Forces Communication and Electronics Association, and in 1992 was elected an associate director, receiving its Chairman's Award as well as its Gold Engineering Medal for his contributions in the area of mine warfare and laser communications. He has received a Gold Medal from the International Eurasian Academy of Sciences, and in 2010 was awarded the N. N. Semenov Gold Medal by the Russian Academy of Sciences for excellence in research accomplishments. In 2011, he was named Outstanding Engineering Alumnus of Rice University.[87]

Diplomat Samuel Winfield Lewis (Class of 1948) is an expert on the Middle East who has contributed articles to the *New York Times*, the *Washington Post*, the *Harvard Review*, and numerous other publications. He graduated magna cum laude from Yale and earned his MA from The School of Advanced International Studies at Johns Hopkins University. The recipient of six honorary doctoral degrees, Lewis had a thirty-one-year career with the U.S. Department of State that included serving as assistant secretary of state for International Organization Affairs, director of Policy Planning, ambassadorial appointments, and heading up the United States Institute of Peace from 1987 to 1993. Lewis sits on the U.S. Advisory Council of the Israel Policy Forum and has been featured in the documentary film *Back Door Channels: The Price of Peace* (2009). A frequent guest commentator on television and radio programs, Lewis is considered an expert on Middle Eastern affairs.[88]

*Pictured at the 2008 Distinguished Alumni Luncheon are honoree Joanne King Herring and her friend Carolyn Farb, two distinguished Houston women.*

Another LHS graduate who has achieved fame because of her work in the Middle East is Joanne Johnson (King Herring Davis). A 1940s graduate, she attended the University of Texas, but left to marry Robert King, a real estate developer. She was an early Houston television star, hosting a talk show on the KHOU and KPRC Houston television stations for fifteen years. Her birthday party for her second husband, oilman Robert Herring, was covered by *LIFE* Magazine.

Herring's role in helping the people of Afghanistan was the basis for the film *Charlie Wilson's War*, and she was the heroine played by Julia Roberts in the film. Herring has received the Freedom Foundation at Valley Forge Award, was knighted by the King of Belgium, and was made a Dame in the Order of St. Francis. Her life is impossible to pigeonhole—it has been social, public, political, theatrical, and philanthropic, a wider-than-normal range of activities, but not so unlike many other Lamar High School graduates.[89]

A spectacular University Interscholastic League (UIL) golfer, Bernard "Bernie" Jay Riviere (Class of 1949) won the unofficial high school golf championship at Cedar Crest Club in Dallas in 1947, but was not chosen for the 1948 Lamar team that won the thirty-six-hole medal play team trophy. In 1949, however, Riviere won the first UIL-sponsored championship at the San Antonio Country Club with a score of 148, birdying the last hole on the second eighteen to finish with a 73, two strokes ahead of teammate Don Addington. Riviere failed to qualify for professional golf, but did the next best thing by going into the golf course architecture and construction business with PGA golfer Dave Marr. The firm's pride and joy is its renovation of Memorial Park Golf Course.

## AFTER WORLD WAR II

When the Japanese surrendered on August 14, 1945, Houston celebrated with a downtown parade. During World War II, the city's industry expanded more than could have been imagined, changing Houston's economy from rural to urban. At the Senior Cabinet meeting held on March 31, 1947, Principal Moyes offered a proposal to change the traditional gray cap and gown to one of the school colors. The Cabinet chose light blue. Thus, a new tradition was established.

The William J. Moyes Chapter of the Quill and Scroll was established at Lamar, though the club has since dropped the principal's name. This organization is an international honorary society for high school journalists. The "H" Association, composed of athletes who have earned a letter in at least one of the Interscholastic League sports, was also created. Coaches

*This memorial plaque lists all of the Lamar students who were casualties of World War II.*

Hal Mickelson, J. E. Dickson, Donald Longcope, and J. D. Vaughn served as sponsors for this athletic organization, which honored all lettermen, recognizing their contributions to Lamar's athletic competitions.

With postwar enthusiasm, the senior class minutes of the Class of 1946 recorded its decision to hold a real prom. Plans were made to rent a ballroom, hire an orchestra, and print a program. After a vote of 102 for and fifty-nine against, they decided to have a "Program Dance." The first, sixth, and twelfth dances were reserved for one's date, and the number of stags allowed was to be decided at a later date. The dance programs had blank spaces for the rest of the dances to be filled in by friends and admirers.

The Texas City Disaster was the most newsworthy event in 1947. Loaded with chemicals, a French ship docked in Galveston Bay exploded, setting off a series of additional explosions that killed more than 500 people and caused $50 million in property damage. The *Lancer* reported that Lamar boys, "too numerous by far to list," came to the aid of the stricken area.

The Class of 1947 is still a close-knit group. Class members told *Houston Chronicle* journalist Claudia Feldman that they attribute their kinship to having been together during the war, experiencing everything from rationing to wearing homemade dresses. Feldman describes the members she interviewed during their 2012 reunion as "patriotic, optimistic and really innocent." As one class member said, despite the war, this was a "happy time to be a teen," living in "simple times."

*Jimmy Brill's Pow Wow Dance Card lists his partners. Normally the girls had the dance card, and the boys filled it out, but this was a dance given by a boys' social club.*

*The 1947 girls' bowling team, left to right: Emily Bertelsen, Carlita Wolbrett, Dakota Ehman, Carolyn Douglas, Grace Grierson, and Jackie Herron won first place in the citywide Junior Chamber of Commerce Bowling Tournament.*

Chapter Three: The 1940s | 65

*Apple crates, packing boxes, and scrap wood are piled to an unbelievable height for the 1949 bonfire.*

Lancer *photographer Charlie West (Class of 1949) poses with comedians Bud Abbott and Lou Costello backstage at Houston's Metropolitan Theater. (Courtesy of Charlie West)*

*All of the students gathered to watch the bonfire ignited and enjoy the mountain of fire located just behind the school. In 1949, this exciting event was held on the Thursday preceding the Friday night game played against Milby High School.*

## A Tumultuous Decade Ends

In 1948, the World War II Freedom Train finally reached Houston. The red-white-and-blue diesel Streamliner had begun its journey in Philadelphia and traveled 37,160 miles to visit all forty-eight states. President Harry Truman's idea to help celebrate the ending of the war, the Freedom Train drew crowds wherever it stopped so that citizens could examine the Declaration of Independence, the Bill of Rights, an original copy of the Constitution, the Emancipation Proclamation, the Gettysburg Address, the Iwo Jima flag, the German and Japanese surrender documents that ended World War II, and other precious documents and national treasures. Naturally, the Lamar Regimental Band was on hand at Union Station (Minute Maid Park), performing under the direction of Lee Keding.

The 1948 October issue of the *River Oaks Times* magazine echoed the students' memories of this decade:

> A fundamental pillar of the community—it is picnics in spring, it is football and basketball and dances in the gym. And it is more; it is education and a preparation for greater learning; it is trig quizzes and English themes. It is Lamar High School, with a map of Texas on the façade as big as a house and a spirit that carries all through life.

By 1949, the essence of Lamar had been established by the guiding hand of a principal who served as sponsor of the National Honor Society and conducted all Senior Cabinet meetings. Lamar students had won impressive UIL awards in writing, drama, and speech, as well as tennis and golf.

The City of Houston provided the perfect backdrop for these successes. In December 1949, the decade ended with General Dwight D. Eisenhower as the keynote speaker for the Houston Chamber of Commerce banquet. W. S. Bellows, concluding his year as the Chamber's president, praised Houston's fast-paced growth and the demand for "forward thinking" leadership that prevented the city leaders from having time to "consider the past," a telling commentary on Houston's inattention to the preservation of its existing environment. Bellows predicted that Houston's destiny was "to surge ahead among the major cities of the world." During the coming decade, Lamar High School, which had already established itself as a first-class school, would be part of this growth, and the best was yet to come.

*The Lamar Regimental Band, led by Lee Keding, was on hand at Union Station (Minute Maid Park) to perform for the Houston spectators who crowded aboard the Freedom Train.*

# CHAPTER FOUR
## THE 1950s

*This nighttime view of Main Street Houston at the end of the 1940s captures the city's exciting commercial growth that continued to increase during the 1950s. (Courtesy of Story Sloane Gallery)*

### POISED FOR SUCCESS

During the next decade, Lamar High School leapfrogged over other Houston high schools in academic honors, athletic triumphs, and fine arts awards. The main reasons for their continued success were the factors that propelled the school forward when it first opened: faculty and demographics. Lamar began receiving recognition as a public school functioning as a college preparatory school where 95 percent of the graduates were college bound. One former graduate described the sense among the student body that almost everyone was going to do well in life because Lamar was such a great school.

Principal William J. Moyes, a scholar who inspired integrity and school spirit, was still the voice of the school. He set the course for Lamar, and his unwavering direction inculcated high academic standards. Although few high school principals sponsor a club or organization, Moyes, when Lamar received its National Honor Society charter, decided to serve as sponsor. He served in that capacity for his sixteen years as principal, conveying by his interest and guidance the importance he placed upon scholarship. The principal's sponsorship of NHS was not continued after Moyes retired.

When Moyes left Sam Houston to become Mirabeau B. Lamar's first principal, he had brought with him the nucleus of Lamar's faculty, including the coaching staff and a number of excellent teachers who remained at Lamar for almost three decades, and whose contributions were incalculable. Among these teachers were Misses H. Lel Red and Drew Black Staggs. Miss Drew Black Staggs taught English at Lamar

*The scarcity of photos of Drew Black Staggs indicates that this UT beauty queen was not fond of cameras. This photo appeared in the 1941* Orenda.

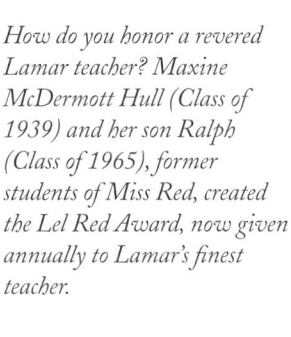

*How do you honor a revered Lamar teacher? Maxine McDermott Hull (Class of 1939) and her son Ralph (Class of 1965), former students of Miss Red, created the Lel Red Award, now given annually to Lamar's finest teacher.*

for twenty-four years and required students to stand to recite their answers. A 1911 graduate of the University of Texas where she was a Bluebonnet Belle, Staggs resided at the Warwick Hotel for the rest of her life. For many years, she sponsored the Lamar honors organization Arrowhead and the *Orenda*. Sandra Nobles Wilson (Class of 1959) remembers Miss Staggs' floral print dresses with eyelet collars, and her mantra for female students, "Gather ye rosebuds while ye may."

Miss H. Lel Red taught mathematics at Lamar for twenty-seven years. The daughter of a prominent Houston doctor who served on the HISD school board for many years, she was in the Rice Institute's first graduating class (1916), and took her MA in Mathematics from Columbia University. Many of her former students still praise her teaching skills and remember her often-repeated admonition: "You should be ashamed to let this problem master you."

Lamar's faculty knew the ropes. They had been a part of the traditions established, and continued taking a lead in preserving the intellectual and moral climate of the school. Dean of women Mrs. Ruth Leavell, a fixture at Lamar for three decades, was a stern disciplinarian and, as one alumna said, caused her the shivers if she just walked by. Librarian Edith Cox, registrar Edith Ferrell, and attendance clerk Mrs. Alice Harrell, along with twenty-one members of the original faculty, were still at Lamar at that time.

Newcomers Lee S. Keding, F. Lee Duggan, Hazelle McCarty, and the legendary Marcile Hollingsworth and Helen Greenwood came to Lamar in the 1940s. Ruth Denney came in 1952. They were significant additions to the faculty who added their expertise to the legacy of superior teaching and achieved iconic status.

Celia Buchan (Class of 1953) in her autobiography called the teachers "first rate," and described their classrooms as "orderly, busy, and sometimes fun."[90] Lamar was the "hot-shot public high school in Houston, as academically rigorous as they got in Texas in the 1950s."[91] Having grown up in a modest bungalow in West University Place, Buchan considered Lamar her "introduction to the life of Texas' super-rich," and though "dazzled" by the lifestyles of her classmates, she soon learned that these class differences, "which nobody acknowledged, were not insurmountable."[92] As an example, she noted that "a girl who lived in a bungalow, sang like Judy Garland, or played a good game of tennis was just as welcome in any group… as a girl whose father was president of Shell [Oil]."[93]

By 1958, Lamar's faculty numbered 104 teachers who had attended fifty colleges. Eighty had master's degrees, and three had doctoral degrees. They taught forty different subjects and sponsored thirty-nine clubs. Lamar's enrollment was now 2,129 students. The faculty strongly supported the students, and all said they loved "to see Lamar win."[94] During the 1950s, more than 300 Lamar students graduated from Rice University, beating the 1940s record of 261. One graduate recalls that when he and his friends received their Rice acceptance notices, they went to the admissions director because one of their friends had received a rejection notice. They convinced Rice to admit him.

*Author Celia Buchan (Class of 1953) was a member of the May Fete Court at Lamar. Elected to Phi Beta Kappa as well as University Sweetheart at UT, she met and married Rhodes Scholar Willie Morris, the acclaimed author of* North Toward Home.

The second important contribution to Lamar's rising star was demographics. The school drew from the upper middle-class subdivisions surrounding Rice Institute: Southampton, Southgate, West University Place, and Braeswood. These were neighborhoods "started by men who were successful in their professions and leaders in the community."[95] Generally speaking, these parents were so pleased with Lamar High School's reputation that, although more and more could afford private schools, they chose instead this unique public school that functioned as a free "prep" school.

## HOUSTON: A CITY WITH GREAT EXPECTATIONS

World War II had brought many changes to Houston, a place now being described as a city with the Midas touch. George Fuermann, longtime *Houston Post* columnist and author of several books about Houston, pointed to "newborn industrial giants" who capitalized on natural gas, which he called the "lusty relation" of oil.[96] Herman and George Brown's Texas Eastern Transmission Corporation, H. Gardiner Symonds' Tennessee Gas Transmission Company, and Claude Williams' Transcontinental Gas Pipe Line Corporation became magnets for white-collar professionals who sought to fill jobs in a city that was now, according to Marvin Hurley, the "dominant market center of the Southwest."[97] In December 1951, General Robert E. Wood, chairman of the board of Sears and Roebuck, correctly prophesied that "within 50 years… Houston will be the fourth or fifth [largest] city" in the United States.[98]

The Texas Medical Center was also undergoing significant expansion. Dr. E. W. Bertner, in a 1951 address to the Kiwanis Club, announced that groundbreaking had begun for the Texas Children's Hospital, St. Luke's Episcopal Hospital, and the M. D. Anderson Hospital for Cancer Research. Three major Houston hospitals broke ground in the same year and opened within three years.[99]

The four-lane Gulf Freeway formally opened in 1952 at a cost of $1.5 million per mile.[100] The city's phenomenal growth was noticed by journalists across the nation. During the 1950s, Houston began acquiring the reputation that has expanded a thousand-fold today. George Fuermann called the city an "air-conditioned Tower of Babel." Fuermann quoted several journalists who were enamored of the city. One described it as "a fascinating and confusing place… a city with its sleeves rolled up, moving with the rhythm of a riveter." In 1955, a reporter for the *London Daily Mail* wrote, "Houston has caused me to lift my ban on the word fabulous." In 1956, the *London Times* wrote that America might "eventually be based on a quadrilateral of great cities—NYC, Chicago, Los Angeles, and Houston." To be a second-generation Houstonian was a distinction in this town where new residents were pouring in.[101]

The "trickle up" impact of the industrial growth which occurred as a result of World War II affected Houston's banks and retail institutions, housing, and commercial construction. During the decade from 1950 to 1960, retail sales increased 90.4 percent and wholesale sales increased 117.6 percent.[102]

The astronomical growth of the airline industry in Houston from 1950 to 1960 was difficult for city officials to keep up with. Six major airlines, two local ones, and an airfreight business were serviced by Houston Municipal Airport, whose passengers increased from 85,000 in 1944 to 538,000 in 1950.[103] Houston International Airport, which opened in 1954 (renamed the William P. Hobby Airport in 1967), was built to handle this increase, but proved inadequate.[104] As a remedy, seventeen businessmen bought 3,126 acres in Northeast Houston, held the property, and then sold it to the City of Houston at cost. Work began in 1962 for the new $100-million airport.[105]

*Houston International Airport (renamed William Hobby Airport in 1967) was erected in 1954 to handle increased air traffic but within a year the facility was deemed inadequate. (Courtesy of Story Sloane Gallery)*

## New Additions to Lamar

Lamar's success was tied to the city's success. Mirroring the city's record growth, Lamar High School was bulging at the seams. In May 1949, the school board had approved a remodeling project at Lamar High School to be completed in 1951.[106] The project included the following additions:

- A soundproof music room for band and orchestra members
- A radio and electronics shop
- Two rooms for mechanical drawing
- One storage room to be used (in a somewhat odd combination) as a music storage room and as an armory room for the ROTC
- A new boys' gym with dressing rooms, lockers, and showers (girls and boys would no longer share a gym)
- Bleachers to seat 1,000 people

As part of the renovation, the outside of the building, including the map—marred by stains from ink and other liquids thrown by rival high schools—was scraped and sandblasted. Kenneth Franzheim, who shared the architectural preferences of the original designers, was the architect for the renovation, and LeBlanc, Inc. was the contractor. The final cost almost equaled the construction cost of the 1937 school building.[107]

The Lamar Class of 1951 numbered a "walloping" 430 graduates. *The Houston Press* printed a photograph of Lamar's senior class with a caption calling Lamar's opening in 1937 "a good year for the school that was out in the country,"[108] and noted that the school had matured with the city. Pictured on the same page was the senior class of the new private college preparatory school across the street. St. John's School held its first commencement in 1951, graduating twenty-five students. These young people had been enrolled by their parents in what the reporter called a "country-day type school," founded in 1946 on seven rolling acres. St. John's headmaster Alan Chidsey, when interviewed about his school, said, "We have no social clubs and the students wear uniform dress," a pointed reference to the differences between St. John's and their rival across the street.

*Sophomores Rob Peebles, Bobby Jean Ray, Mary Petersen, Donald Stewart, and Sally Stedman are proudly eyeing construction on the three-story wing that provided seven additional classrooms and a new gym.*

### A Tragic Chemistry Experiment at Lamar

John Cramer, David Dillman, William Montgomery, Jr., and Ted Strong were second-semester juniors and enthusiastic science students. Cramer had for some time built model rockets. Strong, too, was interested in rockets. Cramer had always mixed fuel in small quantities, but "Strong decided to mix up a full quart jar of his special blend of rocket fuel all at once."[109] On Wednesday afternoon, November 21, 1951, Strong took from the chemistry lab supply room red phosphorous, magnesium, potassium chlorate, and strontium and mixed them in a pickle jar.

Strong and Cramer carried the pickle jar and its highly explosive fuel mixture through Lamar's hallways at the end of the school day, just as students were leaving their classrooms. The two exited on the west side of the building where they joined Dillman and Montgomery in the parking lot. What happened next is not certain. Strong either shook or dropped the pickle jar containing the explosive mixture. At 3:05 p.m., hundreds of students and teachers heard the deafening explosion and saw a brilliant orange flash. Cramer, Dillman, Montgomery, and Strong were blown to the ground.

Four ambulances arrived. Montgomery was not seriously injured. Ted Strong, gravely injured, was rushed to Jefferson Davis Hospital and died shortly after arrival. The other two students suffered horrific injuries. Dillman was badly maimed. Cramer was blown backwards onto the grass, had glass fragments in his face, and suffered mangled fingers. Cramer missed a month of school recovering from his injuries. He describes the unprecedented accident as the "dark side" of the group's enthusiasm for science.

The *Houston Post* said Ted Strong's objective was "soaring to the stars" in a rocket, an ironic twist on the school's motto. The newspaper printed the hand-drawn rocket ship appearing in Strong's Lamar notebook, along with his list of chemicals needed for this experiment.

Strong was said by the *Post* to have "lived" chemistry. A week earlier, Strong's chemistry teacher, Miss Marcile Hollingsworth, had met in conference with Strong and his parents, cautioning the three of them about Ted's interest in dangerous explosives, but Strong, according to the *Post*, was confident of his ability to handle chemicals.[110]

The tragedy momentarily clouded Lamar's unblemished citywide reputation, but it did not put an end to either Cramer's or Dillman's interest in science. Lamar's after-school science club, sponsored by Edna Ruth Miner and Marcile Hollingsworth, continued to be of great interest to these budding scientists. When three Lamar Science Club members went to the 1953 Texas Junior Academy of Science competition at Texas Christian University in Fort Worth, Cramer says, "we made a 'sweep,' winning the first, second, and third prizes in the competition." Cramer won second prize for a paper based on Richard Feynman's quantum-electrodynamics that represented positrons as electrons going backwards in time. Dillman won a first prize for his paper on the chemical identification of minerals. The following year, Dillman entered his first-prize paper in the University of Houston Science Competition, where it won Best Paper. It was published in the *Mineralogist* in October 1952, the first article written by a high school student to appear in this national magazine for geological engineers. Dillman served as president of the Science Club, and Cramer served as treasurer.

Montgomery was elected class poet of his 1953 mid-term class. (Mid-term refers to those seniors who graduate in January instead of June.) His senior class poem was a light-hearted look at his days at Lamar except for these lines, which possibly referred to his friend Teddy Strong: "Our friends whom some again we'll never see… with them forever in heart and soul, for they like us were poured in the same mold."[111]

## Redskins Athletic Victories: The Glory Days

In 1950, Lamar won the University Interscholastic League state championships in both track and basketball as well as the B team football city championship, beginning a decade that brought Lamar unprecedented athletic victories. The 1953 UIL State Championship, Lamar's first state championship in football, was the icing on the cake.

"The King of Swim" was Houston sportswriters' label for Lamar High School. By 1951, Lamar swimmers had won the city championship four times, the state title three times, and the second-place state title twice. A Houston sportswriter noted that it was now expected rather than unusual for Lamar swimmers to take the state championship. These state wins in swimming, held in various Texas cities, were invitational meets, not UIL competitions.

*This handsome swim trophy was a fine addition to Lamar's trophy case. (Courtesy of Will LeBlanc)*

*The 1951 winning Redskins swim team is shown here. The Lamar swim team held the best record of all Lamar sports teams, and during the 1950s captured the state championship or was runner-up every single year.*

*The members of the 1950 football team have forged incredible lifelong friendships.*

The 1950 football team also had a great season, scoring a total of 325 points compared to their opponents' meager twenty-six points. But then they played Reagan for the city championship. An unprecedented crowd of 14,000 gathered at Public School Stadium to watch as the two-touchdown underdog Reagan Bulldogs beat the Lamar Redskins 6 to 0. *Houston Press* sportswriter John Hollis wrote of this momentous game, "Every once in a while along comes a football game in which something happens to lift it out of the plain vanilla and into the ranks of the long-remembered."

How true his words were for the 1950 Lamar teammates who are alive today. When the eight-millimeter tapes of this playoff game were found in the attic of the boys' gym and converted to a DVD, Lamar Redskins letterman back Julio Laguarta, whom sportswriters had called "The Brain," set up a luncheon for Lamar and their opponents, the "spirited" Reagan Bulldogs, to watch a replay. The meeting provided an opportunity for the rivals to get together sixty-two years later and enjoy reliving every play of this memorable game. Tom Biggs and Lew Harpold were excellent players. Eddie Rayburn and Kenneth Paul were named to the All-City team, and Larry Graham achieved All-American recognition.

"A football-fevered attack" was how the Austin High principal explained his students' 1950 attack on the Lamar campus. The rivalry between the two teams had simmered for a long time, fed by numerous encounters. This time Austin claimed they were retaliating for a Lamar raid two nights before in which Lamar students painted "Yea Lamar" in red paint on the sidewalks and building.

Austin's raid was considerably more serious and had to be broken up by the River Oaks Police, who did not arrive in time to prevent damage to Lamar's building: the tops of four concrete benches were ripped off and flung against the front door of the school, and three windows were broken. Police apprehended two of twelve carloads of Austin students. A police search revealed a twelve-gauge shotgun, a pair of brass knuckles, two billy clubs, and a bottle of green paint.

An entire sheet of Lamar school songs illustrated their grudge against Austin. Songs ranged from "Mustang Stew" to the "Horse Meat" yell (Austin's mascot was a beloved horse named Stevie). The most vivid was sung to the tune "Yankee Doodle":

> Stevie Austin came to town
> Upon a scrawny pony,
> He thought football would bring renown,
> But it was all baloney.
>
> Stevie Austin mind your step,
> The Redskins are behind you,
> Stevie Austin, please get help,
> Or leave your scalp behind you.

That year, perhaps because of the Austin raid at their school, the Lamar Redskins football team beat the Austin Mustangs, 52 to 0.

The 1950 B football team, called the Papooses, won the city championship, a fact which helps explain why Lamar remained a gridiron powerhouse for the next two years. Charlie Leyendecker, Jimmy McBride, Rudy Spitzenberger, and Sonny Cutbirth continued as key players and lettermen for the next two seasons.

Houston sportswriters called Larry Graham (Class of 1951) "Lamar's work horse," and he was indisputably one of Lamar's finest athletes. Graham, the son of semi-pro baseball player Lefty Graham, grew up in Southside Place, became a football star, was chosen All-City, and was elected to the sportswriters' mythical All-American Grid Team in 1950.

Graham's finest victories, though, were in track, in which he won Lamar's first UIL state track championships for single events, placing first in both the 120-yard high hurdle competition and the broad jump contest. The 1952 track team handily won the city and regional championships thanks to Sonny Cutbirth, who was the team's high individual point-scorer. Their team points totaled sixty-five, and Reagan came in second with a total of

Coach Hartung smiles with his 1950 State Championship Track Team.

*Lamar's 1950 track team won the city championship as well as the ultimate prize: the UIL Overall Team State Championship.*

only thirty-five points. The team's new coach, Bert Kivell, forecast a strong coming season with six returning lettermen: Bobby Whilden, Joe Bright, Roy Thompson, Jim Johnston, C. B. Stephenson, and Rudy Spitzenberger. Even after Graham graduated, in 1953 the Redskins track team won their fourth straight district crown and their seventh first-place city crown in eight years.

Bobby Whilden, an outstanding runner, won the UIL State Championship in the 220-yard dash in 1953. Three years later he became an Olympic Trials finalist in the 100- and 200-meter competition. Entering the University of Texas on a track scholarship, he led the Longhorns to South West Conference titles in 1956 and 1957. After Whilden took his law degree, he put away his track shoes and joined Vincent & Elkins.

Twenty-five years later, Whilden resumed his track career and has continued to set remarkable records that honor his alma mater. In 2005, at the age of seventy, he won the 100-meter dash in 12.76 seconds, breaking the World Record of 12.91 seconds. At the National Senior Games in Pittsburgh, Pennsylvania, he won the 200-meter dash in the seventy-to-seventy-four age group. The following year, he won the 60-meter dash and the 200-meter dash, setting both national and world records at the National Masters Indoor Championship in Boston, Massachusetts. In 2011, competing in Utah in the seventy-five-to-seventy-nine age group, Whilden set another American record in the 100-meter dash. Whilden was honored as a Lamar Distinguished Alum in 2006.

In 1950, headlines read "Lamar—State Champs—Basketball." Sportswriters and spectators who saw Lamar's game with Alamo Heights called Lamar "the Best Basketball Team in Texas High Schools." Lamar's seventy-eight-point win was the highest score ever registered in a state tournament. Hoopster Phillip Kidd, the "fiery red-headed Lamar forward," was the unanimous choice of local coaches for the All-City basketball team, along with "Slim" Tommy Hill, once described in the *Houston Post* as a bundle of energy and a scoring leader. Both players also made All-State, and Donald

*The 1956 track team was undefeated and untied in ten straight meets. Its superb relay team included Captain Bobby Parks, Wayland Whipple, Bill Gallagher, Wayne Dunlop, and Most Valuable Team Member Frank Price.*

Longcope, who had been coaching basketball at Lamar for thirteen years, was named basketball's Texas Coach of the Year.[112]

The 1952–1953 basketball team finished in second place behind Austin High School, the city champs. But a star who would seriously impact the 1953–1954 Redskins football and basketball seasons was on the horizon. Walter Fondren III, a back for the football team and a guard for the basketball team, was warming up his act. Fondren was already being called the "big gun" in Lamar's defensive lineup. The 1956 basketball season brought Lamar another second-place city win, this time behind Milby, but the Redskins players were well represented on the *Houston Post*'s All-District team. Kenny Bell and Richard Tinsley were both selected. Tinsley, the city's high point-scorer, made the team because of his good long shots, rebounds, and constant "hustling," and Bell was the team's "dynamo ace dribbler."

## THE 1953 LAMAR REDSKINS FOOTBALL TEAM

The year 1953 remains a benchmark for Lamar football history. The Lamar Redskins not only won their first state championship in football, but also gave the City of Houston its first state win as well. Houston had been "denied any part of the state championship since 1920,"[113] when Heights High, as Reagan was often called, and Cleburne shared a co-championship after a scoreless deadlock.

When Lamar won the semifinals, guaranteeing them a chance to win state, Peewee Whitley, owner of Highland Village Barber Shop, offered the forty-two-member team and their four coaches free haircuts on the eve of the game. All forty-six accepted his offer.[114]

*Pictured at left is the state championship football trophy Lamar received.*

Between 17,000 and 20,000 spectators came to Rice Stadium at 2 p.m. on December 19, 1953, a cold, rainy Saturday, to watch this never-to-be-forgotten event. Spectator Lynn Zarr (Class of 1959), then twelve years old, says it was his earliest memory of Lamar. The game's turning point occurred when Walter Fondren and Mickey Smith, each weighing 160 pounds, completed an all-important twenty-eight-yard pass. Lamar's 33-to-7 victory against the powerhouse Odessa team was such a rout that Coach Bob Schulze felt comfortable sending every member of the team in to play, so that each was able to experience this "once in a lifetime opportunity." Fondren, who went on to play football for the University of Texas, was chosen All-Southwest Conference Halfback in 1955 and elected to the University of Texas Hall of Honor in 1983.[115]

*Walter Fondren (Class of 1954), who excelled as a runner, passer, kicker, pass receiver, and defender, was chosen Most Valuable Player in the city and the state. He was honored as a Distinguished Alum in 2001.*

*The Lamar golf team received this trophy when they won the city championship in 1953. (Courtesy of Will LeBlanc)*

Lamar's state championship won Hall of Fame status for their coach, Rice graduate Bob Schulze. The following year, Schulze left Lamar to become the athletic director in the Conroe Independent School District, and later joined Darrell Royal as an assistant coach for the Longhorns.

## Golf and Tennis

Lamar High School students always excelled at golf and tennis. These are the sports many of their parents enjoyed playing and undoubtedly encouraged their children to learn, hence their popularity at Lamar. The tennis team won first in city from 1952 to 1955, placed in every tournament throughout the decade, and opened its 1959 season with seven nationally ranked players. Karl Kamrath, Jr. consistently won matches during his three years at Lamar, as did Jonathan Day and Jimmy Bertrand.

In golf the story was the same, with Lamar taking city, if not district and region, most years. The 1957 team included a young man who later, as an adult, was elected to the Texas Golf Hall of Fame. As a Lamar golfer, Homero Blancas (Class of 1957), along with Bill Kohlhausen, Paul Brindley, and Bob Brent, advanced to win fifth in state. Blancas grew up in modest quarters on the grounds of the River Oaks Country Club, where his father was a greenskeeper. When he was eight years old, he began caddying, and over the years worked hard to become like the players he saw shooting in the 70s.

Five years after Blancas graduated from Lamar, he shot a 55 on a par-70 course in the Premier Invitational Amateur Tournament, "a day of golf like no other," Dan Jenkins later chronicled in *Sports Illustrated*.[116] When

Blancas turned pro in 1965, he was chosen Rookie of the Year and went on to win four PGA Tour events. In 1973, he was a member of the Ryder Cup team. He joined the Senior Tour when he turned fifty and won the 1989 Doug Sanders Kingwood Celebrity Classic.

## GIRLS' ATHLETICS

Women athletes today may have a hard time grasping what girls' sports were like in the 1950s. It was twenty years before the passage of Title IX, and there were no scholarships or accolades for girls who played sports. Despite the lack of opportunity for a free ticket to college, Lamar girls' teams competed enthusiastically and successfully in the city, if not the state. In 1951, LHS girls won their first city championships in both volleyball and archery. Their city title victories continued throughout the 1950s. Carol Childress won first place in individual scoring in archery, helping to secure the girls' city archery title in 1957. The Lamar girls' swim team also consistently placed first in the city.

*In 1952, the "Pinball Punks Cherokee III League" composed of Lolly Anderson, Margaret Diamond, Carol Whitehurst, Sara Moers, and Captain Jerilyn Rice won the Texas State Junior Championship bowling trophy given by the Texas Women's Bowling Association.*

## THE RESERVE OFFICERS TRAINING CORPS

From the 1940s to the 1950s, the Reserve Officers Training Corps was a very popular organization at Lamar. World War II fueled its membership in the 1940s and the Korean conflict fueled it in the 1950s. Many of the students planned to go to Texas A&M, and ROTC training gave them a jump on the Aggie program. In HISD every high school had an ROTC battalion made up of their two or three companies. The combined battalions made up the Houston Regiment, and Lamar provided the Regimental Band.

Lamar had three companies. Classes were held daily in the mornings, and

*The varsity bowling team composed of Captain Mary Rostrom, Candy Walling, Sheryl McKelvy, Cynthia Gude, Nancy Noble, and Betty Sears posed with the Houston Senior High School Bowling Championship trophy they won in 1952. (Courtesy of Will LeBlanc)*

students were required to wear uniforms three times per week. Classroom activities consisted of inspections for weapon proficiency (disassembly and reassembly, usually blindfolded), marching, and studying the ROTC manual used nationwide.

Most college ROTC programs gave credit to students who took ROTC for three years in high school and extra credit to those who were officers. Officers were elected by members according to superiority in the skills taught. The school ROTC programs were run by an Army lieutenant and a sergeant, both veterans of World War II and Korea. School assignments were coveted by ROTC instructors, who "rode out their service years toward retirement."[117]

*Clem Barrere's ROTC awards are displayed. A partial identification includes, top row, left to right: Junior Chamber of Commerce Medal, Drill Platoon Patch, Academic Award Wreath, and Bettes Award Medal. Second row: Expert Marksmanship Medal, Epaulets, Outstanding City Cadet medals, Rifle Team Marksmanship Medal, and a whistle worn by members of the exhibition Drill Platoon. (Courtesy of Clem Barrere)*

*For nearly twenty years, Lamar provided the Regimental Band for all of the ROTC events in the city. In 1956, this band was changed into a traditionally uniformed school band, but it remained an all-male band.*

The girls who were elected sponsors, a highly coveted honor, were permitted to march with the three companies, wearing uniforms similar to those worn by the Women's Army Corps (WAC) in World War II even though they were not officially members. They were also allowed to organize their own rifle team and usually outshot the boys.[118] Their real duty, however, was to be secretaries for each of the three companies. The lieutenant and sergeant on the Lamar faculty each had his own "sponsor secretary," as did the student battalion commander and the battalion adjutant. ROTC student competitions usually resulted in twenty-four ribbons, medals, or both per student, awards that had to be recorded in triplicate, an enormous amount of paperwork in the days before copy machines. The female sponsors maintained these records, and the "typewriters were burning all the time."[119]

In 1956, graduating senior Clem Barrere, Jr. was chosen Outstanding Third Year Cadet in all the ROTC units in the Houston high schools, an award based on written, oral, and practical competition. He was promoted to cadet colonel and was made regimental commander of all of the ROTC units in Houston, and was also given a gold watch. He received the Bettes Award given to the outstanding third-year cadet and was awarded the Map Reading Efficiency Ribbon. After graduation from Lamar, Barrere entered Yale and graduated with a degree in chemical engineering. He later earned his PhD at Rice.[120]

In 1956, Lamar's Regimental Military Band was changed into a regular school band. Interest and participation in ROTC had begun to decline in the mid-fifties as the Korean conflict was settled and public interest in the military waned. The new peacetime programs required only six months of active duty for draftees, and college deferments were automatic. By 1956, Lamar students realized the inadvisability of a military career, with little probability of war in the future.

## Lamar's Top Fan Retires

Principal William J. Moyes announced that 1953 would be his last year as principal of Lamar High School. Former students, current students, faculty, and the community responded with accolades, a Texas-style barbecue, and rewards. The event, held at Rice Stadium, was organized by Howard Tellepsen, Sr., who had been Moyes' student at Central High School and was soon to be elected president of the Houston Chamber of Commerce; Frank W. Sharp, 1952–1953 president of the Lamar High School PTA and the developer of Sharpstown; and E. T. Shaw, charter member of the Lamar Dad's Club.

The tribute drew a crowd of 2,000 who watched as Mayor Roy Hofheinz presented Moyes with the keys to a new, two-toned green Oldsmobile 88 "so that he can do a little traveling."[121] Among those who told stories was Harry Pepper, who was a student at Sam Houston High School (Class of 1930). Pepper vividly remembered when he went to jail for ramming the front of a downtown Houston drug store with his Model T Ford. Worried that he would also be expelled from school, he was surprised when Moyes instead handed him his Latin, history, and algebra books and told him to spend the time in jail studying so he could catch up with the work he missed and still play football. *Houston Post* columnist Morris Frank, master of ceremonies, told stories about Moyes and cracked jokes about the school board. The Lamar ROTC Marching Band played for the occasion under the direction of Lee S. Keding, and a catered barbecue dinner was served after the program. The *Lancer* headline read, "Thousands Honor Moyes on Eve of Retirement."

One of the most historically valuable gifts Moyes received was the book put together by Lamar's Palamar Club and dedicated to "the principal we have loved and admired, whose understanding and guidance have challenged the students of Lamar High School to greater accomplishments." This handsome embossed book is an historical treasure that contains the senior class presidents' commencement addresses, the class poems, and the class wills from 1937 to 1953. The class will, a high school tradition, was always written by the seniors and assembled by the class lawyer. Here is a sample of a typical class will:

> To the students remaining we leave a school we both helped and hindered: helped by the records we have established and upheld; scholastically, in speech and drama, and in sports; and hindered by our wear and tear on the building and grounds and on the nerves of our teachers.

*At Moyes' retirement party, Mayor Roy Hofheinz gave him keys to a new, two-toned green Oldsmobile 88 so he could "do a little traveling." Mr. and Mrs. Moyes pose with their new automobile.*

Ralph O'Leary's *Houston Post* column, "Titled Texans," called Moyes small, wiry, and elfin-like.[122] The reporter quoted the scholarly principal, who loved Lamar and Lamar football, as saying he had missed only two of Lamar's football games in sixteen years. William J. Moyes (the "J" stands for Joy, his mother's family name) expressed his preference for teaching over administration "since the principal sees only the top and the bottom of the enrollment, missing a chance to better know those in the middle group."[123]

Later in 1953, school officials designated Moyes as Lamar's principal emeritus in recognition of his service to the school. He died on July 1, 1959, at the age of seventy-six. Moyes once said, "Nothing is more interesting than classroom work. Contact with the youngsters when they are learning is an inspiring job."[124] Mr. J. H. Wright left his job as HISD personnel director and returned to Lamar, where he had been assistant principal under Moyes. Wright was the school's second principal and served from 1953 until his retirement in 1957.

## Lamar Continues to Polish its Image

By no means were athletics Lamar High School's only claim to fame during this decade. Drama students, taught by Ruth Denney, won first place in the state UIL One-Act Play Championship for five years, the only Texas school ever to have done so.

Additional state wins included the UIL Ready Writing Championship, twice, with Joan Bartheleme and Bob Ball placing first in Copy Editing. In the Speech and Debate category, Lamar took many UIL state victories. In 1954, Jimmy Brannon won the Boys' State Declamation Championship. Patsy Heard and Carmen Stallings were Extemporaneous Speaking champions in 1954 and 1957. Lamar won five Team Debate state championships: 1951, 1952, 1953, 1955, and 1958. The Columbia Scholastic Press Association held its thirty-second annual contest at Columbia University in NYC, and Lamar High School, with 909 points out of a possible 1,000, won first place. Lamar regularly won this award for the next two decades. The *Lancer*, which sold at a bargain seventy-five cents per semester, received a superior rating for its sports coverage and news stories. In the National Scholastic Press Association's contest held at the University of Minnesota in Minneapolis, the *Orenda* placed as one of the top ten high school yearbooks in the nation.

*Top, left to right: Dorothy Dobbins, Graham Campbell, Roy Hofheinz, Jr., Jimmy Wychoff, and Joan Field look with pride at the speech trophies they won in 1953.*

*Bottom: These debate trophies are only a sampling of the many which have been won by Lamar's Forensic League during the school's seventy-five-year history. (Courtesy of Will LeBlanc)*

Academically, Lamar overpowered other Houston high schools during the 1950s. During this decade, usually over half of Houston's high school seniors who qualified to apply for National Merit Scholarships were Lamar students. In 1957, Lamar received a superior Texas Education Agency (TEA) rating. W. R. Goodson, director of the school accreditation division, spent half a day at Lamar with Principal Wright. Very impressed with Lamar's rating as a college preparatory school, Goodson was surprised the school could also offer an outstanding athletic program, an award-winning dramatic program, and a well-recognized newspaper and yearbook.[125]

"What Makes Them Good?" asked *Time* Magazine in 1957. The article outlined steps taken by Robert Marschner, a school board president in Homewood, Illinois, to determine the factors that make a superior high school. Homewood was planning a large new high school and wanted to "do things right." Marschner wrote to the principals of thirty-five public high schools and three private schools that had nationally ranked records of excellence.

"Old-fashioned hard work," the educational level of the community, and the quality of the faculty were the answers Marschner received. The principals also pointed to the importance of having a good library, grouping students according to ability regardless of the danger of "injuring their young psyches," and giving frequent examinations and long hours of homework.

Mirabeau B. Lamar High School and Dallas' Highland Park High School were the only two Texas schools on the list of thirty-eight.[126] Lamar's inclusion was not surprising. A 1956 graduate recalls stories, presumably told by college admissions representatives, that Lamar and Highland Park were the two top academically rated high schools, including public, private, and parochial. According to his research, "only ten of the 654 graduating seniors in 1956 did not go on to college, and 8 percent of the entering fall freshmen at Rice Institute that year came from Lamar." Ivy League colleges became more interested in Lamar, and in November 1957, nine sent representatives to visit with Lamar students. Houston alumni representatives from Barnard, Bryn Mawr, Mount Holyoke, Radcliffe, Smith, Vassar, and Wellesley came, many offering generous scholarships. Duke University and Washington University in St. Louis also visited the campus. Lamar High School was definitely now considered a public high school that graduated superior students. As one student stated, "Everyone in Houston knew that Lamar would be a serious contender in whatever category [we entered], and the thrill of being on top was worth the envy we generated."[127]

## Who Were These Superior Students?

Not all were "stars" in high school, but all admit that they graduated with a solid academic foundation. Alums say they did not drink or smoke, much less do drugs, and their most daring adventures were skinny-dipping in someone's pool or playing a "torrid game of spin the bottle."[128]

The following are a few of the Lamar graduates from the 1950s who left high school and went on to make national and occasionally international names for themselves in science, medicine, government and law, business and public service, finance, and the arts.

## SCIENCE

The decade of the 1950s is known as the "Golden Age of Science Education."[129] The National Science Foundation, created in 1950, was the leader in this movement that addressed the science teacher manpower shortage, and the concern that many high school science courses were inadequate in light of changes occurring in science and technology. The world of electronics was born during the decades from 1938 to 1958. Author Tom Green said prior to that time, "microprocessors were science fiction."[130] He termed this the "decade of the bright boys." Green was referring to participants in the Whirlwind Project, located a stone's throw from MIT and "rivaled only by the Manhattan Project," but this title aptly describes Lamar High School's emerging scientists.[131]

*Bob Wilson repaired radios and televisions for spending money and helped friends with their amateur radio transmitters. In 1978, forty-two-year-old Wilson was awarded the Nobel Prize for his discovery of cosmic background radiation.*

Robert Woodrow Wilson (Class of 1953), one of the youngest winners of the Nobel Prize, provides one example of a Lamar "bright boy." Wilson grew up in West University Place and describes his high school career as "undistinguished, except for math and science." The *Orenda* entry under his senior class photo lists his only activities as band and ROTC, no National Honor Society or Arrowhead! Wilson called his father an "inveterate do-it-yourselfer" with a keen interest in the relatively new field of electronics. He encouraged his son's tinkering with radios and televisions.[132]

Rice Institute, a college for which he says he was barely qualified, woke him up academically. For his Rice senior thesis, he built a regulator for a magnet for use in low-temperature physics. Graduating with honors in physics, Wilson took a summer job at Exxon, where he obtained his first patent. He entered Cal Tech to obtain a PhD in Physics and met a Cambridge astronomer who suggested he go into radio astronomy, which he says offered a nice mixture of electronics and physics. After graduation in 1962, he took a job with Bell Laboratories at Crawford Hill, Arizona, and in 1976 became the head of Bell's Radio Physics Research Department. When he was awarded the Nobel Prize in 1978, Wilson was only forty-two. The award was given for his discovery of cosmic background radiation. In 1979, Wilson was elected to the U.S. National Academy of Science, and is also a member of the American Astronomical Society, American Physical Society, and the American Academy of Arts and Sciences. His honors include Phi Beta Kappa, the 1977 Henry Draper Award, and the 1977 Herschel Medal. Wilson is a distinguished scientist whose achievements honor Lamar High School.[133]

Another physicist from the Class of 1953 is John G. Cramer, who describes himself as having been a skinny, non-athletic kid who had little money, no car, no girlfriend. He sold his senior prom ticket to a junior. Cramer says his friends were "smart" kids.[134]

*John Cramer, physicist and science fiction novelist, is a Fellow of the American Association for the Advancement of Science and of the American Physical Society.*

Cramer recognized his interest in building things and experimenting as a student at Lanier Junior High. From his avid reading of science fiction, he says he discovered that "there were people called scientists who were well paid to do what I would gladly do for free, and I decided to become an experimental scientist."[135]

Cramer says biology teacher Edna Ruth Miner and chemistry teacher Marcile Hollingsworth offered an after-school science club, which he joined. He considers this Lamar Science Club to have been a "very important part of my intellectual development in high school," and expresses regret that these after-school science programs no longer exist.[136] He won the citywide Bausch & Lomb Science Award.

When he was a senior, Cramer went to Principal Moyes and asked to take engineering drawing and machine shop courses in place of the required study hall. Moyes agreed, provided Cramer's grades did not suffer. This college-bound student was an anomaly in an industrial arts class, but metal shop teacher Arthur Herring understood what he wanted to learn.

Cramer was appointed lathe foreman, and Herring proudly displayed the optical spectroscope he built. Cramer credits his success in engineering classes at Rice to this instruction. As a physics graduate student he could "immediately produce detailed technical drawings of apparatus for the machine shop to build" and could walk into the machine shop in the middle of the night and make what he needed "on the fly" in the middle of a run on the accelerator.[137]

His experiences with Lamar English teachers were "mixed." They did not consider science fiction written after H. G. Wells to be "suitable for reading assignments and book reports." His English teachers appreciated neither his terse essays nor his use of irony and sarcasm. Despite this, Cramer recognizes Lamar High School as "providing excellent preparation" for his later career and is grateful for the "high quality of the teaching that was available" to him.

Today, Cramer is professor emeritus of physics at the University of Washington, officially retired, but still teaches one physics course each year. He continues to do physics research in quantum optics. A member of many scientific societies, Cramer is known for his "Transactional Interpretation of Quantum Mechanics" and his two science fiction novels, *Twistor* (1989) and *Einstein's Bridge* (1997). Cramer also works with the Brookhaven National Laboratory and a lab in Geneva, Switzerland. In addition to publishing articles in many scientific journals, he writes a science column in *Analog Science Fiction and Fact Magazine*. Cramer attracted mainstream press attention when he likened the sound of the Big Bang to "a large jet plane 100 feet off the ground, flying over your house in the middle of the night."[138]

William H. "Hank" Carter (Class of 1957) had a relatively undistinguished high school career except for his success in music. He played cello and was chosen for the UIL All-State Orchestra. In college, engineering and physics became his lifelong passions, and he took his BS, his MS, and his PhD in Electrical Engineering from the University of Texas. As part of his graduate work, Carter designed one of the first lasers in Texas. During his postdoctoral work at the University of Rochester, he examined the nature of laser light, holography, digital image processing and analysis, and coherence theory. With physicist Emil Wolf, Jr., he was a co-discoverer of the quasi-homogeneous source model.

The *Washington Post* obituary chronicled the twenty-two years he spent at the Naval Research Laboratory in Washington, D.C., where his research provided practical military and civilian applications such as weapons systems and medical imaging. His love for the cello, developed in high school, continued, and he played with the Alexandria, Virginia Symphony, other orchestras, and chamber music groups until his death in 2009.[139]

Wendell Mendell (Class of 1958) is a physicist who vividly remembers LHS physics teacher Brad Gentry, a man for whom he had great respect. In 1957, Gentry adopted an advanced physics course as an additional option for his "bright boys." This was a course called PSSC Physics, developed in 1956 by the Physical Science Study Committee (PSSC), a group of MIT scientists who wrote a course outline for a new type of high school physics curriculum. The pilot version of this study, which is what Gentry must have used, consisted of a text, a teacher's guide, a lab manual, and some equipment. The MIT committee was disappointed when few science teachers in the United States showed interest in the new course. The fact that Gentry, who taught physics at Lamar for twenty years, was aware of this accelerated curriculum and was willing to teach this advanced course to his students, demonstrated his interest in providing them with the best.

Mendell, who decided to take the PSSC course even though he says he was not one of Gentry's physics "brains," remembers two of his classmates who hid their chess game under the lab table so they could play in class. They were discovered when one of them forgot where he was and loudly exclaimed over his move. Mendell swears that Mr. Gentry, who was vigorously writing on the chalkboard, must have known what they were doing, but since they were two of his prize pupils, or since he sponsored the chess club, he chose to ignore them. Surely Lamar was one of few schools where students surreptitiously played chess in their Major Works Physics class.

Mendell made a perfect score on the College Board Achievement Math Test, and the following credentials indicate his mastery of physics:[140] BS, Cal Tech; MS, UCLA; and PhD in Space Physics and Astronomy, Rice Institute. He spent thirty-three years working as a planetary scientist at NASA and has been elected a member of the International Academy of Astronautics. The editor of many scientific publications in the field of planetary science, he currently reviews and creates strategies for manned and unmanned planetary explorations. His 2005 paper, entitled "The Vision of Human Spaceflight," is a concise summary of man's progress toward the acceptance of space travel, and an understanding of the need to use our "space neighborhood," in light of the "population explosion that is changing our home planet in fundamental ways." Mendell predicts that "wars over terrestrial resources may be less than two generations away."

*Charles Prescott, runner-up for Most Representative Boy at Lamar, is now an internationally honored physicist.*

Charles Prescott (Class of 1957), a classmate of Mendell's, played in the Lamar High School band and was chosen for the UIL All-State Orchestra. A member of the Junior Academy of Science, he also served as president of the Astronomy Club. Prescott received an Honorable Mention for Most Representative Boy at Lamar, and the caption under his class photograph reads "Charles Prescott, often found surrounded with thistle tubes, beakers, and a rubber apron—handy with the slide rule, equations, and a physics book."[141]

After graduation, Prescott took his BS at Rice and his PhD at Cal Tech. He has spent his entire career at the Stanford Linear Accelerator Center, Stanford University, where he is now physics professor emeritus. In 1988, he received the prestigious W. K. H. Panofsky Prize in Experimental Particle Physics. In 2001, Prescott was elected to membership in the National Academy of Science for his original research. He has also been elected to the American Academy of Arts and Sciences, one of the highest honors awarded to a U.S. scientist.

Laurent Hodges completes the roster of 1950s Lamar graduates who became nationally known physicists (three were in the Class of 1957 alone). At Lamar, Hodges was a member of Kachina, the Radio Guild, the Texas Junior Historical Society, and National Thespians. He says his favorite teachers "tended not to be the ones in math and science," admitting the curiosity of this fact, since science has been his life's work. Frances Nesmith encouraged his interest in American history. Hodges feels that Lee Duggan was the teacher who influenced him more than any other. He praises Duggan for always asking a lot of questions and encouraging his students to think critically, and credits him with fostering their interest in the "great political (and social) questions."

Hodges' recollections of physics teacher Brad Gentry differ from others. To Hodges, Gentry was "sarcastic, laid back, very congenial but not particularly inspiring." Hodges feels that the better students recognized Gentry's lack of depth in the subject matter and notes there were many questions he could not answer and he did not care to research solutions. When Hodges took an applied math course at Harvard University, he reevaluated Gentry's teaching methods. His college professor said he had conducted an experiment to determine how students learn best. This professor decided that students who had to go over their notes and correct errors tested better than those who had been given "absolutely-correct notes." Giving Gentry a margin of doubt, Hodges suggests that, because he knew his students were so bright, he may have thought they learned better if he did not give them perfect answers.

Hodges had no intention of becoming a physicist. Chemistry was his love. But after receiving his AB in Chemistry and Physics at Harvard, graduating summa cum laude, he switched and took his PhD, also at Harvard, in Physics. His research interests are "theoretical solid state physics and energy and environmental physics." He has authored a textbook, *Environmental Pollution* (1973, 1977), and several other books. Currently, he is professor emeritus of physics at Iowa State University and lives in a solar-powered home which he designed.

## Medicine

Thomas M. Biggs (Class of 1951) distinguished himself at Lamar in science, literature, and athletics. He was a member of Arrowhead and NHS, won the Harvard Book Award, and also lettered in football and track. After graduating from Rice Institute and Yale University, he took his MD from Baylor and specialized in plastic surgery, which has been his life's work.

Biggs is a world-renowned physician and a Life Member of the American Association of Plastic Surgeons. He has authored over fifty publications in medical journals and presented more than 150 papers at professional meetings. His awards include "Homage" from the Brazilian Society of Plastic Surgery, the title of "Grandfather" by residents in Guadalajara, Mexico, and the Most Distinguished Surgeon Award from the Houston Society of Plastic Surgery.[142]

E. Brad Thompson (Class of 1951), a classmate of Briggs and a fellow member of Arrowhead and NHS, was also a debater and a member of the chorus. After Lamar, he took his undergraduate degree from Rice, his MD at Harvard University, and did postdoctoral studies at the University of Cambridge in England. For twenty-two years at the National Institute of Science, Thompson researched biological chemistry and genetics. In 1985, he moved back to Texas to serve as chairman of the Biochemistry and Molecular Science Department at the University of Texas Medical Branch in Galveston, where he was appointed professor emeritus. He left in 2003 and went to the Center for Biomedical and Environmental Genomics at the University of Houston's Department of Biology and Biochemistry. His nonscientific interests include choral music, an activity he began at Lamar, together with ocean sailing, triathlons, gardening, and P. G. Wodehouse.

The interests of Michael "Mike" Hattwick (Class of 1959) while at Lamar were band, orchestra, and debate. Hattwick was also Student Council president, sophomore class president, and cheerleader. He earned his BS at Harvard and his MD from Baylor College of Medicine before leaving for the United Kingdom, where he took an additional degree at the University of London. Back in the U.S., he worked for the Center for Disease Control in Atlanta, Georgia, as director for several important divisions until the early 1970s, when the CDC sent him to England, where he served as registrar and visiting lecturer at St. Thomas' Hospital Medical School and became a licentiate of the Royal College of Physicians. Hattwick now practices in Fairfax, Virginia, and in 1994 founded NoVa Healthcare, working to provide consultation for physicians and healthcare organizations. Hattwick is an outstanding Lamar graduate and an internationally recognized physician.[143]

## Government and Law

The second-youngest man to serve as Harris County district attorney (the youngest was Peter Gray in 1842), Carol Vance (Class of 1951) took office as an appointee of Governor John Connally. He ran for the office in the next election, was elected, and ran unopposed in all subsequent elections, serving from 1966 to 1979.

*Honoree Carol Vance is pictured at Lamar's 2003 Distinguished Alumni Luncheon. When Vance retired as district attorney, he was succeeded in 1979 by Johnny B. Holmes, Jr. (Class of 1959).*

Vance's innovative contributions to the job of running a large district attorney's office have been emulated nationwide. After leaving office, Vance asked state officials to implement a Christian faith-based prison ministry at the Jester II Unit in Fort Bend County. This unit has now been renamed the Carol S. Vance Unit, and Vance continues to do prison ministry at this facility.[144]

Fred Hofheinz (Class of 1956), Houston's only second-generation mayor, served one term from 1974 to 1978. His father, Mayor Roy Hofheinz, served as mayor from 1953 to 1955, while Fred was a Lamar student. Fred Hofheinz was a Lamar debater, member of NHS, and was elected class lawyer. He was also a pole-vaulter and lettered in track.

A Rhodes Scholar finalist, Hofheinz earned a BA and PhD from the University of Texas and received his law degree from the University of Houston in 1964. Since leaving office, he has taken an active role in Houston's civic and charitable affairs. He practices law and manages oil and gas interests here and abroad.[145]

*Mark White, former governor of Texas, spoke to the crowd of alumni and students at Lamar's seventy-fifth-anniversary celebration.*

Former governor of Texas Mark White (Class of 1958) is another Lamar graduate who pursued a political career. White loved his three years at Lamar but said participation in football was out since he weighed only 135 pounds, and regrettably he was too short for basketball. Civics teacher Ernest Mills "stirred" his interest in politics. White took his BA and LLD degrees from Baylor University and began his political career as state assistant attorney general in 1966. He was elected the forty-third governor of Texas, serving from 1983 to 1987. Since then he has considered entering Houston politics, but has given up the idea and spends his time practicing law. When interviewed as a 2002 Distinguished Alumnus, he called Lamar a treasure in Houston, a school that represents the best in public education.

Judge Lynn Hughes (Class 1959) currently serves as a federal judge. He took an undergraduate degree from the University of Alabama, his Master of Laws at the Virginia School of Law, and his Doctor of Jurisprudence at the University of Texas Law School.

Hughes was appointed in 1985 by President Ronald Reagan to the United States District Court, Southern District of Texas. Hughes belongs to the Judicial Election Nominations Committee and served on the Texas Supreme Court's Task Force on Revision of the Rules of Civil Procedure from 1991 to 1995. His civic contributions include working with the Rift Valley Research Mission and serving as an Ethics lecturer for the American Association of Petroleum Geologists.[146]

## Business and Public Service

Burt McMurtry (Class of 1952) and his wife Deedee Meck (McMurtry) (Class of 1952) both feel very fortunate to have gone to Lamar, a school which provided such good preparation for college. After graduation, both went to Rice, where Burt took a BA in English and a BS in Electrical Engineering. They married a week after their graduation and moved to California. He pursued a research career at Sylvania working in the microwave tube division. McMurtry started part-time graduate work at Stanford University, where he took his MSEE and PhD, but continued at Sylvania, where he did laser research and development. In 1969, he formed a venture capital business, which he ran until 1995. During his twenty-six-year career, McMurtry formed two other venture capital partnerships and their portfolios include Adaptec, Altera, Compaq, Intuit, Microsoft, and Sun Microsystems, among many others. He served for seventeen years on Rice University's board, eleven years on the Stanford University board, and seven years on the board of the Carnegie Institution of Washington, D.C. Honors include Fellow of the Institute of Electrical and Electronic Engineers, Gold Medal and Distinguished Alumnus awards from Rice, and the Gold Spike Award from Stanford. Today, the couple's philanthropic contributions include the McMurtry Residential College at Rice and the McMurtry Art and Art History Building at Stanford (scheduled to open in 2015).

Dr. Donald Haragan (Class of 1954) is an academician who laughingly claims he attended every major university in the state until they finally made him president of one. He began by earning a BS in Meteorology at the University of Texas, an MS from Texas A&M, and returned to the University of Texas for a PhD in Civil Engineering. Recognizing Texas Technological College and Lubbock as areas of growth, he began teaching there and has never left. He served as provost for ten years, and as president for five. His influence has resulted in the establishment of the University Honors College, the International Culture Center, the University Writing Center, and the Texas Tech Press. In 2003, he became a charter member of the Board of Directors of the Civil and Architectural Engineering Academy of Distinguished Alumni at the University of Texas. He serves on several non-profit boards and is currently the head of the Honors College and the president emeritus of Texas Tech.[147] In 2009, Haragan was honored as a Distinguished Alumnus of Lamar High School.

David Hamilton (Class of 1957) is a businessman who has made money in trucking, real estate, and food services. At Lamar, he was an athlete, a scholar, and a leader. He lettered in football and basketball, was a member of the National Honor Society, and was junior class president. After graduation, he took his BA at Rice and his MBA from Harvard Business School. When he married Catharine Cline, an Amarillo oil heiress, "his only asset was his intelligence."[148] Friends have noted that he often reads a book a night and has total recall. He has used his business sense to "make a fortune."[149] Hamilton and his wife were asked in Versailles if there was anything to be done about the palace gardens there, which had fallen into disrepair. Out of a love of all things French, they founded the "American Friends of Versailles," an "elegant group dedicated to the pursuit of beauty," after this visit. The palace gardens, an UNESCO-declared treasure, has greatly benefited from the philanthropy of the Hamiltons.[150]

Judy Ley (Allen) (Class of 1957) was a student who participated in every activity at Lamar and excelled in all of them. During her senior year, she was secretary of NHS, president of Cherokee, *Lancer* staff editor, lettered in volleyball and track, and was elected cheerleader.

After Lamar, she earned her BA from Stanford in 1961, and in 1963 was one of the first women to receive an MBA at Harvard—even harder, she says, was finding a job. Architect John Carl Warnecke hired her, and she became manager of his New York office. While there, Ley became interested in wine and wrote a book, *Which Wine? The Wine Drinker's Buying Guide*, organizing a national book tour to promote the book, which sold over 100,000 copies. Back in Houston, Ley has had a successful business career as asset manager of Allen Investments, a family company. Former director of the Federal Reserve Board in Dallas (1999–2006), the Advisory Board of Governors of Rice University, and chairman of the Round Table of the James A. Baker Institute for Public Policy, Ley is an advisory trustee of the Houston Ballet Foundation and trustee of the Museum of Natural Science. She has supported and served as honorary chair of FIRST Robotics, an organization that sponsors national competitions for students who are interested in science and engineering. Combining non-profit community organizations with financial institutions, this respected Houston businesswoman, reminiscent of her days at Lamar High, is still able to do it all.[151] In 2011, she was honored as a Distinguished Alumna of Lamar High School.

*Judy Ley (Allen) (Class of 1957) told Dr. McSwain that Lamar needed Robotics, a program combining engineering and creativity. She is holding a photo of the LHS Robotics team she helped to fund.*

*Charlie Fogarty, or "Mr. Woodshop," runner-up for Most Representative, had already built two boats before he came to Lamar. After graduation, he started the U-Frame-It stores, saying he helped invent the do-it-yourself craze. The Steamboat House restaurant is this businessman's latest venture.*

## STAGE STRUCK IN TEXAS

In 1952, the same year Ruth Denney came to Lamar, the talented Ryba twins, Joan and Jane, who captivated the Houston public with their charm, beauty, and brains, graduated from Lamar and entered Rice Institute. While students at Rice, they appeared in New York City on the Herb Shriner television show *Two for the Money*, their first introduction to national show business. Phi Beta Kappa graduates, these Rice cheerleaders attracted Bud Adams' attention, and they became the "Oiler Twins." Joan says this assignment was the "greatest job two girls could have had at that time." They wore custom-made suits with "discreet logos on the pockets" (costumes quite different from today's football team representatives), attended the games, and made television appearances to promote the team.[152]

*Lamar co-eds Jane and Joan Ryba were nearly identical, but singer Dean Martin said he could tell them apart in profile because the tips of their noses were different. (Courtesy of Joan Ryba)*

Their mother's fondness for Las Vegas had already acquainted them with the city. They entered a contest, held by Jakie Friedman, Carolyn Friedman Farb's father, to be Texas Copa Girls for the Sands Hotel, to lure gamblers to Vegas. They won, and the Texas Copa Girls were costumed in gold cowboy hats, boots, and showgirl costumes trimmed in fox fur. This began their show business career. Although they took time out to appear in stage shows and a Hollywood film, most of their time was spent working or having fun with almost every famous entertainer in the

*Well-known Las Vegas showgirls, the Ryba twins pose with comedian Red Skelton. (Courtesy of Joan Ryba)*

United States who came to Las Vegas, including Dean Martin's Rat Pack, Joey Bishop, Danny Kaye, Jack Benny, Jack Lemmon, and many others. When they left Las Vegas, they spent twenty-six years in Chicago working trade shows and conventions—an eventful life for these Lamar graduates.[153]

The other show business triumphs by Lamar students during this decade must be attributed to Ruth Denney, a Midwestern farm girl who graduated from Ohio Wesleyan and came to Texas to teach drama at Lamar in 1952. The benefits Lamar reaped from Denney's tenure are incalculable. Denney's directorial talent and her ability to spot and encourage budding drama students brought forth an outpouring of stars unlike anything that had previously occurred in any public school in this city and this state and, perhaps, the nation.

Her previous teaching experience was in Zanesville, Ohio, at a tiny high school where she consistently won state honors. She said her initial experience at Lamar was a "rude awakening" when her cast lost to Reagan High School at her first UIL contest. The Thespian banquet's 1954 skit promised, "We'll get to state by fifty-eight!" They did not have to wait that long! Denney's first win occurred in the spring of 1955, when the Lamar production of *Our Town* won the UIL championship, with Joanne Sweet taking first in state as Best Actress and Bob Crutchfield as Best Actor. Crutchfield was called "the Voice" by his fellow students at Lamar and went on to have a successful career as senior vice-president of Universal Studios from 1987 to 1997. Denney and her students continued their winning streak for the rest of the decade.

*This was the album cover for the recording of Lamar's musical* Annie. *(Courtesy of Will LeBlanc)*

Tommy Sands had a role in *Our Town* and had already starred in Denney's 1955 production of *Annie* with Pat Becker, who played Annie Oakley. Both Sands and Becker are pictured on the show's album cover.

At age fifteen, Sands had already been signed to an RCA recording contract. He left Lamar to pursue his career and became an overnight teenage idol. He sang "Friendly Persuasion" at the 1957 Academy Awards ceremony, appeared in several films, made a number of records, and was awarded a "star" on the Hollywood Walk of Fame for recording.

During the production of *Annie Get Your Gun*, Paula Ragusa (Class of 1955), who later took the name Paula Prentiss, says she joined Denney's drama class out of curiosity, but it could also have been because of her crush on Tommy Sands, who she thought was a Tony Curtis look-alike. She says she worked for a whole semester to affect a slouch, since Sands was about a foot shorter than she. In *Annie* she had a bit role and her stage directions were to dance around the fire with the other Indians. In the final rehearsal, she decided to make her role more interesting and began twirling away from the group. Denney called her over to make it clear that her improvisation was not acceptable and told her, "You should not be in my drama class." Prentiss says she learned a valuable lesson in discipline that has guided her for the rest of her life.

By 1959, Prentiss was appearing on Broadway in *A Hatful of Rain* when she was discovered by a talent scout who sent her to Hollywood to play in *Where the Boys Are*. Her breakthrough occurred in

## CAST

**PRESENTED BY**

Drama Department
Music Department
Art Department
Physical Education Department

|  |  |
|---|---|
| Annie Oakley | PAT BECKER |
| Frank Butler | TOMMY SANDS |
| Dolly Tate | MARTHA CRAIG |
| Winnie Tate | BEVERLY MONTGOMERY |
| Tommy | JIMMY KELLEY |
| Little Jake | BOBBY MILLER |
| Jessie | FRAN MARYE |
| Minnie | MABLE SIMS |
| Buffalo Bill | SONNY BAUMGARTEN |
| Pawnee Bill | ALAN SWEETON |
| Charlie Davenport | BOB CRUTCHFIELD |
| Sitting Bull | BOB BLAINE |
| Heap Big High Pockets | TOMMY TUNE |
| Wilson | HUGH McBRIDE |
| Mrs. Schyler Adams | KAY BRAZELTON |
| Mrs. Sylvia Porter | JAN HILL |
| Mac | WAYNE SPEER |

**DIRECTED BY**

Mrs. Ruth R. Denny — Drama
Mrs. Virginia Stecher — Chorus
Mrs. Kitty Lowry — Dancing
Miss Geneive Filson — Art
Mrs. H. L. Sandel — Costuming
Mr. Edward Trongone — Orchestra

**DANCERS**

*Indians*
Betty Bush
Sue Sellors
Paula Ragusa
Melba St. Clair
Patricia Johnson
Patti Pollard
Suzanne Lewis
Jo Anne McConnell
Anne Ragusa

*Western*
Nan Moreland
Cleo Britain
Emory Kelley
June Schneider
Frances Linke
Dixie Clark
Sunny O'Neil
Marsha Meredith
Sally Sultan
Tommie Lu Storm

*Jazz*
Faye Veyon
Mary Hatch
Sally Shaffer
Martha Starling
Suzanne Summers
Carolyn Clayton
Nancy McKewen
Dorothy Furton
Jean Elliot
Sally Kate Marshall

**WESTERN CHORUS**

Edna Sample
Sandy Rowell
Carolyn Eacley
Judy Weigand
Jane Sullivan
Marsha Gaunt
Betsy Murphy
Debbie Hill
Babs Wilcox
Carol Kinney
Lyda Hord
Kay Womack
Jo Rae Simmons
Melinda Robinson

*Queen,* MARSHA GAUNT *and Beauties,*
Ann Ragusa
Carol Kohler
Fran Marye
Sally Shaffer
Joni McConnell
Gail Pontikes
Dolores Scofield
Leone Guthrie
Carolyn Clayton

*Sailors*
Dick Goff
Tim Albans
Tommy Overstreet
Jerry Wright
Kenton David
Dennis Hill
Johnny McCoy
Wayne Weachman

**EXTRAS**

*Squaws*
Cynthia McDonald
Ann Suggs
Cecile Wilson
Judy Wahlers
Benita Williams
Barbara Castell
Light Bailey
Nancee Kirk
Carol Hudson
Donna Snow
Barbara Bayer
Peggy Tuggle

*Side Show*
Diane Rego
David Woodard
Pat Roten
Edna Rogers
Jane Sullivan

**ORCHESTRA**

Allen Gorden
Gene May
George Berry
Jim Black
Alan Sweeton
Mike Rieves
Stan Drain
John Vance
Dick Pentecost
Lindsey English
William Day
Marion Jenkins
Larry Stevenson
Hubbard Miller
John Gemotes
Gainer Lindsey
Bob Durst

Student Director . . . June Lee
Script . . . Martha Craig, Barbara Farren, June Lee
Cue Girls . . . Suzie Hamilton, Carla Griffin
Stage Crew . . . Bob Gentry, Chilton Bryan, Steve Spencer, John Drake, Charles Green, Ferg Ginther
Lights . . . Jimmy Orr, Jimmy Keenan, Jimmy Danenbaum
Lobby . . . Anne Whitty, Joanne Sweet
Props . . . Gaye Irving, Carol Hurst, Judy Robinson
Costumes, Design . . . Tommy Lu Storm
Costume Committee . . . Carolyn Shearer, Barbara Farren, Diane Martin
Make-Up . . . Pat Wargo, Mary Lelia Crane, Deanna Rochelle, Retta Moddy, Sherry Speer, Kathy Lacy, Beverly Parker, Annes Geis, Trulla Harrison
Head Usher . . . Vann Wilson
Tickets . . . Connie Clendenin

**BOYS' CHORUS**

Sherrell Stewart
Walter Bloxsom
Dick Goff
Milo Kearney
Jerry Wright
Billy Armer
Jimmy Vrba
Jerry Russell
Dennis Hill
Bobby Roberts
Johnny McCoy
Hart Peebles
Tommy Samuels
Jim Springer
Mike Taylor
Roy Glasscock
Kenton David
Tommy Overstreet
Stephen Smith
Tim Albans
David Knapp
Alan Engberg
Bob Dunnam
Bill Landfield
Wayne Weachman

*Annie had a one-hundred-member cast, including four performers who achieved national fame: male lead Tommy Sands, Paula Prentiss as an Indian, Tommy Tune as Heap Big High Pockets, and Tommy Overstreet, who sang as a sailor and in the mixed chorus. Bob Crutchfield became an executive at Universal Studios. (Courtesy of Will LeBlanc)*

1964, when she starred with Rock Hudson in *Man's Favorite Sport*. This role brought her comparisons to Katherine Hepburn and gave her a reputation as a "kooky screwball." Along with Candace Bergman, Jane Fonda, and Stephanie Powers, Prentiss is considered to have paved the way for actresses who wanted roles as assertive career women and social advocates.[154]

Denney's next UIL win was the play *I Remember Mama* in 1956. The following year, *Years Ago* also won state, and Betty Knauth won first in state for her acting. In 1958, Lamar again won state, with *A Roomful of Roses*, Denney's favorite of all plays. The judge stated that it was the best play Lamar had ever done.[155] *LIFE* magazine writer Eliot Ellisofon, who came to Austin for the UIL contest, agreed. The *Lancer* quoted him as saying, "this beats any summer stock production I have ever seen."[156] *LIFE* photographer Jane School was also brought in to check out Lamar's production.

*Ruth Denney loved providing her students with speech and drama opportunities and turned the students' morning announcements and devotionals into the Radio Guild, whose members conducted celebrity interviews that were aired on local radio stations.*

The subsequent *LIFE* Magazine article, "Stage Struck in Texas," stated that more Texans are associated with drama than any other state, and Ellisofon concluded that everyone in Texas must be "under the spell of dramatics." His words were somewhat prophetic, considering that Houston is today second only to New York City in its number of theater seats. *LIFE* Magazine displayed a small photo of Lamar High School's *A Roomful of Roses*, identifying it as a family comedy competing in the state contest held in Austin by the University of Texas.[157]

That year, Denney took the cast of *Roses* to Purdue, Indiana, to perform a forty-five-minute excerpt for the National Drama Conference. Lamar was one of seven high schools in the nation invited to perform, the only school selected from Texas. According to Denney, this was the biggest honor awarded to a high school drama department.[158] She said she liked going to Purdue with her "tops in state" cast, and the students who went still remember this bus trip to Indiana.[159]

The administration recognized Denney as a superior faculty member and gave wholehearted support for her little "jaunts to Austin" (UIL competitions) and trips to Purdue for the national competition. Faculty members have indicated that Ruth Denney could get pretty much anything she wanted from the administration, as well as from her students, even though some officials did not totally understand what she was doing. When Principal Watts once observed her students in a rehearsal, he remarked, "Well, they sure do know their lines."

The Drama Department's activities occurred in The Little Red Theater, which Denney called Lamar's answer to Broadway. This structure began life when HISD was getting ready to haul off one of the temporary buildings. Denney stopped them: "No, no, I want to use it for a theater." She had the building connected to the one she already occupied, arranging them in a *T* shape and opening walls to provide room for an audience and a theater-in-the-round stage. The students were thrilled, and during that summer they painted the exterior a bright red and the interior black.

This building became a home for countless Lamar drama students, those who performed as well as those who worked behind the scenes. "Denney's Demons," later known as "Demons and Dolls" to include female helpers, was a diversified collection of amateur carpenters, electricians, light men, and set builders who held the Drama Department's productions together with "masking tape and baling wire." They wore baggy white overalls during performances when moving sets on stage, but black overalls for their everyday nitty-gritty work. This group installed recessed lights, "stereophonic" sound, and air conditioning. They were the jack-of-all-trades students who "oiled the machinery" of Denney's productions.

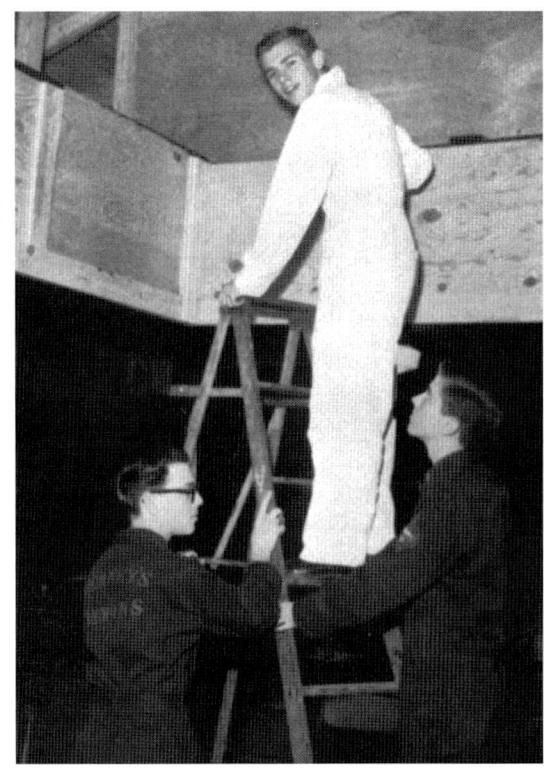

*Denney's Demons wore white overalls during performances, but black overalls for their everyday work. They kept Ruth Denney's shows glued together.*

The actors and actresses revered Denney, who they say treated them as peers, listened to them, and was quick to applaud when they did a good job. They respected her high standards, and her rule that if you did not do it right, you were out. When she said to "walk the chalk," she meant just that.

Carlin Glynn (Masterson) (Class of 1957) credits Denney for her career as a professional actress and says Denney was her anchor, a teacher who made a tremendous difference in her life.[160] Glynn, who is the mother of actress Mary Stuart Masterson, made her Broadway debut in *The Best Little Whorehouse in Texas* and won a Tony for Best Featured Actress in a Musical in 1979. Glynn was in several movies, including *Sixteen Candles* and *A Trip to Bountiful*. In 1982, she won the Laurence Olivier Award and has taught acting at Columbia University.

High school musicals have been part of the American way of life for the past seventy-five years. Ruth Denney's productions still live in the recordings that were made, and also in the memories of the cast members and crew.

A musical depends on good music, and a newcomer to the faculty provided Denney with a willing partner who more than met her expectations. Edward Trongone came to Lamar in 1954, hired as conductor for both the Lamar Orchestra and what was the only military band in Houston public schools, the all-male ROTC Marching Band. His idea of what a school band should be, and his passion for jazz, led him to move Lamar's music program in a new direction. He separated the Lamar Band from the ROTC unit[161] and outfitted them in blue uniforms styled like those worn by other Houston schools. Lamar's band was still all-male, but they no longer wore the khaki-and-olive-green military uniform.

Trongone formed a stage band that Ned Battista (Class of 1957) says was really a swing/jazz band, but these names for innovative music would not have been permitted by the administration.[162] When Trongone heard Battista play at San Jacinto High School, he persuaded him to transfer to Lamar so he would have more advantages. Battista says this decision was a turning point in his life. Trongone gave him the advice that has guided his career, telling him not to draw lines between "good" music and "bad" music, but instead, to play all styles. His successful career indicates his diversity. Battista is the founder and conductor of the Houston Pops, now known as the American Pops, who in 1993 performed the music of Cole Porter in Japan. He has been a guest conductor for many acclaimed symphony orchestras around the country, including Boston Pops, St. Louis, Calgary, and Vancouver. In addition to his conducting career, he has composed music in every category from symphonic works to jazz. Battista is assistant conductor of the Houston Ballet and still conducts his Pops Orchestra.[163]

*Edward Trongone's stage band was composed of Bob Wright (not pictured) on the piano, drummer Dave Barry, and in the front row: John Scarborough, Everitt Frizzel, Hubbard Miller, and Bob Durst. Second row: Barry Roberts, Kimball McMahon, and trumpeters George Williams, Ned Battista, and Mike Reeves. (Courtesy of Ned Battista)*

Max Neuhaus (Class of 1957), another one of Trongone's students, as a senior won a percussionist seat in the All-City Orchestra. After graduation from Lamar, Neuhaus went to New York, where he roomed with classmate Ned Battista, who was attending Julliard. Julliard did not recognize jazz, and this by now had become Neuhaus' passion. He enrolled in the Manhattan School of Music to study jazz percussion. In 1964, he made his solo debut at Carnegie Hall and, supported by a Rockefeller grant, served as artist-in-residence at the University of Chicago.

By the time he was twenty-eight, Neuhaus had moved away from percussion to become an important pioneer in the field of sound art. In a 2006 interview with Menil Collection director Josef Helfenstein, Neuhaus said he did not want to spend the six hours a day required to maintain his ranking as "the best drummer in the United States." When Columbia Masterworks asked him to make an album, he says he jumped at the chance to permanently record his talent, so that he could leave the world of music performance to become what he wanted to be.

His use of feedback as a musical device is now known as "live electronic music." Neuhaus' philosophy of art arose from his conviction that people's perception of space depends as much on what one hears as on what one sees. As an artist-in-residence at Bell Laboratories, he developed techniques that resulted in what he called a "block of sound." He worked to produce a work of art out of sound, sound that one almost cannot hear. He considered the sound without the place to be nothing. His important but somewhat unknown Times Square Piece was commissioned in 1977. Times Square was a most difficult location, but was set in what Neuhaus felt was the epitome of public places. Helfenstein calls this visually anonymous "sound block," located between 45th and 46th and between Broadway and 7th Avenue (just below the George M. Cohan statue and rising from a subway grate), an "amazing" piece.

Most music emanates from visible loudspeakers. Neuhaus' works of art, by contrast, are three-dimensional aural images that the viewer enters. Neuhaus has permanent sound installations at Chicago's Contemporary Art Museum, Houston's Menil Museum, and many European locations.[164]

By 1958, Trongone's efforts had established the world of jazz at Lamar High School, and his high school orchestra was invited to join the Houston Symphony Orchestra in performing a special concert at the Music Hall. The Lamar musicians played "Concerta for Jazz Band and Symphony Orchestras," the "first time a high school group had ever played this piece with a major symphony."[165] According

*Ned Battista invited Tommy Tune to return to Houston and perform with his Pops Orchestra. The two former classmates are pictured in the Green Room at Jones Hall. (Courtesy of Ned Battista)*

*At the Brownwood Music Festival, the Lamar Stage Band won a special first-place trophy because their performance was so superior to that of the other schools. (Courtesy of Ned Battista)*

to the *Lancer*'s front-page story, the Lamar Orchestra also soloed, playing "Teenage Rhapsody," an original composition written by Ed Gerlach especially for this concert. The Lamar Orchestra was playing all over the state, winning medals and honors in the State Orchestra Contest at the Brownwood Music Festival, where it was given a special first-place award because its performance was so superior to any of the other schools. Shortly before Trongone died, he was able to watch his former pupil Ned Battista conduct the Stratford Symphony in Stratford, Connecticut. After the concert, they visited, and Battista says that the Brownwood Trophy meant more to his former teacher than anything else in his life.[166]

In 1958, ten of Trongone's students won either All-State Band or All-State Orchestra in the UIL competition and were also chosen for Sam Houston State's Orchestra Festival. Ruth Denney never forgot how much she loved working with Edward Trongone. They had collaborated on many Lamar productions, and when she founded the High School for the Visual and Performing Arts in 1971, she persuaded him to join her faculty.

"A female Fred Astaire!" is what Tommy Tune says he thought the first time he saw Ruth Denney. Her elegant brown linen suit and brown-and-white spectator high heels made him think of the suave, sophisticated dancer who was one of his idols. Growing up in Houston, Tune wanted to become a ballet dancer, but he kept growing taller and knew this would never be. He says when he saw Fred Astaire in the movies, he realized he could wear pants and still dance. Tune came to Lamar in 1953, a fourteen-year-old who told his guidance counselor he wanted to take dancing. She told him they had no dance program and sent him instead to Ruth Denney.

One of Denney's gifts was her ability to spot talent in people and bring out the best in them. She immediately realized Tune's potential and gave two Alley Theater tickets to a high school sophomore who had never seen a play, sparking in him a passion that would become his life's work. Tune appeared in every variety show performed at Lamar during his three years there. He acted and sang, but choreography was his specialty. The talents of Tommy Tune were so remarkable that Denney planned musical after musical to give him choreographic opportunities. After he graduated, she brought him back from college to choreograph more productions. In the April 10, 1957 *Lancer*, Tune, then a senior, told the reporter he intended to go to Lon Morris College, having won a $300 dramatic scholarship, and expressed hope that he would "someday become a Broadway choreographer." He was reaching for a star, but his success surely surpassed his expectations.

As he celebrates fifty years in show business, Tommy Tune is still performing, most recently in a cabaret act in New York at the Regency Hotel. He would have preferred the Carlyle Hotel, but said he is too tall for the stage.[167] Tune has won nine Tony awards, eight Drama Desk awards, three Fred Astaire awards, and the Society of Directors and Choreographers' George Abbott Award for Lifetime Achievement. He is also the recipient of The National Medal of Arts, the highest honor for artistic achievement given by the president of the United States. His star is in place on the Hollywood Walk of Fame, and in 2009, Tune was designated a Living Landmark by the New York Landmarks Conservancy.[168] He and Ruth Denney maintained a lifelong friendship, and he says she always came to New York for his openings. She visited him at his home on Fire Island, and he came to Austin and spent time with her on the lake.[169] Tune says Ruth Denney put him on the road to success.[170]

Jim Bernhard (Class of 1955) also started his climb to the stars in high school. An active debater and an editor of the *Lancer*, he was a member and officer of so many clubs, he was a shoo-in to be elected Most Representative Boy of his senior class. As a debater, Bernhard took speech instead of drama, but he got into the productions anyway, often as the narrator.

*Tommy Tune returned to the Lamar stage to perform once more for his classmates and kick off the auditorium remodeling campaign. (Courtesy of Will LeBlanc)*

Following graduation, Bernhard took a history degree from Rice, graduating summa cum laude and Phi Beta Kappa. He was a Marshall Scholar at the University of Birmingham, England, where he took his MA. His career indicates the influence of his electives at Lamar. He is the author of fourteen published plays and has worked as a lyricist, newspaperman, college English professor, actor, theatrical producer, artistic director, concert impresario, television host, and crossword puzzle constructor.[171] An author described as a "word sleuth," Bernhard has written two books, *Porcupine, Picayune, & Post: How Newspapers Get Their Names* (2007), and *Words Gone Wild: Puns, Puzzles, Poesy, Palaver, Persiflage, and Poppycock* (2010).[172]

In his tribute to Denney on her ninetieth birthday, Bernhard expressed regret that he could not be there to wish her happy birthday in person, but said, "Thanks to you, I'm working in the theater," referring to his current production.[173]

A country and western star who has achieved fame in the entertainment world is Tommy Overstreet (Class of 1955), or "T. O." as he is referred to by fans and radio disc jockeys. Overstreet's career as a major recording artist, songwriter, music publisher, and record producer has included twenty-two international tours, twenty albums, and engagements in clubs, as well as major network television shows. His career as a songwriter took off with his top five hit, "Gwen, Congratulations," which went to number five on the *Billboard* country music chart. Four more of his country and western hits have risen to the number five position, and eleven have reached the ranking of top ten singles, along with many that have ranked in the top twenty hits. Overstreet credits his cousin, "Uncle Gene Autry," for his decision to try for a singing career.[174]

### THE CHORALETTES—A SHOW BIZ PHENOMENON

Lee S. Keding founded his one-of-a-kind girls' musical club, the Choralettes, in 1952, the same year Denney joined the faculty. The Choralettes' first big trip was performing at Texas A&M. In 1958, they were invited by the president of the National Broadcast Company to perform for Houston radio station KPRC, a broadcast that was heard on 286 NBC radio stations across the United States.

Ruth Denney and Lee Keding may not have had the most cordial relationship. As one colleague remarked, it was a clash of egos. But students of both teachers frequently collaborated on productions leading to friendships between the Drama Department and the Choralettes. One example is Carol Kinney (Williams), who served as president of the Choralettes and was elected Most Valuable Member. She became the Choralettes' accompanist and treasures this experience. Keding would throw down a sheet of music and say, "Learn this by tomorrow, please."

Williams also played for the variety shows and musicals that Ruth Denney directed. One starred Tommy Tune, who curled himself in a large wicker basket. Williams began playing "snake charmer" music, and Tommy slowly emerged from his hiding place. This brought the house down, though now Tune says he doesn't know how he was able to do this because the basket was not that large. Carol Kinney Williams considers her lifelong friendship with Tommy Tune and her membership in the Choralettes as the two most important gifts she received from Lamar.[175]

Over the years, the Choralettes became known as Lamar's "show troupe."[176] As Williams said, "Keding put Lamar on the map!" When they performed in private for Ed Sullivan, he told Keding, "You would be insane if you ever took these girls out of pastels," referring to their uniforms. These shirtwaist dresses in pale aqua, green, yellow, and pink were color-coordinated to complement their eyes, hair, or cheeks and were worn with pumps and floppy picture hats. In the winter they wore white. Originally, the uniform included wrist-length white cotton gloves, but these were dropped in the 1960s.

Lee Keding was described by *Houston Post* journalist Kathy Lewis as someone who looked more like a character from *The Great Gatsby* than a high school teacher. Lewis wrote a lengthy article on the occasion of the Choralettes' celebration of its twenty-fifth anniversary. The article appeared on the front page of the "Today" section. She described Keding as Lamar's Beau Brummel. This choral director, who truly believed that "clothes make the man," was selected for three years as one of the ten best-dressed men in Houston. His wardrobe included eighty-three suits, thirty-five pairs of shoes, and 500 ties, every one of which had a white background. He was quoted in the *Lancer* as saying, "I like white. I have a white car, a white watch band, and only white shirts and handkerchiefs,"[177] and admitted that ten of his eighty-three suits were white. A stickler for good grooming, Keding was elegant and gentlemanly. He expected the same elegance and good manners from his Choralettes, but his upbeat personality, his kindness, and his smile that stretched from ear to ear made the members love him.

By the 1970s, the Choralettes' popularity and reputation preceded them. They had performed four times at the Orange Blossom Festival in San Bernardino and once at both the New York and Seattle World's Fairs. They had breakfasted with President Lyndon Johnson (1967) and sung the "Eyes of Texas" to the mayor of New York.

*Wearing the white gloves Mr. Keding felt made them look more ladylike, the Choralettes perform at a trade show in the Houston Coliseum.*

Danny Thomas sang with them during his gig at the Houston Oaks Hotel in 1971. They were at the opening of Houston Baptist College and "Dr. Billy Graham smiled as he heard the Choralettes sing."[178] They appeared with Bob Hope for a show at the Houston Music Hall, and John Wayne met them when he came to Houston to promote his film *The Alamo*.

Keding denied that the club was a "rich girls' organization." Girls who could not afford the trips were urged to find sponsors or patrons who ranged from the wealthy women who were the mothers of Choralettes, to the beauty salons where the mothers had their hair done, and to Neiman Marcus and Sakowitz, the stores where they shopped. Bud Adams, owner of the Houston Oilers, was also a patron.

One critic quipped that, if the Houston Symphony had Keding's kind of backing, they could get out of the red. Many schools all over the United States had musical groups, but few if any went on trips like the Choralettes. Even Keding's critics conceded that there was no other group like the Choralettes, calling the group "good-will ambassadors," and Keding, a "promoter from the day one." Over the years, he built a power structure through which he wielded tremendous influence in the school and in the city. During its three-decade history, this girls' singing group, regardless of Keding's traditions that seem outmoded today, had a huge impact on Lamar and Houston.

Not all of the girls were accomplished musicians. They were "stars" because "they were pretty, well-dressed, and well-mannered, not because they could sing."[179] Keding instructed the particularly poor singers to "just mouth the words."[180] They were happy to do so, since "some felt it was as

*The Choralettes vacationed in Hawaii every other year. They stayed in first-class hotels and were given first-class treatment by the airlines that had a VIP room waiting for them in Dallas when they changed planes.*

important to be a Choralette as it was to be a Kappa or Pi Phi at the University of Texas."[181] When performing for *Houston Post* reporter Kathy Lewis in 1976, one of the Choralettes fainted on stage. She was carried off the stage by one of the Choralads, a group of six boys whose job was to move the risers and, if need be, serve as a "catcher."

### OTHER LUMINARIES

James Lee Burke is a 1955 graduate who has become an internationally admired and celebrated literary mystery novelist. Burke is the only author to twice receive the Edgar Award for Best Novel, and he has been named Grandmaster by the Mystery Writers of America. A Guggenheim and Breadloaf fellow, Burke is also a recipient of a National Endowment for the Arts Fellowship. The author of thirty novels and two short story collections, Burke attended Southwestern Louisiana Institute, Lafayette, Louisiana, where he was taught to write by his freshman professor, Lyle Williams.

Before his success as an author, Burke was a social worker, college professor, truck driver for the U.S. Forest Service, reporter, and land surveyor for pipelines. Critics call him a genius, a Faulknerian writer who uses sociological and biblical themes that are also reminiscent of Steinbeck. Three of his novels, *Heaven's Prisoners*, *Two for Texas*, and *In the Electric Mist with Confederate Dead*, have been made into movies. This brilliant author is considered a major influence on the generation of mystery writers who have come after him.[182]

Artist Dick Wray graduated from Lamar in 1952, and Henry Gadbois (Class of 1948) says Wray sat in the back of Norma Henderson's art class and drew comics. Wray studied architecture at the University of Houston but left to go to Europe for two years, a trip that established his desire to be an artist. He finished his education in Germany, returning to Houston in 1959. In 1962, he was awarded the Ford Foundation Purchase Prize.

A painter of abstract expressionistic art, Wray was acknowledged as one of the first Texas Moderns in the 2006 exhibition "Texas Modern: The Rediscovery of Early Texas Abstraction" at Baylor University. This Houston Modernist might have been surprised had he seen the *Houston Chronicle*'s obituary referring to him as "The Old Master of Texas Art."

GeeGee Kamrath Mygdal (Class of 1957), one of Texas' finest sculptors, is the daughter of eminent architect Karl Kamrath, who was an early Lamar tennis star. GeeGee Kamrath demonstrated artistic talent early and was already taking classes at the Museum of Fine Arts when she arrived at Lamar. In high school, she excelled at volleyball and tennis, and praises physical education instructor Elise Hawkins (Class of 1948). But art was Kamrath's passion, and she had tremendous respect for her art teachers Genevieve Filson and Mary Lorena Brown—especially Brown, who encouraged her interest in sculpture.[183] While at Lamar, Kamrath won Gold Key art awards and was vice-president of the art club Wapika.

Kamrath earned her fine arts degree at the University of Texas, studying with famed sculptor Charles Umlauf. She traveled in Europe and had her first bronze sculpture cast while living in Florence, Italy. Upon returning to the United States, Kamrath learned the technique of bronze casting in graduate school at the University of Iowa. Today she is one of Texas' foremost sculptors and her work includes corporate and institutional commissions as well as private commissions for bronze sculptures of many prominent Texans. She has done large-scale pieces at the University of Texas, the Austin State School, Baylor University, and St. Luke's Methodist Church, to name a few. Kamrath was honored as a Distinguished Alumna of Lamar High School in 2007.[184]

## The Importance of Lamar's Faculty

Teachers make a school. All of the research that has ever been done on the importance of fabulous modern facilities filled with computers and lab equipment pales when compared to the impact of a well-educated faculty who employ sound teaching methods and who care about the students. Nowhere is the truth of this borne out more emphatically than Lamar High School during the 1950s.

What speaks to Lamar High School's superior collegiate preparation is graduates who talk about not even needing to buy the chemistry textbook at UT, or about breezing through Math 100 at Rice. The teachers at Lamar unquestionably gave their students an excellent foundation, but they also gave them much more. This was a school where, amidst the teachers' demands of academic discipline, they also taught their students to dream tall dreams.

Interviews with alumni make clear the influence of Lamar's teachers on their lives: "My teachers were my mentors, they were my inspiration… Mrs. Teshner is the reason I majored in English." "Lee Keding determined my major in music and my career as a music teacher…" Miss Hollingsworth was "that wonderful chemistry teacher who provided the foundation for my successful career in chemical engineering." One graduate put a positive spin on Coach Fred Pepper's stern refusal "to put up with any foolishness." Because of Pepper's strictness, "I was prepared for my Fish year at Texas A&M."

Celia Buchan calls Miss McCarty "an upright lady" who taught Celia that books "might be something more than a vehicle for a good grade." Another praises McCarty for teaching him to write, a necessary skill for his business career. John Pundt remembers English teacher Opal Glen Chase, who required a two-page theme written on any subject to be turned in every Monday. Pundt says, "What a foundation for my journalism degree and my newspaper career," to have that kind of discipline drilled into him. Many students praise the teaching of Mabel Scott, whose English classes were designed to give students a good preparation for college.

Katherine Taylor Mize says she still uses one of Helen Greenwood's tools in her own classroom. Greenwood would throw out a topic for discussion, encourage every class member to contribute, and then stop the class and ask, "Now how did we get to this point in the discussion. Let's trace it backwards and see where we started." She challenged them to remember what each student had contributed until they returned to the original subject. Another former student uses Helen Greenwood's name as her computer password. Margaret Buchanan created Sequoyah, a club for writers, to encourage "future literary giants."[185] She inspired them not only to write for pleasure, but also to enter Ready Writing, *Atlantic Monthly*, and *Scholastic Magazine* contests. In 1951, her pupil Joan Bartheleme won the state championship in UIL Ready Writing. A Sheaffer Snorkel fountain pen (ten were given out of 45,000 entries) was won in 1955 by Sequoyah club member Bob Durst, who also received a Certificate of Merit from *Scholastic Magazine*. Miss Buchanan's Sequoyah members' anthology won first place in state that year.

Art teacher Norma Henderson inspired a whole generation of Lamar artists and created the Cartoonists Association in 1952. When Henderson retired, Genevieve Filson carried on her legacy. Few, if any, high schools have a club designed to give budding cartoonists "unlimited opportunities to display their talents" creating cartoons for the front hall bulletin boards.

Filson's students, most of whom were members of the Wapika art club, were encouraged to enter every art contest open to high school students. In 1953–1954, Lamar students won fifty-nine certificates and keys in the prestigious Foley's Department Store competition, seven awards in the City Scholastic Art Contest, and fifty-three certificates and keys in the Local Division of the National Scholastic Art Contest. Three students placed in the National Scholastic Art Contest, competing against 170,000 entries.

The contests, tournaments, games, and athletic events that produced such an overwhelming list of winners in athletics, drama, debate, art, music, science, and ROTC were the product of faculty encouragement and support. A 1956 graduate describes the campus as being "alive" with students before and after school: "Everyone you knew was a member of various clubs and organizations." Lamar was a place where "everyone was encouraged to do everything." Teachers did not arrive late and leave early, but rather spent long hours being a part of the lives of their students and urging them to pursue their dreams. They sent them off to college and urged them to make a difference.

Students could not initiate submissions and entries into public school competitions, much less provide their own transportation to events held citywide, statewide, and even in bordering states. Lamar teachers and parents who helped transport students to these contests took tremendous pride in their students' participation.

Former Lamar students say that they have come to recognize the teachers' selfless involvement with their progress, and most feel that this support was instrumental in their college choices, their career choices, and their lifelong pastimes. One graduate pointed to a Lamar teacher who called her thirty years after graduation to express condolences because she had seen in the newspaper that the

*Gilbert Shelton (left), whose classmates described him as a scribbler. Today he resides in Paris, France, and has achieved international fame as an underground "commix" artist. Commix is Steven Spielberg's term to define multi-layered graphic stories. On the right is club member Ernest Fontaine.*

woman's husband had died. "That's the kind of connection you had with your teachers at Lamar." Another describes the essence of Lamar as a school whose faculty provided "the foundation of learning and an appreciation for the act of learning." And finally, sculptor GeeGee Kamrath Mygdal, reflecting on her high school days, probably speaks for many of her classmates when she says, "How lucky we were to come along at this time" in Lamar's history.

No discussion of the 1950s would be complete without a mention of the tremendous camaraderie that still exists among the graduates of these ten classes. The innumerable breakfast clubs, luncheon groups, bridge groups, supper clubs, birthday clubs, and even cruises, as well as reunions every five years when the norm at most high schools is ten, provide a testimonial to the importance of schooldays at Lamar, where students made friendships that have lasted a lifetime. Lamar students graduated with a sound academic foundation, social skills, and lifelong friendships. Their high school gave them the tools to become leaders and team players, and the inspiration to take an interest in their community and involve themselves in public service.

# CHAPTER FIVE
## THE 1960s

According to Tom Brokaw, "the sixties blindsided us with mind-bending swiftness, challenging and changing almost everything that had gone before."[186] Bob Dylan's lyrics, "The times they are a'changin'," aptly described the momentous social and cultural changes that occurred when a vanguard of hippies or beatniks began to question the philosophy of hard work, respectability, and conformity.

Despite—or perhaps because of—young people's rejection of traditional values, the 1960s have been called an exciting decade, a time when President John F. Kennedy "passed the torch to a new generation of Americans" and inspired them to think that they could make a difference.[187]

These "flower children," who are so often mentioned in any discussion of the 1960s, used their loss of faith in the future after the assassinations of Kennedy and Martin Luther King as justification for their irresponsibility and drug use. Seventy percent of them came from prosperous families with an income of over $7,500 ($284,700 in today's dollars). Lamar students who were similarly privileged could have been influenced by these California-based groups, but this destructive philosophy was generally not embraced by them.

For more than thirty years, Lamar High School had prided itself on tradition, academic excellence, and a rather genteel student body who were derisively referred to as "Tea Sippers" by other Houston high schools. Only by the end of the 1960s were changes beginning to occur as Lamar students adopted the hairstyles and clothing of the new generation and abandoned some of the formality they previously embraced.

In 1961, the City of Houston was "reaching for the stars" as it transformed itself into what was called a "city of the future."[188] Marvin Hurley, the Houston Chamber of Commerce director whose

*The Astrodome is complete. Astroworld and Loop 610 are under construction. Colt 45 Stadium is in the background. Diane Foreman (Class of 1972) worked summers at Astroworld and appeared in* Brewster McCloud, *a film directed by Robert Altman that was shot at the amusement park. David Purdie (Class of 1985) grew up loving this park. When he heard of the demolition, he went daily to the site and shot footage of the amusement park's demise, which he has made into a documentary film. (Courtesy of Story Sloane Gallery)* son Gary (Class of 1960) was a graduate of Lamar, stated, "People from everywhere crowded into Houston… bringing new ideas and viewpoints, newcomers who energized the city into becoming a center of innovation and civic creativity." The Chamber of Commerce worked "to keep in step with the changing requirements of a fast-moving age and a dynamic community" by pumping up research and development programs, schools, colleges, and the fine arts.[189]

Its success in keeping up was affirmed in 1961, when the area twenty-two miles southeast of Houston, a 1,000-acre tract of land "donated" by Rice Institute, was officially designated as the site for the new $60-million space center. Criteria for the selection of a site, aside from the requirement of 1,000 acres of land, were an adequate infrastructure that included water transportation, a labor market that included skilled workers and scientists, educational facilities, plenty of electricity, and a favorable climate.[190] Texas political leadership, provided by Vice President Lyndon Johnson, Congressman Albert Thomas, and Congressman Bob Casey, was undoubtedly a factor in the choice of Houston over twenty other cities.

George Brown, a principal of Brown & Root and chairman of the Board of Trustees of Rice Institute, and Morgan J. Davis, president of Humble Oil, made the land available for the project. Humble donated 1,000 acres to Rice, and Brown masterminded Rice's vote to transfer the property to NASA. What Brown and the university received in return was Brown & Root's being named principal engineering and architectural contractor for the project, and Rice University receiving the bulk of the federal grant money to fund "research programs on space problems."[191]

*According to Hofheinz's biographer, Edgar Ray, the roof of the Astrodome was designed by Lamar graduate Ralph Anderson (Class of 1939). (Courtesy of Story Sloane Gallery)*

On July 2, 1962, the Manned Spacecraft Center opened its doors in Houston. The Houston Chamber of Commerce held a parade through downtown Houston followed by a barbecue at the Coliseum for the astronauts and their families. Less than five years later, NASA's payroll was $50 million, and 125 companies had opened offices in and around Clear Lake.

By mid-decade, a powerful Houstonian created another masterstroke. The formal opening of Houston's futuristic "big bubble" occurred on April 9, 1965. Roy Hofheinz's creation, the Harris County Domed Stadium, packed the spectators in and is said to have contributed $80 million to Houston's economy in just one year.[192] Architecturally, the modernistic dome was innovative and spectacular. Roy Hofheinz's inspiration for the design supposedly began with his visit to the Colosseum when he attended the World Conference of Mayors in Rome in 1955. The genesis of Hofheinz's conception of Houston's dome lay in the Roman arena's circular shape, the papyrus cover pulled over the top on hot days, and the placement of dignitaries on the top row.[193] Hofheinz did talk with Buckminster Fuller about designing a geodesic dome, but Ralph Anderson (Class of 1939), a member of the Houston architectural team that designed the dome, said the Astrodome was no more a geodesic dome "than I am."[194] Anderson should know, since Edgar Ray, Hofheinz's biographer, says he "had the most to do with roof of the dome."[195]

Aside from Ralph Anderson, Lamar's other links to the "bubble" were Hofheinz's children, Roy Jr. (Class of 1953), Fred (Class of 1956), and Dene (Class of 1960). During the 1950s, Judge Hofheinz accompanied Roy Hofheinz, Jr. to a Lamar debate team contest in Denver, Colorado. The senior Hofheinz was so impressed with the event that he advised his younger son Fred, who was entering Lamar that fall, to sign up for debate.[196]

Roy Jr., a brilliant student, received his AB degree at Rice, became one of the youngest Rhodes Scholars in history, and was awarded his PhD at Harvard in 1967. A celebrated scholar whose publications have been translated into four languages, he served as director of the Fairbank Center for Asian Research at Harvard University. Hofheinz' second son, Fred, who is Houston's only second-generation mayor, has been discussed previously. His sister, Dene Hofheinz Anton, claims that the genesis of the Astrodome was a case of "too many rain checks at Buff Stadium." Watching the Buffs play baseball was one of her most enjoyable times with her father. Irritated by rainstorms that interrupted the games, she asked her father, "Why can't we play baseball indoors?"[197] That is exactly what Hofheinz had in mind when he decided to bring major league baseball to Houston. He promised the National League that he would "beat the bad weather especially in summer—the humidity and mosquitoes—by playing inside." Hofheinz's solution was to build the Astrodome. Dene says he sold their home on Yorktown to "buy a ball club," but she admits she enjoyed working with the press and celebrities who came from all over the world to see "the Spaceship that had landed in the Texas Prairie."

A recent article, "Growing Up Hofheinz" in *Houston Lifestyles & Homes*, describes Dene's experiences as daughter of the creator of Astrodomain. Briefly dating Frank Sinatra and meeting stars such as Andy Williams, Dionne Warwick, and Elvis Presley, she went on to be a successful country and western composer who now owns two publishing companies. Dene has won the Helen King Award given by the National Academy of Songwriters and the White Hat Award given by Nashville Songwriters Association International and serves on the Board of Directors of the Texas Baseball Hall of Fame. Her current mission is to save the Astrodome from demolition.[198]

## Ruth Denney's Sixties Stars

Robert Foxworth (Class of 1960) says Ruth Denney and Helen Greenwood "saved" him. These two teachers' faith in him changed his philosophy on life and his future, as well as his attitude toward school.[199] Foxworth was elected president of Kachina, inducted into the National Thespian Society,

*Bob Foxworth (Class of 1960) was kicked out of Bellaire High School, which he describes as full of preppy, snobbish students who were critical of anyone who did not fit into their mold. When he came to Lamar, he said he expected it to be the same, but it was not.*

joined the writing club Sequoyah, and became a feature writer for the *Lancer*, an admirable list of accomplishments for a young man who had before placed no value on school.

Considering Denney's training, it is not surprising that Foxworth's first career choice was the legitimate theater. He began at Washington, D.C.'s Arena Stage, but is best known for the characters he played in *Falcon Crest* and *Six Feet Under*, as well as numerous other roles in Hollywood films and on television.

All Lamar students respected Denney's drama program, and the artistic crowd and the socially prominent students crossed back and forth. Foxworth's lifelong friendship with Dene Hofheinz began when they met in Miss Denney's class.

Harriet Melendy (Class of 1961) was a Lamar graduate who excelled in many fine arts activities, including a state championship win in the UIL Poetry Interpretation contest. She became one of Ruth Denney's stars and felt that this teacher was someone she could trust with anything. Melendy received a scholarship to study at the Alley Theater, and by 1962, she was starring at the Playhouse Theater in *Gypsy Rose Lee* and working at KTHT Demand Radio as the "Velvet Voice." When she married, she dropped her first name and became Melendy Britt. Her successful theatrical career has included everything from a L'Oreal hair color advertisement where her line was, "Because I'm worth it," to the voice of "She-Ra/Princess Adora" from the *She-Ra: Princess of Power* television series.

*Harriet Melendy was described by the 1961* Orenda *as "one of the finest actresses Lamar has ever had, outstanding in serious, comic, or musical presentations."*

Ellen Smith (Class of 1964) is better known today as Jaclyn Smith. A dancer when she came to Lamar, Smith easily added acting to her talents. She loved Denney's Little Red Theater and joined Kachina and the Modern Dance Club. While a junior at Lamar, she acted in Theater Inc.'s *Gentlemen Prefer Blondes*, but her goal was still to be a dancer, and that was her major at Trinity University.[200]

She left Trinity and headed for New York, hoping to dance with a ballet company, but only found work in modeling, television commercials, and magazine advertisements. She was the Breck Shampoo girl for several years and then she and Farah Fawcett became the spokeswomen for Wella Balsam shampoo.

Twelve years after graduating from Lamar, Smith got her break when she played a private investigator with Farah Fawcett and Kelly Garrett in *Charlie's Angels*. A smash success, the show ran five seasons, and the rest of her career has been filled with successful television movies, more television series, and guest appearances in various productions. Smith is now described as an actress/businesswoman who pioneered the concept of celebrities developing brands for clothing, home products, and cosmetics.

Ruth Denney's *Ah, Wilderness!* was her last state win, but she set the record for being the only director to have won the state UIL competition five times. Andy Rembert and Maureen MacEntyre won state awards for Best Actor and Actress in this Eugene O'Neill play. Rembert describes the annual field trip to Austin for the UIL competition as anything but fun and games. A harrowing test of time, the cast and crew had to set up the props, perform the play, and dismantle the set in a strictly ruled number of minutes. He remembers one performance where the "stage manager started the count-down as we were finishing the performance."[201]

*Jaclyn Smith says that for her, Ruth Denney was high school. Smith is shown with her mentor Ruth Denney and fellow dancer Tommy Tune.*

According to her former students, Denney was a teacher who "looked for and found the best in each of us." Her compassion and charisma provided her with an uncanny ability to sway young people. As one student said, "She talked to you and you stayed talked to." Denney became like a mother to them as she pulled her casts together and took them to the moon.

This Midwestern farm girl, who came to Texas and remained at Lamar High School until 1966, inspired her students to "reach for the stars." After leaving Lamar, Denney fulfilled her own dream by creating Houston's High School for the Performing and Visual Arts (HSPVA). Since she lacked the credentials to be principal, she was appointed director, then was tapped by the University of Texas Department of Theatre and Dance, where she taught for twelve years. When she died a week before her ninety-third birthday, she was called a "legendary Texas theater educator" and one of the most influential arts educators this state has ever had. The stage in the Ned S. Holmes Performance Hall is named for her.

## Lamar's Faculty and Students Continue to Excel

In May 1963, three years after Robert Foxworth graduated, Helen Greenwood, the English teacher of whom he thought so highly, was honored by Harvard University for her "excellent work as a teacher."[202] The Distinguished Secondary School Teacher Award was presented to her during the Harvard commencement exercises held in June. Greenwood was one of four teachers in the nation awarded this honor.

*Lamar teacher Helen Greenwood, who moonlighted as an Alley Theater actress, was persuaded by Ruth Denney to teach a nighttime private acting class for Tommy Tune, Carlin Glynn, and others at Greenwood's home.*

Her former student Gene Clements, a magna cum laude graduate of Harvard, nominated Greenwood for the award, and another student, Keith Shepherd, wrote her this letter of congratulation that was quoted in the *Lancer*:

> Thanks mainly to your preparation, I have been able to take honors English courses here at school [Washington University–St. Louis]. I am majoring in English and journalism and hope to do graduate work in political science after I graduate in 1964… this award from Harvard has only confirmed what I already knew.

Students speak of Miss Greenwood's oft-repeated comments, "You are beginning to develop a delightful style," and "This shows depth of feeling," making them feel as if they could write and had thoughts worth expressing. Her positive words of encouragement and gifted classroom presentations undoubtedly account for Greenwood's tremendous impact during her twenty-four years at Lamar.[203]

Ready Writing awards, American Chemical Society awards, foreign language medals, science fair honors, and mathematics honors are a testament to Lamar students' superiority. In the UIL Ready Writing competitions, Bob Ball won gold medals in the district, region, and state competitions. He won first place in the National Second-Year French Contests the following year. Senior class president, he was a 5.0-GPA member of Arrowhead who also won a National Merit Scholarship, one out of 1,000 awarded nationally. After graduation, he entered Yale University, where he made the freshman Dean's Honor List.[204] His classmate Suzanne Martyr won national in the First-Year French Contest. The following year, Lamar again took home the first-place awards for the National First- and Second-Year French Contests.

In 1960, the Lamar science team placed first in the American Chemical Society's contest examination, and David Vinson was the grand-prize chemistry winner in the Greater Houston Science Fair. Gray Jennings led Lamar's chemistry team to a first-place win in the 1961 American Chemistry Society competition. The top 10 percent of the chemistry classes competed in a contest for American Chemical Society scholarships. For four consecutive years, the Lamar team placed first in this contest.

Two of Lamar's chemistry teachers deserve some credit for these students' wins. Marcile Hollingsworth and Florine Carr conducted a "Sunrise Chemistry Class" from 7:00 a.m. to 8:00 a.m. for twenty-two days prior to the contest.[205]

Hundreds, if not thousands, of Marcile Hollingsworth's students praise her for teaching them to love chemistry, for providing instruction that made it unnecessary for them to buy the freshman chemistry textbook in college, and for inspiring many to choose chemistry as their career. An examination of her credentials validates Hollingsworth's lifelong commitment to excellence. She earned her BS in Chemistry at the University of Texas and was awarded membership in the freshman honor society, the honorary pre-medical society, and Iota Sigma Pi, the honorary chemistry society.

*Fellow chemistry teachers Marcile Hollingsworth, right, and Florine Carr, wife of Coach Carr, left, worked tirelessly to educate and inspire thousands of Lamar students. (Courtesy of Florine Carr)*

*Marcile Hollingsworth is pictured in her chemistry classroom. She served as a WAC in World War II and was promoted to lieutenant general.*

Over the course of her thirty-six-year HISD career, Hollingsworth has received the following awards: Delta Kappa Gamma named her a Texas Key Woman Teacher in 1961, the Texas Chemical Council named her the Outstanding Chemistry Teacher in 1963, and in 1975 she received the Grady Park Award from the Science Teachers Association of Texas. In 1985, she received a plaque for Outstanding Contributions as well as an Honorary Life Membership in the Science Teachers Association of Texas. She has received the Award of Distinction, the Twentieth Century Award, the Grand Prix Award, and the Gold Medal Award from the Texas Retired Teachers Association.

Described as a "compassionate, organized, highly intelligent individual," Hollingsworth has mentored many teachers as well. Lamar was fortunate to have her on its faculty for fifteen years (1951 to 1966) before HISD appointed her as the supervisor of science. When HISD opened its state-of-the-art science center in 2001 on 2.4 acres, the facility was named the Hollingsworth Science Center. This splendid facility used for science curriculum training is a fitting tribute to this respected Lamar chemistry teacher.

In addition to chemistry, mathematics has always been a priority at Lamar. Mrs. Marjorie Eason's Major Works Calculus class produced numerous math exam

*At the dedication of the Hollingsworth Science Center, Superintendent Kaye Stripling said, "This facility is a tangible tribute to Marcile Hollingsworth, a great educator who devoted thirty-six years to the betterment of science education." (Courtesy of Rique Carson)*

winners during the 1960s. From 1962 to 1964, Lamar students Gray Jennings and Stephen Swenson made the highest team scores in the city and won an achievement award for one of the highest team scores in the Southwest. The Lamar team won an engraved plaque for being in the top 10 percent of the nation seven times. In 1965, Mrs. Eason was invited to attend a meeting of one hundred United States educators in Pennsylvania to spend four days exchanging ideas about math curriculum developments and listening to speakers.[206]

By 1961, forty-one Lamar alumni held doctoral degrees in the sciences, according to the National Academy of Sciences. (The National Research Council announced having conducted "a study of the high school backgrounds of people who received third-level research degrees."[207])

The collegiate success of three Merit Scholars from the Class of 1962 was reported in a 1967 edition of the *Lancer*. Lee Hogan graduated in the top 2 percent of his class at Georgia Tech, Sydney "Buddy" Buttrill graduated from MIT with a degree in chemistry and a minor in physics, and Louise Connally studied math and zoology as a pre-med student at the University of Texas, graduating Phi Beta Kappa.[208] Looking at the outstanding careers of Hogan, Buttrill, and Connally underscores the superiority of Lamar's graduates.

> "TOTAL AIR-CONDITIONING PROMISED BY APRIL 1970"
> —*Lancer*, May 1, 1969

Lee Hogan (Class of 1962) was allowed to skip his freshman year at Georgia Tech and after graduation completed his MBA at Harvard University. He served as president and chief operating officer of Houston Industries from 1993 to 1997 and as director of operations for Reliant Energy in Asia, Europe, and Latin America. Hogan was president of the Board of Directors of St. Luke's Hospital and board member of the M. D. Anderson Cancer Center, The Texas Medical Center, and the Salvation Army.[209] Hogan was honored as a Distinguished Alumni of Lamar High School in 2005.

In 2007, following retirement from his successful career, Hogan joined St. Martin's Episcopal Church Leaders' Quest Program and traveled to South Africa. Hogan founded the Anglican Health Network to apply the leadership lessons he learned on his quest and currently directs the Surplus Medical Equipment Program. He has made five trips to Africa and calls his Leaders' Quest experience a "wake up call" that has helped him "examine how my own plans for helping my community compare" to those of the leaders he has met.[210]

S. E. "Bud" Buttrill, Jr., who is a consultant for various high-tech companies, says his greatest strength is his "ability to solve problems and make systems work." After graduation from MIT (1966) with a degree in chemical physics, he took his PhD at Stanford (1970). The math skills he learned at Lamar High School placed him one semester ahead at MIT, which he says was a huge advantage. Also, Hollingsworth had provided extra chemistry labs for him. The greatest gift he says he received from Lamar was studying under Helen Greenwood, who taught him how to write. According to Buttrill, many scientists lack the writing proficiency to communicate their ideas. He has continued his work in chemical physics and to date has been granted twelve U.S. patents with one pending, has authored over thirty-five papers in refereed journals, and has presented more than sixty papers at professional meetings.[211]

Louise Connally (Strong) (Class of 1962) has had a remarkable career in medicine. She is professor of cancer genetics at M. D. Anderson Cancer Center and holds a joint appointment as professor in the Department of Breast Medical Oncology. Devoting her life to the study of the relationship between genetics and cancer, Strong has received the following awards: Ashbel Smith Distinguished Alumna of the University of Texas Medical Branch in Galveston (1997), the Distinguished Texas Geneticist Award from the Texas Genetics Society (1997), and the Charles A. LeMaistre Outstanding Achievement Award in Cancer at the University of Texas M. D. Anderson Cancer Center. In 2006, she was honored as one of the Distinguished Alumni of Lamar High School.

E. Linn Draper, Jr. (Class of 1960) was a National Merit Scholarship semifinalist, National Honor Society member, American Chemical Society examination winner, business manager of the *Orenda*, and vice-president of Pow Wow. He received a BA and a BS from Rice University and his PhD from Cornell University. He served on the University of Texas faculty as director of the Nuclear Engineering Program, but left academia to join Gulf States Utilities. Appointed president from 1987 to 1992, in 1993 Draper became CEO of American Electric Power, a company that serves more than 3 million customers in seven states. His honors include member of the National Academy of Engineering, member of the Cornell University Council Board, member of the University of Chicago's Board of Governors for the Argonne National Laboratory, president of the American Nuclear Society, and chairman of the Nuclear Energy Institute.[212]

Scott Caven (Class of 1960) earned his BBA and LLD from the University of Texas, working for Governor John B. Connally as a legal assistant. In 1969, he entered the brokerage business at Goldman Sachs, serving as vice-president and then regional manager for Houston, South Texas, and Mexico. Governor Bill Clements appointed him as chairman of the Texas Growth Bond Board of Trustees, and Governor Ann Richards reappointed him, as did Governor George W. Bush. Caven has been active in many organizations at the University of Texas, appointed to the Board of Regents by Governor Bush and then elected chairman of the board in 2007. He has also supported the TIRR Foundation, the YMCA, the Houston Symphony Orchestra, and his church. A man who has shared his talents with Houston and his state, Scott Caven was chosen as a Distinguished Alumni of Lamar High School in 2010.[213]

David Dewhurst (Class of 1963), a name familiar to all Texans, earned his BA from the University of Arizona while playing college basketball. Following service as an officer in the U.S. Air Force, Dewhurst worked for the Central Intelligence Agency and the U.S. State Department. An early developer in the electric cogeneration business, he founded a Texas-based energy and investments company, earning a reputation as an innovative and successful businessman.[214]

Dewhurst began his public service career as commissioner of the Texas General Land Office. After 9/11, he was appointed by Governor Rick Perry as chairman of the Governor's Task Force on Homeland Security. Today he serves as lieutenant governor and president of the Texas Senate and is a Distinguished Alumnus of Lamar who believes that "education is the key to any child's future."[215]

Also in the Class of 1963 were two men whose lifelong friendship was solidified by their three years at Lamar. Ned S. Holmes and his friend W. McComb "Mac" Dunwoody both took business degrees from the University of Texas. Both pursued careers in investment banking. Holmes worked in New York City at Morgan Guaranty Trust, but returned to Houston in 1971 and entered the commercial and multi-unit residential real estate business. He currently works with a United Kingdom company in the development and management of companies in Houston, Atlanta, Denver, Orlando, San Diego, and other U.S. cities. Holmes' community involvements and honors are many and include serving on the City of Houston Planning Commission, the Greater Houston Partnership Board, the Southwestern Regional Board of the Institute of International Education, and the Urban Land Institute Board, as well as commissioner of the Port of Houston. His generosity to Lamar High School can be seen by gazing up at the sign on the meticulously renovated auditorium. Without Ned Holmes, Lamar would have a much different look, for this man has repaid his alma mater many times for the education he received within these walls.[216] In 2000, he was honored as a Distinguished Alumnus of Lamar High School.

*Right: Distinguished Lamar Alum for 2000, Ned S. Holmes is shown at the dedication of Lamar's new auditorium with classmate and Alumni Association supporter Betsy Sauer (Class of 1962).*

*Below: The interior of Lamar's Ned S. Holmes Performance Hall includes 1,000 new upholstered chairs, a new stage surface, curtains, carpeting, a sound system, and lights. Tommy Tune returned to dedicate the facility on October 21, 2009. (Courtesy of Will LeBlanc)*

Mac Dunwoody graduated from the University of Texas with honors. Working first in Boston, he returned to Houston, where he started the Corporate Finance Department of First City National Bank. Today he is the co-managing general partner of Inverness Management, but Dunwoody has also worked tirelessly for many years to provide scholarship assistance for inner-city students. He co-founded Imagine College, a program that has provided scholarship opportunities for more than 5,000 young disadvantaged students.[217]

## ATHLETICS

The *Lancer*'s sports column was written by Peter Roussel (Class of 1961), a student whose father, Herbert Roussel, was the drama, music, and film critic for the *Houston Post* for thirty years. Having grown up in a newspaper-oriented family, he says his goal was to be a professional sportswriter. But shortly after graduating from the University of Houston in 1965, Roussel was hired by U.S. Congressman George H. W. Bush to be his press secretary and continued to serve him when he became ambassador to the UN and chairman of the Republican Party. Roussel remained in Washington, D.C., serving as a presidential aide until 1981, when President Reagan appointed him deputy press secretary. In 1983, the University of Houston honored him as a Distinguished Alumnus, and in 1986 chose him for the first Distinguished Communications Alumnus Award.[218] Roussel was honored as a Lamar Distiguished Alum in 2000.

An academically superior athlete is the dream of every high school coach. Don Longcope, Lamar's venerable basketball coach, and Brad Gentry, the school's tennis coach, undoubtedly were excited when they first met Lamar Roemer. In 1962, this NHS honor student was also Lamar's outstanding tennis champion, winning state as the UIL Class AAAA singles champion. He played in the U.S. Open seven times and was honored as an NCAA All-American scholar athlete. Lettering in both tennis and basketball during his three years at Lamar, he was honored along with teammates Jerry McGhee and Howard Tellepsen in the basketball All-City selections. After graduation, Lamar Roemer went to Trinity University, where he was captain of the tennis team during its four-year winning record. He earned his PhD at Texas A&M in Geologic and Geophysical Oceanography and has a successful oil and gas business.[219]

*Tennis star Lamar Roemer competed at Wimbledon and was one of the nation's top-rated junior tennis players. (Courtesy of Lamar Roemer)*

Including Roemer's win in 1962, Lamar won four UIL State Championships in tennis from 1960 to 1967. Lamar's doubles team, composed of Dale McCleary and Leslie Berkes, won the UIL State Championship in 1960–1961, Gordon Herbert and Frank Jones won the doubles UIL State Championship in 1962–1963, and George Taylor won the championship in the singles category in 1966–1967.

Two 1963 graduates who shared their love of football at Lamar were Randy House and Bill Poland. House says he was too small and lightweight to think about playing, so he proudly became Lamar High School's first "Little Red" mascot. After graduation, he attended Texas A&M, where he was a Distinguished Military Graduate. He was commissioned into the U.S. Army and served two tours in Vietnam, continuing his military education at the Ranger School, the Airborne School, the Rotary Wing Flight School, the Army Command and General Staff College, and the National War

*Olympic medalist swimmer Cynthia Potter (Class of 1968) was the first woman athlete to address the U.S. Congress.*

College. Among his many medals and awards are the Defense Distinguished Service Medal, Defense Superior Service Medal, Legion of Merit, Distinguished Flying Cross, and a Bronze Star. House retired as a lieutenant general and continues to serve as an advisor to the U.S. Army and the Department of Defense.[220]

Bill Poland (Class of 1963) lettered in football and baseball his junior and senior years at Lamar. He took his BSME at Georgia Tech, followed by an MBA at Stanford in 1971. Poland remained in California and entered the field of real estate management. In 1979, he founded his own company, Bay West Group, a business that has developed several million miles of light industrial and garden office buildings. Poland is past chairman of the San Francisco Convention and Visitors Bureau, along with other community involvements. In 2007, Bill Poland and Randy House were both honored by Lamar High School as Distinguished Alumni.

Olympic swimmer Cynthia Potter (Class of 1968) made a name for herself in sports at a time when there were few opportunities open to women. Title IX was still five years away, and professional

*In 2007, Bill Poland and Randy House were both honored as Distinguished Lamar Alumni. Here they are shown with the other 2007 recipients. Left to right: Doug Pitcock, Lauren Anderson, Randy House, and Bill Poland.*

and collegiate sports, except for golf and tennis, did not include women. Potter was a diver, but no diving programs for women existed at any colleges when she graduated from Lamar. When offered a spot on the men's diving team at Indiana University, she took it.

From then on, Potter won honor after honor. In 1970, 1971, and 1977, she won World Diver, and then National Champion twenty-eight times. A member of four Olympic diving teams, in 1976 she won the Bronze Medal in Montreal. In 1987, she was inducted into the International Swimming Hall of Fame. Potter regularly works as a commentator for the Summer Olympics and proudly announces on national television that she is a graduate of Lamar High School in Houston, Texas.[221]

*Lamar's baseball field was named for Bill Poland, an excellent Lamar athlete and generous Lamar supporter.*

Swimming continued to be a sport in which Lamar consistently excelled, but while the team won the city title most years, no UIL State Championships are recorded until Kate Green (Class of 1969) won the girls' one-hundred-yard butterfly championship in 1969.

The annual Football Banquet in 1964–1965 honored Corbin Robertson, Jr.'s outstanding contributions to Lamar's Redskins football team. The six-foot, two-inch, 200-pound senior, who lettered two years in baseball and three years in football, was a scholarly athlete who was also a member of NHS. As a senior, he had won the City Baseball Batting Award, and for two years was chosen as a member of the All-District football team. His father, Corbin Robertson, Sr., was emcee for the banquet. Corbin Jr. (known at Lamar as "Corby") received the E. T. Shaw Award for the Most Valuable Lineman and the Captain Award. *Lancer* staff member Jeff Young reported that Corby accepted the awards just as graciously as he catches passes, "pausing each time to thank all in his now-famous manner of accepting praise."[222]

## A COLLEGE PREPARATORY HIGH SCHOOL

A brief comparison of Lamar High School's graduation requirements with those of Reagan High School,[223] a typical HISD secondary school, indicates the difference between a school where 98 percent of the students went on to college and one where that percentage was considerably lower.

In math, both schools required two units for graduation, but Lamar suggested this consist of one and a half units of Algebra and one year of Plane Geometry, which actually added an extra semester. Reagan allowed General Math and Commercial Arithmetic, courses not even taught at Lamar, to satisfy the mathematics requirement.

At Lamar, students had to take two units of science, biology, chemistry, and physics, or a combination of the three. At Reagan, only one science unit was required. The Lamar handbook

*Front row: Elsa Rosborough (Class of 1942), Jeanette Clift George (Class of 1942), and Sherry Woodard Williams (Class of 1979). Back row: Corbin Robertson, Jr. (Class of 1965) and Walter Fondren III (Class of 1954). These Lamar graduates were honored as Distinguished Alumni in 2001.*

recommended students use at least two electives to take extra math, social studies, foreign language, and science. Reagan's handbook contains no guidelines for elective choices.

Lamar offered four years of Latin, Spanish, French, and German. Reagan offered two years of Spanish and Latin. In 1960, Lamar began offering shorthand, "a new course which offers a good way to take your notes and save time in college." Reagan's yearbook speaks of the opportunities in the business world for graduates. Reagan counselors received many phone calls from businesses wanting to hire "top students" to come to work after graduation. Lamar probably did not receive such calls.

At Lamar, students could join an astronomy club, an art club, a library club, a writing club, and a rodeo club. They could join a radio club that broadcast on a local radio station, and they could participate in three different drama activities. For Lamar students interested in agriculture and livestock, two clubs, FFA and the Rodeo Club, both of which had close ties with the Houston Livestock Show, enabled students to be a participant in the parade and other activities of this popular citywide event.

In April 1961, *Lancer* articles provided examples of the speakers who came to address Lamar's student body. During one week, they had the opportunity to hear lectures by Dr. James McCord, president of the Princeton Theological Society, who spoke about President Kennedy's newly established Peace Corps. Dr. W. W. Sawyer, professor of math at Wesleyan University, spoke about the importance of taking the mystery out of math. Lamar economics students heard lectures by Texas National Bank executives.

The "Voice of Lamar" was celebrating its third anniversary by 1962. Changing the name from the Radio Guild to the Radio Club, this remarkable bi-monthly radio program aired on the University of Houston station KUHF-FM. The club was designed to "further students' interest in radio and television fields." A "Velvet Voice" contest sponsored in 1962 generated the funds for the club to buy a new tape recorder.[224]

All Houston high schools had students who handled the daily public address announcements. At Lamar, however, the members expanded their scope to include citywide on-air programming and called themselves a "welcome relief" from the regular disk jockey's "quick wilting jokes or news flagrantly tainted with local color."

The sponsor of the Radio Club was Mary Junger. When she was not teaching at Lamar, Junger was an opera singer who performed at the Music Hall. She was also an actress and played leading roles at Theatre Inc. At Lamar, she conducted workshops, coaching the members of the club on interviewing, announcing, acting, producing, and writing.

Under her tutelage, the Lamar club members produced taped interviews with the Kingston Trio, Red Skelton, John Wayne, Jeanette Clift (Lamar Class of 1942), Senator Strom Thurmond, and political commentator David Brinkley. The Radio Club's radiocast on Friday, October 5, 1962, was a student discussion about the domed stadium.[225]

Hamilton Beazley (Class of 1961) was vice-president of the Radio Club as well as president of Sequoyah, the writing club. He received Honorable Mention in the *Atlantic Monthly* Writing Contest for his short story, and had a story published in *Scholastic Magazine*. Beazley took fourth place in the National Spanish Exam and was treasurer of the National Forensic League. A member of Arrowhead and NHS, he received a National Merit Scholarship Letter of Commendation.

After graduation from Lamar, Beazley received his BA in Psychology from Yale, his MBA at Southern Methodist University, and his PhD at George Washington University. Today he is a nationally recognized author, university professor, and consultant on power, creativity, and entrepreneurship. In an interview, Beazley said his high school English teacher "encouraged me to write essays and short stories and tutored me in how to write well."[226]

*The Lamar Rodeo Club's purpose was to add color and spirit to Lamar by furthering its Texas heritage through participation in parades, outings, barbecues, and socials.*

The English teacher to whom he referred was Helen Greenwood. He deeply appreciated her teaching and has visited her grave in Navasota, Texas. Beazley is pleased to have signed a contract with Disney's Hyperion Press, which in 2014 will publish his first fiction work, a young adult novel.

The use of the excellent library facilities supported the academic pursuits of the students at Lamar High School. By 1962, the library had grown from fewer than 1,000 volumes to over 15,000 and subscribed to 117 magazines. Members of Wowapi, the library club, kept the shelves in order, handled circulation, and decorated the library's traditional Christmas tree.

Lamar's biology museum "ranks with Houston's Best."[227] Lamar's museum, maintained by biology teacher Laura Anderson, featured specimens of "land, air, and sea life." One exhibit featured the feet of birds, from a tiny hummingbird's foot to that of a massive owl. Water tanks contained various sea creatures including a whole tank for squid and octopi. The specimens had all been acquired with the permission of the Fish and Game Department.

The Lamar Astronomy Club, composed of "star gazers," was the only high school astronomy club in the Southwestern United States. It also had Houston's only privately owned observatory (pre-Burke Baker), constructed in Addicks, seventeen miles west of Houston, by members who used donated

*During the 1960s, the Lamar Library was visited daily by more than 400 students and teachers.*

building materials.²²⁸ The club's two telescopes were among the finest in the city. Originating in 1955 during a period of intense interest in science education, the Astronomy Club offered members a place to meet where they could observe, time, and record phenomena, meteors, and comets. The group boasted that, as the largest astronomy group in the area, they were "the authority on astronomy for Houston."²²⁹

*One of the library's most revered traditions was decorating its Christmas tree.*

In 1961, Paul Knauth, president of the club, represented Houston at the National Science Foundation's Astronomy Institute. Only thirty high school juniors in the United States were invited to attend this event. In August, club members spent a week at McDonald Observatory to observe the annual Perseid meteor shower. By 1963, the members were turning their recordings in to "the meteor research program of the Canadian Astronomical Society, where the combined information of the world's atmosphere is compiled by computers."²³⁰

In addition to supporting "star struck" astronomers, Lamar also provided opportunities for students interested in music and theater. A vocalist who was one of Lee Keding's Choralettes,

Elizabeth Newnam (Class of 1961), remembers the excitement of riding on a float down Pennsylvania Avenue in Washington, D.C., where they had come for the Cherry Blossom Festival. A serious musician who took private voice lessons, Newnam recognized that Keding was a talented organizer and promoter, but not really a musician. Newnam took her BA from Randolph Macon and an MA in music from Florida State University, and has taught voice lessons in Kentucky and Texas. But music is only one part of her life. In 1989, Elizabeth Newnam was ordained an Episcopal priest. Today, she credits Margaret Buchanan, her English teacher at Lamar, as the person who taught her to write and thereby "prepared me for the rest of my life."

Newnam has served as the vicar of St. George Church in Canyon, Texas, as well as at St. Barnabas and other Episcopal churches in San Francisco. She has worked as a social worker with the Lighthouse for the Blind and founded an interdenominational consortium of eleven churches in Canyon to help supplement the lives of impoverished residents.

Margo Sappington (Class of 1965) spent her time at Lamar in Kachina, the National Thespian Society, and the French Club. She was also a member of Arrowhead and the French Honor Society. Less than ten years after leaving Lamar, she was nominated for a Tony award as Best Choreographer and a Drama Desk Award for Outstanding Choreography for her work in the play *Where's Charley?*. Sappington choreographed and performed in the original production of *Oh! Calcutta!*, and in 1971, she choreographed her first of many ballets.[231] She was honored recently as a Lamar Distinguished Alum.

Edward Carson "Casey" Williams (Class of 1965), while a student at Lamar, was reportedly the first Greg Noll custom surfboard dealer in Houston. He joined Artisans, the art club at Lamar,

*Pictured on the float at the Cherry Blossom Festival in Washington, D.C., are the Choralettes, who participated five times in this event.*

*Houston native Francie Mendenhall, one of Dean Martin's original Golddiggers, is posed on Martin's left. (Courtesy of Francie Mendenhall)*

*Dick Walters (Class of 1963), past president of the Lamar Alumni Association, is talking with John Daugherty (Class of 1962), who was honored as a Distinguished Lamar Alum in 2000. Daugherty is a respected Houston realtor who devotes much of his time to community service and is a strong supporter of Lamar.*

and his media was photography. After graduation from UT, he received his MFA in Photography at the San Francisco Art Institute. The following years were spent teaching photography at various colleges around the country. He started the Photography Department for the Glassell School of Art in Houston. His work is part of the permanent collections at museums in Paris, New York, Houston, Dallas, and Austin. His death from encephalitis caused by the West Nile Virus occurred in January 2013, while his show "Within" was still on exhibit at the Holly Johnson Gallery in Dallas, as his *Houston Chronicle* obituary points out.

Francie Mendenhall (Class of 1969), a Houston native whose parents owned Houston's Playhouse Theater, says she was born on the stage. After developing her acting and singing skills in Norma Lowder's Mixed Chorus at Lamar High School and the school's production of Gilbert and Sullivan's *The Mikado*, this nineteen-year-old became one of Dean Martin's original Golddiggers. After her stint in Las Vegas, she appeared on Broadway with Pearl Bailey in *Hello Dolly*. Her successful career in musical theater included roles on television and work with Tommy Tune and Peter Masterson, who co-directed her as Miss Mona in four productions of *The Best Little Whorehouse in Texas*.[232]

### THE OPENING OF ROBERT E. LEE HIGH SCHOOL

HISD ignored the superior education Lamar High School offered its students, the awards amassed in athletics, scholarship, and the fine arts, and the honors that made this school tops in the city, and decided that the enrollment of Lamar (with 1,500 fewer students than the school now has) had become too large. They whittled it down to size by chopping off a portion of Lamar's district to create Robert E. Lee High School, a school that had a splendid beginning but short-lived success.

"It was as if a Berlin Wall was erected at the railroad tracks crossing Westheimer at Highland Village," according to Mike Journeay (Class of 1964). Though no physical barrier was erected, Lee's opening in the fall of 1962 took away all of the students who lived in Tanglewood, Briargrove, and the other subdivisions west of Highland Village and south of Buffalo Bayou. The fact that enrollment in Kincaid School's Class of 1963 was the largest in the school's history is probably not coincidental.[233]

Lamar Principal Dr. Woodrow Watts left Lamar in 1962 to open the new Robert E. Lee High School.

Most of the students, both those who remained at Lamar and those who had to transfer to Lee, were a close-knit group that looked upon the opening of the new school with great sadness.[234] One alum says this division of Lamar students ripped the heart out of club memberships and close friendships, and altered family legacies as Lamar parents saw one offspring graduate from their alma mater and the other from Lee. Bellaire High School had opened seven years earlier, and while subtracting many fine students from Lamar's class rolls, it did not have the same shattering impact.

HISD added insult to injury by moving Lamar's principal, Dr. Woodrow Watts, to the new school, replacing him at Lamar with Harold Costlow. Watts took nineteen of Lamar's key teachers with him to Lee. Watts stated that his goal for Lee was to build a "good strong academic program [like Lamar's], including Major Works classes [like Lamar's] and the four major foreign languages, Latin, Spanish, French and German [like Lamar's]."[235]

No doubt, Lee would have a fine Foreign Language Department, since Watts, following usual HISD procedure, took the French, Spanish, and Latin teachers with him. In addition, he took four superior English teachers—Jennie Teshner, Mabel Scott, Willas Melton, and Vivian Wilson—and two of Lamar's finest math teachers—Gladys Pushard and Edward Adams, each of whom has been mentioned by three decades of alumni as Lamar math teachers who made a tremendous difference in their lives. Mr. Adams, who sponsored the National Honor Society, the Christian Student Union, and the Astronomy Club, was an especially important faculty member whose transfer left a void. Gifted music teacher Rosamund Glosup, who sponsored two organizations, Mixed Chorus and the Lamar-O-Liers, also went, along with Edward Trongone, the respected band and orchestra conductor.

The teachers were certainly not forced to leave. Their choices were, perhaps, motivated by geography, the opportunity to move to a brand new school, loyalty to Principal Watts, uncertainty as to what Lamar's new principal's style of management would be, or a desire to start anew and perhaps gain a higher position. Regardless of their reasons, the result was the same, a loss for Lamar.

While Lee's opening enrollment of 900 may have necessitated some faculty reduction at Lamar, the *Lancer* article "Costlow Reveals Plans for Lamar" made clear the effects of Watts' raid. "Although we are suffering a great loss due to the teachers who are leaving to go to the new Robert E. Lee High School, the ones who are taking their places [new teachers] are equally capable." Clearly, Lee's teacher base was assembled at the expense of Lamar's faculty.

In 2012, Lamar High School and Bellaire High School are still growing and thriving, while Robert E. Lee High School is effectively gone. HISD made a momentous decision based on 1962 demographics when they decided to split Lamar. The lines for the Lee district included a mixture of middle-class to affluent upper-class family homes (Tanglewood and Briargrove), along with apartment projects that all too soon became unstable and undesirable. Many of the parents who lived in what were formerly Lamar-zoned neighborhoods withdrew their teenagers and enrolled them in private schools.

*Helen Weinberg came to Lamar in 1937 and remained for twenty-seven years, teaching government and sponsoring the* Orenda, *for which she received the Scholastic Press Gold Key award from Columbia University.*

### The Costlow Regime

Harold Costlow had a reputation for being able to organize fine teams who functioned individually. As his new assistant principal, he chose Lon Wheeler, previously a science teacher at Lamar. In 1964, however, Lamar's faculty suffered three more unavoidable losses. Miss Lel Red, mathematics, Miss Nell Morris, Spanish, and Miss Helen Weinberg, civics, retired from teaching. Each had served since 1937, when the first Lamar student walked into the "halls of fresh paint."[236] Their combined experience at Lamar totaled eighty-one years, and all three said they did not regret a day of it.

Miss Morris, the sponsor of Arrowhead since its beginning, said, "When Lamar was born, there was nothing out here but flat land." A hard rain flooded the campus so often they called it "Lake Lamar." A former student praised Miss Morris for her total control of the class, which resulted in listening and learning, giving them a great foundation for two more years of Spanish in college. Miss Weinberg had been the business sponsor of the *Orenda* since its origin. Miss Lel Red, Miss Morris, and Miss Weinberg said their formula for teaching was good, hard work.

*Principal Harold Costlow was beloved by Lamar teachers and pupils alike.*

In May 1969, "Clothier Mrs. Sandel" ended her thirty-one-year career as the home economics teacher at Lamar. The last of the original group who came to Lamar from Sam Houston High School with Mr. Moyes, Sandel was the first sponsor of the cheerleaders and continued this duty for twenty years. Some of the top home economists and interior designers in Houston were her former pupils. Upon retiring, Mrs. Sandel said she hoped she had inspired her "girls," because they had certainly been an inspiration to her. She called herself a "sentimental lollipop about Lamar."[237]

## POLITICS AT LAMAR HIGH SCHOOL

Lamar was the only school in Harris County to have a state legislator on the faculty. Henry Cushing Grover was elected to serve as a Democrat in the Texas House of Representatives in 1960, 1962, and 1964. Members of Lamar's faculty have been active in local politics, but Grover actually served as an elected official in the Texas legislature, balancing his legislative terms with HISD's semesters while he was teaching at Lamar.

In 1966, Grover changed to the Republican Party and was elected to the Texas State Senate from District 15. From 1957 to 1964, he taught American history and civics to his students, whose knowledge of social science was surely augmented by having a teacher who was getting firsthand experience in the workings of their state government. He left Lamar to pursue his political career full-time, led the field in the gubernatorial Republican primary in 1972, and competed against Dolph Briscoe in the general election, losing by only 100,000 votes. His political fortunes never recovered from this setback, and his political philosophy, which remained staunchly conservative and pro-life, ended his public service career. Called a statesman rather than a politician by his wife, Grover died of Alzheimer's disease in 2005. Of the eight House positions in Harris County, Grover's was the only one represented by a member of the teaching profession.[238]

*Homemaking teacher Bebe Sandel made the first Big Red out of chicken wire, papier mache, and oil paint. She and her helpers hid it in a student's garage.*

The *Lancer* excitedly announced, "If you thought you saw Mr. Kennedy in the halls of Lamar on Wednesday, September 13—you were right!" In the fall of 1961, Miss Inez Bryan's civics class heard a lecture delivered by Mr. Edward Kennedy, younger brother of President John F. Kennedy, who had come to Houston to speak at the ribbon-cutting of Sharpstown Center. Claude Hooten, Jr. (Class of 1950), a lead architect for the mall, invited his former Harvard roommate and lifelong friend Edward Kennedy to speak at the event and asked him to also speak at Lamar High School.

Kennedy told the Lamar students that his roommate had talked so much about Lamar, he wanted to come to the school. He spoke to them about the importance of education, especially the importance of educating the people of Latin America to build a "strong protection" against communism.[239] His visit to Lamar is poignant considering his brother's assassination in Dallas two years later.

A drawing by David Amidon on the front page of the December 19, 1963 issue of the *Lancer* depicted five men of different nationalities hanging their heads in sorrow. The caption, "The World Cried," referred to the assassination of President John F. Kennedy on Friday, November 23rd. A *Lancer* editorial tried to explain the "indescribable shock and numbness which gripped every man, woman and child… accompanied by a deafening silence as [they] tried to comprehend the full meaning of the century's most horrible crime." The editor praised the "president's vitality, his concern and understanding of the people around him, and his faith in God," and concluded with, "A president has died and a little bit of us has died with him." Even the *Lancer*'s sports page contained an article entitled "Kennedy Was Great Sports Enthusiast." President Kennedy read "the sports pages just like he did the international news." The article referenced his love of sailing, softball, and touch football at Hyannisport or on the White House lawn. Though his back problems could have made him a spectator, he "played in pain and showed the soft and flabby American the way of a man with guts."[240]

While the Lamar students mourned the loss of President Kennedy, in 1964, in a straw vote conducted when President Lyndon Johnson—who had served since Kennedy's death—ran for election, 921 votes were cast for Goldwater and 739 for Johnson.

Congressman George H. W. Bush gave the commencement address for the Lamar Class of 1968. The *Lancer*, in a front-page story, announced that Bush, a respected member of the House of Representatives since 1966, was "the first Republican ever to represent the county [Harris] and the city of Houston."[241] Eleven years later, Bush was sworn in as the forty-first president of the United States.

## Lamar: A Party School

A *Lancer* editorial in April 30, 1964, "Lamar, Party School," deftly refuted a claim made at a recent party attended by students of an unnamed rival school that Lamar was nothing but a party school. The *Lancer* editor, citing the 98.6 percent college admissions rate in 1963 and 95.7 percent in 1964, announced that thirty or more of the seniors planned to attend Rice University, and that Lamar had won more "Woodrow Wilson Fellowships than any other schools, public or private." The Woodrow Wilson Fellowship, sponsored by the Ford Foundation, was awarded to graduates based on their achievements since high school. Lamar led the State of Texas in the number of graduates who won the Woodrow Wilson Fellowship award in 1964 and 1965. The editor also pointed to the seventeen National Merit Scholarship finalists and five valedictorians, and said that "Lamar was rated as one of the top twenty-five schools in the entire nation whereas the rival school was not even mentioned."[242] The fact that in 1962, the American Physics Society ranked Lamar as one of the top ten high schools in the nation, was more than they wanted to hear, and the rivals reportedly slunk off dragging their tails.

## THE ART OF MAKING MUSIC

In the spring of 1961, during Edward Trongone's last full year at Lamar, the Lamar Stage Band traveled to Enid, Oklahoma, where they won first place at the Tri-State Festival, the largest competition held in the nation. To finance their trip, the members mowed lawns, washed cars, and held a band concert. All of their musical arrangements were written by Ned Battista (Class of 1955), who was studying music at the University of Houston.

The Lamar Orchestra continued its excellent record despite Trongone's departure. In January 1964, they traveled in zero-degree weather to Chicago, where they won a first-place award at the Midwestern Band Clinic. Their director, Mr. Lantz, won the Gold Medal of Honor, awarded only once before in seventeen years.

Rosamund Glosup taught music at Lamar from 1957 to 1962. She sponsored the Lamar-O-Liers and the Mixed Chorus, and in 1962 formed a new group of male singers. The Cavaliers sang light music as well as serious music but didn't seem to have lasted long, probably because Mrs. Glosup left at the end of the year to go to Lee High School.

*Lamar's Choraliers are being televised by KPRC, c. 1961. Their sponsor, Rosamund Glosup, is in the foreground leading her singers. (From the Rosamund Glosup Scrapbook)*

A "Dutch" treat was offered by fifty-five Lamar-O-Liers on live television for the Houston Trade Fair on September 23, 1963. Apparently, it was a program honoring Dutch businessmen. The Dutch Consulate furnished costumes for the show, and KLM airlines flew in fresh flowers from Holland especially for the Lamar-O-Liers program. Led by Norma Lowder, the chorus sang some of the songs in Dutch, and the television coordinator used "electrical windmills" which "added to the Dutch atmosphere."

"Chorus to make National TV" was the *Lancer* headline in December 1966, when the Mixed Chorus, accompanied by sponsor Norma Lowder, left for New York and Washington, D.C. In New York, they made a videotape for coast-to-coast television under the direction of the former owner and manager of Carnegie Hall. A concert with the Pageant of Peace was scheduled on the White House lawn in connection with the lighting of the national Christmas tree. Returning to New York, the group performed at Rockefeller Center in front of the sixty-five-foot Christmas tree. Afterwards, they were luncheon guests of Rockefeller Center and were given a tour of the buildings.[243] Brandon Smith says these trips with Norma Lowder were splendid.

While the Mixed Chorus, the Lamar-O-Liers, and the Choralettes continued performing, by mid-decade the music world at Lamar began shifting. In January 1965, the Physical Education Department and Palamar replaced the May Fete with a Hootenanny. A popular fundraiser, the show ran for two performances.[244] A group that called itself "The Dream Machine" was the headliner for the January 1968

*Glosup's Cavaliers was a newly formed boys' chorus. Top row: Aubry Fisk, Bill Erwin, Lee Wolf, Ernie Gammage, Gary Patterson, Darryl Schroeder, Jim Gradwohl, and Tom Greacen. Middle row: Johnny Augsburger, Earle Peel, Johnny Ramsey, Jess Hines, Charles Kollenberg, John Friery, and Kit Werlein. Front row: Ed Bravenec (accompanist), Bill Buchan, Larry Johnson, Andy Rembert, Tom Booth, Holly Fisk, Charles Cayce, Rick Wells, and Stanton Evans. Patterson is now Lamar High School's director of professional development and fine arts programs. (From the Rosamund Glosup Scrapbook)*

Hootenanny. It sang tunes popularized by the famous recording star Aretha Franklin, offerings that were a departure from music previously heard at Lamar.[245]

Coach Duke Lane reminded students that the proceeds from this fundraiser were the baseball and basketball teams' only financial support and each team cost about $1,200 for just one year.[246] The coaches had formed a group called the Hooteneers, who performed with the help of the band director. A description of their act was not reported by the *Lancer*.

"The popularity of folk music is a blessing for Lamar students," the *Lancer* announced in the May 5, 1966 issue. Al Morrison, Susan Giles, Carolyn Baer, and Mike Miller were pictured in the article as a group of students who had performed at local coffee houses. Baer had auditioned for the New Christy Minstrels.[247]

In addition to folk songs, soul music also came to Houston, bringing a whole new "family of dances." The "Shing-a-ling" and the "Funky, Funky Broadway" were two dances enjoying popularity in 1968. A *Lancer* article quoted Lamar English teacher Iris Loep, who said her interest in teenage dances arose from the "numerous inquiries of curious adult friends who expected her to be informed because of her close association with the younger generation." She learned the Shing-a-ling, which she described as a "shuffle of your feet while doing the two-step," from her students Jan Journeay and Candy Caldwell.[248]

Houston's answer to the popular *American Bandstand*'s Dick Clark was a man named Larry Kane. He advertised his Dance City USA in the *Lancer*, promising it was a "new Concept, something For everyone." Specifically, the ad mentioned classes for the "New Go-Go Dances."[249] Kane, born Harry Lieberman, from San Jacinto High School's Class of 1953 and a cum laude graduate of the University of Houston, started his show in 1959 as a Houston version of *American Bandstand*. Many of the local dancers were Lamar students and alums.

*Students singing popular folk songs such as "Where Have All the Flowers Gone?" and "Blowin' in the Wind" perform in the Hootenanny, the popular variety show that took the place of the May Fete.*

*The Larry Kane Show* was aired live on Channel 13 and syndicated live to New York City, Los Angeles, Nashville, and over one hundred other markets. Because of Kane's large following, Houston was the only city that never showed Dick Clark's program while Clark was on the air. Attracting a line-up of professionals such as Hank Williams, Jr., Dionne Warwick, the Supremes, the Lovin' Spoonful, Roy Head, and even Tony Bennett, Kane's show became a "barometer that influenced radio airplay and such national publications as *Billboard* magazine." Every show began and ended with Kane's favorite song, The Beatles' "All My Lovin'."

Until the mid-1960s, Lamar's world was still idyllic. Alan Pike (Class of 1962) describes his days at Lamar as a time when "we were at peace, life was good, and exquisitely simple." By the end of the 1960s, television shows like *Leave it to Beaver* and Norman Rockwell's drawings were just memories of a world that no longer existed.[250]

Journalist Linda Ellerbee, also a member of the Class of 1962, reiterates Pike's description of their Lamar High School cocoon. "We were a pretty ignorant lot" who took little notice of world events and the integration that was coming to the South. She describes herself and her classmates as "Post-War babies" who grew up in a prosperous "city on the make," where their middle-class parents had come to make their fortunes or at the very least to "do well." Ellerbee feels that few if any of the students took notice of Rachel Carson's *The Silent Spring*, their apathy mirroring that of many who were not disturbed by Carson's indictment of environmental habits. According to Ellerbee, Lamar students were more concerned

*Students eating lunch on the lawn.*

*The 1960 senior class officers—girls with short curly hair and skirts that extend to mid-calf, and boys with flat-tops, and everyone wearing white bobby socks—contrasts with those pictured eight years later.*

*By 1968, girls wore their hair long, either straight or with flips, short skirts, and no loafers or white socks. Boys had Beatles haircuts and/or sideburns. Their positioning on a parapet contrasts with the more formal portrait sittings of all previous classes.*

about "Liz and Dick" or "Southwest Conference football scores" than they were about the Cold War.

Despite their carefree innocence, however, or perhaps because of it and their instinctive acceptance of whatever coursework the teachers assigned, students at Lamar got a "first class education for free." At Lamar, Ellerbee says she read everything from Sartre to Shakespeare. Margaret "Tiny" Wisdom exposed her to national politics, Ruth Denney opened the world of dramatics, and Mabel Scott provided superb writing instruction that enabled her to make a name for herself as a journalist. Ellerbee suggests that her class may have been the "last generation to get the chance to be so carefree, so oblivious, so silly, so joyous—and so innocent."[251]

By the end of the decade, millions of young people across America were sporting a new look: hairstyles and clothing popularized by the "love children." Lamar students abandoned the formality they previously embraced, choosing new traditions to replace old ones and creating a very different atmosphere at Lamar.

A comparison of photographs and verbiage from *Lancer* newspapers and *Orenda*s from 1960 to 1969 provides a look at Lamar's adaptation of the new culture and social habits of this decade. In looks, speech, and behavior, Lamar began changing as some students became watered-down versions of "hippies." The 1960 *Orenda* photo of the senior class officers shows four conservatively dressed young people who are positioned in a traditional setting.[252] In the 1968 *Orenda*, the senior class officers have abandoned the traditional dress, hairstyles, and formality of the earlier group.

Few Lamar students became hippies, but many copied modified versions of their clothes, hairstyles, and language. The captions in the 1968 yearbook indicate this transformation: "Mass Confusion," "Psychedelic Seniors," "Sing Out," "Stand Up and Holler!" and "Don't Fence Me In."

"Tennies Here Tennies There—And Everywhere." As early as 1963, some Lamar students actually showed interest in wearing tennis shoes outside of gym classes, automatically subjecting them to ridicule by many of their fellow classmates, according to a tongue-in-cheek article in the *Lancer*:

> When an individual is seen strolling in his tennis shoes he is not trying to be an exhibitionist, but he is actually a representative of a conservative movement interested in the advancement of the tennis shoe, and accordingly, in the welfare of his society.

The reporter, Publius, ridiculed the new fad of wearing a tennis shoe "on every foot" and anxiously awaits the success of the "tennie Crusade" which will overtake the "mentally insecure, leather-soled adolescent."[253]

"Down with Pappagallos," was the rallying cry of those who joined the fictional "Students Against Pappagallo" organization. These soft, flat "must have" shoes that came in all of the current preppy colors were criticized because they wore out quickly. A reporter slammed those who criticized the popular (and expensive) shoe brand just because of the brief lifespan of its product.[254] The gist of the article was "Who cares if they are not durable?"

The 1961 *Lancer* announced scholarship recipients and an article entitled, "Good Grades are Great!" in which Emilie Stude is praised for her 4.8 grade point average, and Alan Nash, who was the class valedictorian, for his 5.0 average. The only serious subject addressed is an editorial that challenges students to quit smoking.

Eight years later, drug abuse was the front-page *Lancer* article, quoting speakers who recently came to Lamar High School for a program on drug abuse. A doctor spoke about those who use illegal drugs and their psychological and physical dependency on them. An attorney spoke to the students about the legal ramifications of drug possession and use. By the end of the decade, drug use among Lamar students was a reality.

By 1968, the *Lancer* included an editorial section to bring "new ideas for the school's improvement," and to attack "old problems from a more realistic viewpoint."[255] "Grades: Unfair Device?" criticized the reliance on grades as a measure of learning, and students who might be "fooled into thinking they are better than the next person," a revolutionary idea for Lamar students, to whom grades had been an important barometer of their success.

New courses added to Lamar's curriculum indicate the transformation from a serious college preparatory format to a school that better reflected the everyday lives and interests of its students. Computer-oriented math, a business law course, and a bookkeeping course indicate a different focus for some. A Distributive Education store, carrying school supplies, candy, and paperbacks, opened in October 1969, providing DE students with hands-on experience in operating a commercial establishment. DE students, though many undoubtedly would go to college, were not taking college

*Twenty-two of the first Arrowettes, Lamar's new drill team, are pictured in 1968.v*

*Jo Lynn Dover was chosen as the first Arrowette captain of the Reserves.*

preparatory courses, and they attended school during the morning and worked in the afternoon at a store of their choice.

The Pacifica radio station opened in 1969, bringing a "new type of radio" to Houston, though not as "shocking" as some had expected. The station did not care about sponsors or the size of its audience. Much of its staffing relied on volunteers, and Lamar students who worked there included Bob Ebersole, Philip Davis, Debbie Saccomano, and Kaye Bennett.[256]

## More Curriculum and Club Changes

The most astounding *Lancer* headline in 1968 was "Former Burbank Coach Helps Plan Drill Team." One of Lamar's most defended traditions was being abandoned. Lamar had always been the only Houston high school without a drill team. The article said by the fall a "performing" group would be in place. The sponsor, Mrs. Avis Kernahan, was already working with a group of junior girls on rules, uniforms, and membership. A *B* average and a *G* in conduct were to be required along with a faculty recommendation and members would take drill team in place of physical education, requirements duplicating those of Houston's other high school drill teams. The new group, called the Arrowettes, would be a dance team with twirlers. The Lamar Marching Band would provide their music. The reasons for starting a drill team: to improve student attitude and the football team's spirit.

One tradition was reestablished at Lamar in 1969 when *Viewpoint* was published. Many teachers and students had mourned the loss of the annual anthology composed of student writing published by Sequoyah, the writing club. Faculty member Jean Nipper was able to resurrect this cherished Lamar student publication. The *Lancer* noted, "For the first time in several years, Lamar will have a literary publication." Lamar's Ready Writing Club had worked out the details of categories and judges. Lamar teachers would select entries which would then be read by Rice and University of Houston professors.

## WATER SPORTS

"Surfer Girl at Lamar?" the *Lancer* discussed Lemoine Lutey's hobby. She had already won nine trophies during her three-year surfing career and in 1967 won first place in the Texas Surfing Championship held at Port Aransas. A member of Locked 'n' Surf Club, a club with six female members who were sponsored by a local surf shop, Lutey spent weekends practicing in Galveston and summers on California beaches. When interviewed about her plans for the future, Lutey said, "I hope to surf all of my life."[257]

Lutey was not the only Lamar student interested in surfing. By 1968, a regular column, "Surf Talk," written by Craig Wells, appeared in the *Lancer*. Wells makes reference to the First Annual Port Aransas/St. Joe's Island Competition. Calling the contest results a series of "ups and downs" for Lamar students, Wells mentions his own victories in the quarterfinals and his defeat in the semifinal heat.

"Brandenburger Known on Skis Around the World," was the title of a *Lancer* article in March 1969, written about a Lamar senior who contended with competitors from all over the world. At age sixteen, Bubba Brandenburger ranked second in water-skiing at the Internationals at the Mexico City tournament, and at a water-skiing event in San Antonio, he broke the world record for boys' jumping. Unfortunately, he suffered a broken finger when he hit a ladder while skiing backwards in the Shamrock Hotel swimming pool, causing him to miss the national competition in 1968.[258] In the summers, Brandenburger performed at Sea-A-Rama in Galveston when he was not teaching astronauts and their families how to water-ski. Walter Cunningham, Edward White, Mrs. White, and Gus Grissom's son were among his students.[259]

## THE CLOSING OF THE DECADE

At Lamar High School in 1969, some young men and women had more on their minds than water sports. In addition to wearing tennis shoes and ridiculing those who spent money on the short-lived Papagallos, these young people talked about an unprecedented idea: "Student Power," a name attached to a new course at Lamar that signaled a different way of thinking about education. Announced by the *Lancer* in February 1969, this non-credit "humanities" course was offered to all students who signed their names on a petition circulated by seniors Carol Noel and William Fox. The two leaders took their list to Principal Costlow to show student support for the course.

The *Lancer* stated, "What was a list is now a class." Miss Greenwood and Mrs. Wolfe taught the class in what was called a "free atmosphere," meaning the course did not concern itself with grades or tests. The topics covered were drama, art, philosophy, music, architecture, and science, each section lasting about three weeks. Honor students and respected members of Lamar's faculty were excited about this course, and the students' enthusiasm aligned them with young people across America who challenged educational conformity. Lamar had come to a dividing line regarding the future of the school and decided to put one foot into the new world that beckoned.

The 1960s brought revolutionary changes to this thirty-two-year-old school, but greater changes lay ahead as HISD finally implemented the law of the land and integrated its schools. To quote from an article that appeared in the November/December 1974 issue of *Texas Monthly*, Lamar was a "public high school whose public was about to change."[260]

# CHAPTER SIX
## THE 1970s

During the 1970s, young people across America coped with changes in their world that they had once taken for granted. The Vietnam War was an overwhelming influence. The killing of four students at Kent State University shattered trust in police officials and fostered disillusionment. The Watergate scandal damaged faith in government. In the late 1960s, students across the nation began to lose interest in school. The 1970s brought increased apathy and weakened school spirit. Ted Barrow (son of Thomas Barrow, Class of 1941), editor of the Kinkaid School's student newspaper, decried his fellow students' apathy: "This disinterest *must* not continue in the future of this class or this school." Kinkaid's biographer Susan Santangelo pointed out the apathy not only at Kinkaid "but at almost every educational institution in the country."[261] Certainly, it was true for Lamar.

Students at Lamar were no longer as interested in social clubs or rooting for the home team. Of the girls' social clubs, two of five folded, and membership in boys' clubs dwindled. Students went to after-school jobs instead of hanging around for club meetings and activities. They were ready to discard the social values their parents took for granted. The grading system, the traditional classroom setting, clothing, hairstyles, music, dance forms—all were questioned, and students' rebellion was often described by parents and teachers as "doing their own thing."

An excerpt from the *Orenda* illustrated students' thinking. A paragraph entitled "Find Out For Yourself" described students' feelings about the educational process.[262] Stating their preference for "hands-on" experience instead of traditional methodology, Lamar students were no longer satisfied with "second-hand information," whether in the chemistry lab or the metal shop. Language labs at Lamar were applauded because they gave students the opportunity to "listen to tapes without interference" and to learn at their "own rate of speed."[263]

*Susan Cooley's (Class of 1970) black tooth photo from the* Orenda *is an example of 1970s Lamar students parents described as "doing their own thing."*

Students wanted independence and the opportunity to make their own way. When the voting age was lowered from twenty-one to eighteen, a Lamar senior made Houston history by running for the HISD school board. Karl Doerner III was a River Oaks resident whose father graduated from Lamar in 1947. His father had been an honor student, drum major of the Lamar band, and had formed a very popular Lamar dance band.

The *Lancer* announced Karl Doerner III's candidacy, described his platform, and printed a disclaimer that "his [Doerner's] views do not necessarily represent those of the Lancer staff."[264]

Doerner's platform recommended a lower student-teacher ratio, de-emphasis on letter grades and testing, and greater student involvement in HISD through the formation of a student advisory committee. He also planned to persuade "progressive educators to come to Houston" and hold "seminars on national education to promote new ideas for HISD."²⁶⁵ Needless to say, Houston voters rejected this eighteen-year-old candidate.

*Eighteen-year-old Lamar High School senior Karl Doerner III filed as a candidate for the HISD school board.*

Three out of every five marriages ending in divorce resulted in one in five children living in a single-parent home.²⁶⁶ Whether as a result of divorce, a need for extra income, or the influence of the women's movement, the "new" working mother created a generation of latchkey children and teenagers who received less parental attention. In more and more families, no longer was someone waiting at home to provide discussion of the school day or guidance and support for assigned schoolwork. At Lamar and across the nation, student grades and national test scores began dropping. Students were coping with a changing world, and the educational scene in Houston was about to undergo even more changes.

## The Process of Integration

Integration came slowly to Houston. When the Supreme Court handed down its decision in *Brown v. Board of Education* on May 17, 1954, Houston was the largest segregated school district in America. It took twenty years for Houston schools to be fully integrated, but it was a reportedly peaceful integration. In 1958, Hattie Mae White was the first African American elected to the HISD school board, and she served until 1967.

Judge Ben Connally ruled that desegregation in Houston schools must begin in September 1960, but his edict resulted in only twelve black children attending a school in which they were the minority. Other measures were needed to meet the court's mandate.

In the meantime, "white flight" began, as some parents moved to the suburbs to avoid integration.²⁶⁷ Others, if they could afford it, moved their children to private schools. In 1970, a breakaway school district located inside the loop was proposed by a group of parents living in the western section of Houston. For the next eight years, supporters of the proposed Westheimer Independent School District (WISD) kept alive some parents' hopes that segregated schools could be preserved.

WISD was a proposed new school district consisting of a twenty-three-square-mile area to include "about eight thousand students."²⁶⁸ WISD undoubtedly drew much of its financial support from the affluent parents of Lamar and Lee High School students, parents who believed segregation was the only way to preserve their "free" college preparatory school.

The idea for a separate independent school district may have come from Dallas, Texas, where the prestigious and award-winning Highland Park High School was not and never has been part of the Dallas Independent School District. Instead, the school had always had its own district, the Highland Park Independent School District, a neighborhood school district with only one high school, a couple of middle schools, and some elementary schools, whose enrollment is and always has been 99 percent white.

The movement in Houston was led by former HISD board member Robert Eckels and interim WISD board chairman Joel Coolidge. The new district's concern was reportedly HISD's "decline in the quality of education."[269] But the courts did not accept this and ruled against WISD, calling it an obvious attempt "to disrupt HISD's successful desegregation."[270] HISD fiercely opposed the new district because it could ill afford to lose the 10.8-percent property tax income from this valuable area that contained most of the high-dollar homes in Houston.[271] Also of concern, the rumblings from East End and West University Place made HISD fear that there would be other breakaway neighborhoods if WISD accomplished its goal.[272] The Houston Teachers Association went to federal court to stop the formation of WISD because it felt hiring in the new district would discriminate in favor of white teachers.

In 1977, the U.S. District Court in Houston heard a ten-day trial. Judge Finis T. Cowan ruled against WISD, and "permanently enjoined the advocates of WISD from creating and implementing their school district."[273] Cowan's basis for his decision was that WISD would hire only white teachers, would cripple the resources of the central city district by taking away tax funding and white students, and would impede the desegregation process. WISD appealed Cowan's decision in federal court, which once more ruled against WISD in November 1978.[274]

Billy Reagan was hired as the new superintendent of HISD in 1974, bringing closure to the subject of desegregation in Houston schools. Implementing his "magnet school" concept, which included "tuition waivers and free transportation" for out-of-district students, Reagan used compromise and tact to solve the integration problems that had existed for over a decade. In 1984, Houston's U.S. District Court finally declared that "all vestiges of the dual school system [in Houston] had been eliminated."[275]

## Lamar Weathers the Storm

The 1972 yearbook describes Lamar as a place where "students representing diverse Races, outlooks, and ideals strive to be individuals and whole within themselves."[276] "It's Different at Lamar," said an article written by Shari Loe in the January 12, 1973 issue of the *Lancer*. Loe addressed the subject of school integration in what she called "human terms." She interviewed black transfer students from Jack Yates High School and Jesse H. Jones High School to find out their reasons for coming to Lamar. Most cited the chance for better learning. One explained, "At Yates I wasn't doing anything and making *A*'s, now I have to work to get *C*'s. If I were at Yates, I probably wouldn't be in school right now, I'd be skipping." One junior said, "I found out that what I'd heard about white people wasn't true—or at least it hasn't happened to me yet." The reporter said that all sophomore transfer students and the rest of the juniors "agreed with that statement." One senior girl was happy to get away from Yates' "fashion model" emphasis on clothing that she felt took the place of education. Most seconded the opinions of the underclassmen and said "the learning situation was better here." The reporter cited the black students' "optimism" about coming to Lamar, and their overall acceptance by white students as an indication that "things look like they're heading in the right direction."[277]

State Senator Barbara Jordan, an African American, was invited to address the entire Lamar student body in 1977 as a tribute to Black History Week. Jordan briefly discussed the legalization of slavery by the U.S. Constitution and the problems it created, but said she was more concerned about the present than the past. She expressed hope that America would live up to the promise of a "land of the free, a home of the brave." A question-and-answer session was held afterwards, and Jordan told the students she was influenced to enter politics when a black woman, Judge Edith Sampson, spoke at Phyllis Wheatley High School, where Jordan was a student.[278]

The cultural sophistication and self-confidence of Lamar students was indicated by a student candidate for the HISD school board, by left-wing *Lancer* reporters photographed campaigning for McGovern, and by Carol Noel, daughter of a conservative judge, spending her summer working for the Head Start program in New Mexico. These actions explained new attitudes and helped to explain why integration caused scarcely a ripple among the student body.

Despite enormous change brought to Lamar by integration, the harmonious blending of the students was clearly indicated in the 1972 *Orenda*. Black transfer student Joseph Scott Gamble was elected cheerleader and Most Popular Senior Boy, and senior photographs of black students who graduated with him indicated that most had joined social and/or service clubs and participated in many extracurricular activities.

D. C. Phillips taught biology at Lamar for twenty-seven years. His precarious perch on a seesaw indicates the fun-loving nature of this beloved teacher.

"Pomp and Circumstance," Gregory Curtis' description of Lamar High School's new racial breakdown, based on his visits to the school and interviews with students and teachers, appeared in a *Texas Monthly* article in 1974. Curtis concluded that there were some "whites who don't like blacks and blacks who don't like whites," but their animosity did not produce angry groups who confronted each other. Blacks who didn't want any social association with whites tended to isolate themselves from "all school activities." Curtis also mentioned that black students were earning honors and being elected to class offices. Though some thought integration would end the school, Lamar maintained its integrity, its record of excellence, and some of its traditions while the entire student body assumed a new identity that no one had foreseen.

One unpleasant side note concerned HISD's desegregation redistricting of the southwest Houston area, resulting in redrawn lines for Lamar and Robert E. Lee High School. Redistricting resulted in a lot of unhappy students—especially seniors, for whom no exception was made. The captain of the football team and a newly elected cheerleader were transferred out of their home school and, as had happened with the opening of Lee High School in 1962, clubs were altered and students uprooted. Redistricting did not result in improved integration, and many disgusted parents moved their teenagers to private schools.

## FACULTY MEMBERS WHO MADE A DIFFERENCE

Biology teacher D. C. Phillips, who sponsored Key Club and the cheerleaders, took the job of guarding the school mascot to heart. The would-be thieves were students who attended Lamar's archrival, Robert E. Lee High School. Both schools frequently stole or attempted to steal either Lee's "Uncle Bob" or Lamar's "Big Red,"

*Being responsible for the safety of Big Red, a larger-than-life papier-mache red and blue figure with rolling eyes and a frightening grin, was a serious job. Lamar's mascot was modeled after that of the Cleveland Indians football team.*

a life-sized papier-mache figure. Phillips and members of the Key Club moved the mascot around to different hiding places during the month preceding the game. The week before the Lee game, Phillips slept in the teachers' lounge to protect Big Red from a school break-in. The day of the game, Phillips and his Key Club members transported the mascot to the game in a special trailer.

Phillips' penchant for drama and fun was evidenced by his appearances at pep rallies posing as a Redskins football player dressed in an oversized sweatshirt and introduced as "Speedy Phillips," the Lamar player who had "warmed the bench 600 games in a row."[279] Lamar students loved Phillips' frivolity and his passion for their school, because as sophomores they had known only too well his other side—a terrifying Major Works Biology teacher who inspired, prodded, and put the fear of God into incoming sophomores with his demanding labs and text mastery requirements. Studying for one of Phillips' biology tests was said to take priority over all other class assignments. Despite his rigid requirements, or perhaps because of them, former students praise Phillips. One student, citing the effectiveness of his excellent explanations, described Phillips' bumblebee dance which taught them how bees know where the nectar is and what to do with it. The record number of his students who achieved advanced placement in biology and who have chosen careers in science attest to his teaching success.

University of Texas graduate Iris Loep emphasized that she still enjoyed teaching after sixteen years at Lamar. As a sponsor of the student-written literary magazine *Viewpoint*, Loep enjoyed the opportunity to "help students stimulate their creativity." In 1978, the magazine received a first-place rating by the Columbia Scholastic Press Association's literary competition in New York. Loep also sponsored the *Orenda*, recognizing it as an important "marker in time" that recorded both national and community information.[280]

For more than fifteen years, Trula Meglasson and Pam Young taught civics/economics classes to seniors who still remember their excellent teaching. In 1973, Meglasson was selected to receive the Valley Forge Teachers Medal, a national honor sponsored by the Freedoms Foundation at Valley

*Louise Fuller taught English at Lamar for thirty years and sponsored the* Lancer *for most of that time.*

*Ernest Brew, a hardworking and popular assistant principal, served at Lamar for twelve years.*

Forge, Pennsylvania. Chosen by a jury of Supreme Court justices, presidents of service clubs, and presidents of patriotic societies, Meglasson was recommended by her minister, her immediate supervisor, and others. George Strake, national trustee of the Freedom Foundation, presented her with the award.

### ANOTHER CHANGING OF THE GUARD

Principal Harold Costlow died of cancer at a local hospital in 1976, after nineteen years at Lamar, fourteen of these years as principal. Avidly supporting school organizations, Costlow had also been active in HISD, serving as president of the Houston Principals Association and as a committee member of both the National and Southern Associations of Secondary Principals. The *Lancer* dedication to him read:

> Even before you enter the building you can tell something is wrong. The flags are at half-staff and a blanket of sadness seems to hang around the area. When you enter you can hear it in the voices and see it in the faces of the students. The classrooms are quiet with sorrow.[281]

During Principal Costlow's tenure, vocational programs and reading courses were added, and he planned several of the school renovations. All but eight members of the then-current faculty had been hired by Costlow. The 1976 *Orenda*'s "In Memoriam" for their principal stated that "Lamar was Harold Costlow's life" and the 10,000 students whose lives he touched "will never forget him."[282]

Another significant change that occurred at Lamar was the retirement of Miss Louise Fuller. Sherry Evans (Class of 1957) describes her memories of Fuller's influence:

> She was a delight, a serious taskmaster who loved teaching, loved students, loved seeing us grow under her tutelage… Miss Fuller had a magical way of instilling in us the firm belief that Lamar was the best school on the planet, and the *Lancer* was the best school

newspaper on the planet. Heck, we probably thought the *Lancer* was better than the *Post*, *Press*—or *Chronicle*—all because of Miss Fuller.[283]

Her students paid tribute to their "boss" and said, "We don't know what we will do without you, Miss Fuller."[284]

## OUTSTANDING ALUMNI

In 1973, the *Lancer* ran two articles devoted to illustrious alumni Elsa Rosborough, Paula Prentiss, Tommy Sands, and Dene Hofheinz. The article concluded by asking, "Who from the class of '73 will write his or her name in the pages of history?" It is interesting to review the accomplishments of some of the seventies graduates who did just that.

The Class of 1970 produced "stars" who made a name for themselves in a wide variety of careers. Lisa Tuttle (Class of 1970), whose genres include fantasy, horror, feminism, and books that feature gender issues, found her passion as a teenager. She spent her years at Lamar as assistant editor of the *Lancer* and writing for *Viewpoint*, where she served as director of the short story competition. She also belonged to the Creative Writing Club and the Ready Writing Club.

Outside of school, she founded and edited the Houston Science Fiction Society's magazine *Mathom*, and by 1971 had sold her first short story, published in *Clarion II*, a respected national anthology edited by Robin Wilson. After graduation from Syracuse University, Tuttle moved to Austin, where she wrote for the *Austin American-Statesman* daily newspaper and founded the Turkey City Writer's Workshop. The author of fourteen novels, four non-fiction works, and four short story collections, Tuttle sometimes uses the pen name Maria Palmer. She moved to London in 1981 and later to rural Scotland.[285]

John Gray is another 1970 Lamar graduate whose writing has brought him national recognition. In 1992, his book *Men are From Mars, Women are From Venus* was published and became a bestseller and was translated into forty languages. This phenomenally successful book has inspired audio and video recordings, weekend seminars, themed vacations, a one-man Broadway show, and a television sitcom.

Brandon Smith (Class of 1970) spent his high school years further developing the passion that he has pursued all of his life. Smith was a child actor at the Alley until he grew too tall to play a juvenile role. He chose to go to Lamar because of Ruth Denney, but after his mother Chris Wilson, a well-known Houston actress and theater owner, bought a house in Highland Village to be in the Lamar district, she learned Denney was leaving to found a high school for the performing and visual arts (HSPVA). Smith found himself at Lamar with Mendenhall and other experienced young actors who basically ran the Drama Department for Denney's young and inexperienced replacements. At Lamar, he was president of Thespians and Kachina as well as assistant stage manager of Norma

*During his fifty-year theatrical career, Brandon Smith has appeared as a character actor whose credits include films such as* Born Free, RoboCop 2, The 40-Year-Old Virgin, *and television series* Lonesome Dove *and* Walker, Texas Ranger.

Lowder's Mixed Chorus. He was active in UIL One-Act Play contests, was chosen for the All-Star Cast in 1968, and won Best Actor in 1969. He says these tournaments taught him how to audition and not freeze up. Instead of traditional college work, he went to Europe, where he studied at Jacques Lecoq School of Mime and Theatre in Paris, the East 15 Acting School in London, and the Old Vic Theatre School in Bristol.

In Hollywood this character actor has appeared in over one hundred films and television series. He lists his special skills as a proficiency with dialects, snow skiing, miming, horseback riding, fencing, and stage fighting. Successfully earning a living as an actor for more than fifty years, Smith says Lamar offered him a rich fine arts experience that helped him hone his skills.[286]

Jamie Rhodes (Class of 1970) holds two UT degrees, but wears Aggie T-shirts in his job as director of new ventures for the Texas A&M University Systems. His job as director of the Angel Capital Association is to create commercial opportunities for Texas A&M professors, researchers, and budding entrepreneurs. He connects these groups with what the *Austin Business Journal* calls "the right sources of funding and advisers to create what he envisions as a 21st-century version of Silicon Valley in Central Texas."[287] Rhodes says his start-ups enhance the reputation of Texas universities by attracting investment money outside the state. He says he is "having fun working with the Aggies."

Mike Godwin (Class of 1970) began his writing career at Lamar as a staff member of *Viewpoint*. While in law school at UT, he edited the *Daily Texan* newspaper. His legal practice is in the field of Internet law and he is a Policy Fellow at the Center for Democracy and Technology in Washington, D.C. In 2003, MIT Press published his book *Cyber Rights: Defending Free Speech in the Digital Age*. He is called the champion of the preservation of free speech in the digital age, and MIT Press says, "Godwin shows how the Constitution should apply in cyberspace." He is also a columnist for *American Lawyer* magazine.[288]

Godwin has achieved something of a legendary status on the Internet through his enunciation of "Godwin's Law of Nazi Analogies," frequently referred to on the Internet simply as "Godwin's Law." Godwin himself defined it, as follows: "As an online discussion grows longer, the probability of a comparison involving Nazis or Hitler approaches one."[289]

*Ellen Wright (Clayton) took her BS from Duke University, her MS from Stanford University, her MD from Harvard University, and her JD from Yale, an unprecedented collegiate record even for a Lamar graduate.*

John Culberson (Class of 1975) describes himself as a "Jeffersonian Republican." A graduate of West University Elementary School, Lanier Middle School, and Lamar High School, Culberson worked as the *Lancer* photographer. He took his BA from Southern Methodist University and his JD from South Texas College of Law. While in law school, Culberson was elected to the Texas House of Representatives, where he served until 1999, and in 2000 was elected to represent the 7th Congressional District of the U.S. House of Representatives following the retirement of Bill Archer. His congressional assignments include the Appropriations Committee, and he is a member of the Tea Party Caucus.[290]

Ellen Wright (Clayton) (Class of 1970) collected many awards and honors at Lamar, where she was named as a National Merit Scholarship semifinalist and recipient of the American Chemical Society award. After graduating from high school, she began her impressive postsecondary academic career. Excelling in both law and genetics, Clayton is internationally respected and holds appointments in both of these disciplines at Vanderbilt University. There she has founded the Center for Biomedical Ethics and Society. Her published works include two books and over one hundred scholarly contributions to medical journals and textbooks. Clayton has been an advisor to the National Institute of Health on topics such as children's and women's health and the "ethical conduct of research involving human subjects."[291]

Emily Fourmy (Cutrer) (Class of 1970) is another academician who began as an outstanding student at Lamar High School. Her high school honors include Arrowhead, National Honor Society, National Merit Letter of Commendation, and serving as treasurer of her senior class. After leaving Lamar, she entered the University of Texas, where she earned a BA in American Studies and an MA and PhD in American Civilization. She has pursued a successful career in academic administration and on January 9, 2013, was appointed the fourth president of Texas A&M University–Texarkana. Dr. Richard Box, Board of Regents chairman, remarked that he was "glad to have found someone with Dr. Cutrer's experience and academic knowledge to lead our Texarkana campus."[292]

Samuel Miller (Class of 1970) played football, lettering in JV in 1967 and Varsity in 1968 and 1969, but still found time for his studies. After graduation from high school, Miller went to Johns Hopkins for his BA and then back to Houston for his MD at Baylor College of Medicine. He served as intern, resident, fellow, assistant, and associate professor at Harvard Medical School and Massachusetts General Hospital. His specialties are microbiology, immunology, and genome sciences. He is director of the University of Washington's Enteric Research Investigative Center. Among his honors are the Squibb Award from the Infectious Diseases Society of America and election to the American Academy of Microbiology, the American Society of Clinical Investigation, and the American Association of Physicians.[293]

*Brigadier General Michael Longoria is shown with the 2009 Distinguished Alumni honorees, Houston historian Dorothy Knox (Houghton) and Texas Technological University's president emeritus Don Haragan.*

Brigadier General Michael Longoria (Class of 1974) was also an outstanding athlete at Lamar who lettered in football all three years. He was chosen captain of the football team and Most Valuable Player. Most of his classmates were probably unaware that Mike Longoria took ballet lessons to improve his agility as a quarterback. He also lettered three years in track. As a junior, he represented Lamar in Washington, D.C., in U.S. Representative Bill Archer's Student Intern Program. The criteria for his selection were a *B* average, an interest in government and political science, and "willingness to report his experience back to his class."[294] He was elected president of his senior class and the Key Club's governor of the Texas-Oklahoma District.

After graduation from Lamar, Longoria was accepted into the Air Force Academy, where he graduated in 1979 with a degree in economics and international affairs. He earned master's degrees in organizational communication, national security, and airpower art and science. A five-time recipient of the Bronze Star, Longoria is the most combat-experienced officer in the Air Force and the senior parachutist in the USAF, having made 705 jumps. When interviewed for Lamar High School's Distinguished Alumni award, Longoria credited D. C. Phillips' mentoring and the Key Club for providing leadership opportunities.[295]

Gregory Michael Senofsky (Class of 1974) was an outstanding science student at Lamar where as a junior he took first place in physics and won special awards from the U.S. Army, Air Force, and Navy at the Fourteenth Annual Science Engineering Fair. His science fair win enabled him to go to the International Science Fair in San Diego, where he presented his project "An Independent Study of the Transversely Excited Atmospheric Pressure Laser."[296]

After graduation, Senofsky attended Yale University and graduated from Rice with a BA. He took his MD at Baylor College of Medicine and interned at the University of Virginia's Medical Center. He is a breast surgeon who performs 600 breast operations a year, specializing in sentinel node mapping and surgical treatment of cutaneous melanoma. The author of *The Patient's Guide to Outstanding Breast Cancer Care* and many journal articles in his field, Senofsky founded the Breast Institute in Valencia, California, and is director of the Sheila Veloz Breast Center, also in Valencia. He is Chief Resident in General Surgery at the University of California, San Diego, a Fellow at the University of Miami, and a clinical faculty member of the Department of Surgery at UCLA School of Medicine.[297]

Ronald Watson "Ron" Henley (Class of 1975) spent his years at Lamar honing his skill as a remarkably talented chess player. Already awarded a "Master" rating, he served as president of Lamar's Chess Club and led the club members to state championships during his junior and senior years. He received the first chess college scholarship to attend the University of South Florida.

*Newscaster Sherry Woodard (Williams) was master of ceremonies and honoree for the 2001 Distinguished Alumni Luncheon.*

By 1980, Henley was awarded the "International Master" title and in 1982 at Surkarta, Denpasas, Indonesia, he won the "Grand Master" title. He has won international class tournaments and has authored a number of educational chess books, as well as narrating more than sixty chess videos and online chess lessons.

Kathy Ruiz (Class of 1975) has become one of Houston's most celebrated chefs. In 1979, she graduated from the University of Manhattanville in Purchase, New York, with a degree in biology, planning to follow the path of her father, a Houston eye surgeon.[298] Her love of cooking, however, led her to the kitchen. Her specialty is New American Cuisine and she has been featured on the PBS *Great Chefs of the West* series. Having owned and/or managed restaurants on the Yucatan Peninsula and in Houston, Ruiz is now the corporate executive chef of Houston-based Landry's Restaurants, a chain of 300 restaurants in Houston, Kemah, and Galveston. In 2003, Kathy Ruiz was honored as one of Lamar High School's Distinguished Alumni.

Sherry Woodard (Williams) (Class of 1975) was a member of the National Honor Society and Arrowhead, as well as a National Achievement Scholarship semifinalist. She was a member of Mirabeau, the French Club, and the Backgammon Club, and was elected as a Junior Class Favorite, cheerleader, and member of the Homecoming Court.

After graduation from Lamar, Woodard earned a journalism degree from Texas A&M and began working for KTRH News Radio in Houston. She began her television news career at WGPR-TV in Detroit and then moved to television station WKBD-TV to host a live morning talk show. In Dallas at KXAS-TV she worked as a reporter and an anchor and then returned to Houston to work for Channel 39 and Fox 26. Today, Sherry Williams has her own show, *News Saturday Morning*, at KHOU-TV Channel 11 from 7:00 to 9:00 a.m. She is also a roving reporter on occasion and went to the New Orleans area to cover Hurricane Ike. The Associated Press, the Dallas Press Club, the Houston Press Club, and United Press International have honored her, and in 2002 she was honored as a Lamar Distinguished Alumna and has served as master of ceremonies for the annual luncheon.[299]

## WHAT MAKES LAMAR HIGH SCHOOL UNIQUE?

Student diversity was the explanation given by the 1977 *Orenda* for Lamar's uniqueness. Enrollment was 25 percent black, 7 percent Hispanic, 3 percent Asian, and the remaining 65 percent Caucasian, the different races contributing a variety of cultures and lifestyles. The *Orenda* stated,

*Alvis Prince (Class of 1976), second from left, now a retired special agent for the U.S. Secret Service, is pictured with the other 2002 Lamar Distinguished Alumni honorees, Olympic swimmer Cynthia Potter, Governor Mark White, and investor Mac Dunwoody.*

"There is no typical Lamar student," and asserted that this diversity "gives each student a head start for living successfully in the adult world."³⁰⁰

Twenty-nine years after her graduation, Juana Gregory (Bernard) (Class of 1976) expressed her own feelings about this diversity:

> Lamar in the 1970s, evolved into a very diverse group of kids. While we all had our differences, social, cultural, racial, and economical, we learned in time to get along and accept these differences, thus forming solid, lasting cross group bonds. I have always believed that Lamar better prepared me for the diversity at a big public university, better than those who experienced a more sheltered, less diverse school experience. I clearly remember feeling fortunate that I had gone to Lamar.³⁰¹

Bernard's views reflected the tremendous changes that had occurred in the world since the cocoon-like experience of Lamar students during the 1950s and the 1960s.

Assassinations, a controversial war which many young people did not support, and an unprecedented political scandal that went all the way to the White House—all these were covered in living color on the television sets that had by now found their way into 99 percent of the nation's homes. The effect of these tragedies, along with the integration of Houston schools, transformed this academically superior college preparatory school into a high school that now sought to prepare its students for the real world, no matter what that world constituted. At the beginning of the seventies, the *Orenda* acknowledged that some seniors would go to college and others would "find jobs to earn a living." Unlike graduates of previous decades, who were largely impervious to outside influences and problems, students at Lamar during the 1970s talked about their school as a "microcosm" where everyone "seems to mesh together in a cohesive unit, each respecting the other, but each going in his own direction."³⁰²

Lamar's central location has always made it a desirable destination for new students and the implementation of new programs. The addition of programs such as education for the deaf, for speakers of English as a Second Language (ESL), and for the mentally disabled, plus a brand new freshman class, caused the *Orenda* editor to describe 1978 as "Lamar's year to be Movin' Up."

By the end of the 1970s, Lamar was called "One Nation: Many Tribes" by the 1979 *Orenda*. The white, black, Hispanic, and Asian racial categories included immigrants from Vietnam, Iran, New Zealand, and Ecuador, and Lamar was now described as "a melting pot" where students could mingle and work with classmates who taught them different ways of life and who produced "a very remarkable and interesting student body."³⁰³

*Lamar scholar Alan Wilson's Science Fair project was a blood-type study composed of data he had gathered during his summer job at Herman Hospital's Histocompatability Lab. He went on to earn his BS at MIT and his MBA at Harvard.*

## Student Apathy Has Died

In addition to praising the diversity at Lamar High School, the 1979 *Orenda* ended the decade with the pronouncement that the contagious "Redskin Pride" resulting from the band's taking first place during the "Battle of the Bands" had put an end to student apathy.[304] The editor claimed that "students discovered a spirit within themselves of which they had never been aware" that had led to greater support of their school.

The yearbook also announced that students no longer found school "boring," citing more than fifty clubs as well as new electives such as guitar, geology, sociology, psychology, advanced social problems, and music appreciation. Students and faculty "always found something to which they could react pleasantly," and created a friendly atmosphere that "made Lamar a wonderful place to be."[305]

The "Redskin Pride" described above is best illustrated by the fact that two new social service clubs were formed in March 1979, both devoted more to service than to social events. The boys' club Sehcapa was Apaches spelled backward. Their first project was a campaign against littering, which was a widespread problem at Lamar. The girls' club was Taysha, an Indian word for "friendly." Taysha's goals were to "1) Promote school spirit 2) Loyalty to the school and 3) Help improve the outlook of the school." The club also devoted itself to picking up trash around the school. The subject of littering was addressed in a number of *Lancer* articles. There

*Dennis C. Phillips was a guest at the Lamar Distinguished Alumni Luncheon on May 4, 2007.*

was general concern for the school's appearance. "This means you" talked about Lamar's spacious grounds and large tree-shaded areas, and remarked on the school's unusual features, including separate gyms for boys and girls, covered walkways, and original tile in bathrooms and on window sills. The editor commented on the original slate blackboards, which would last forever if oiled regularly, and lamented the general lack of respect for what the editor termed "this [forty-three-year-old] lady."[306]

In 1978, *U.S. News and World Report* called Houston "an explosive roaring juggernaut that's shattering tradition as it expands outward and upward with an energy that stuns even its residents." By 1980, the city was seven times larger than it had been at the end of World War II and was now the fifth-largest city in the United States.[307]

But the decade ahead would put Houston into a crisis mode as dropping oil prices caused a ripple effect in the city's economy. Building permits plummeted, banks failed, and the city struggled to recover. What would be the impact of this citywide recession on the students at Lamar High School?

**1937–1987 Lamar**

**"AT 50"** "GO BIG RED"

# CHAPTER SEVEN
## The 1980s and 1990s

The eighties brought dramatic changes to the City of Houston. In 1981, Houston's first female mayor, Kathy Whitmire, was elected. In 1983, 155 new office buildings were constructed, including Transco Tower, the tallest building in the world built outside a central business district. The same year, voters approved building the George R. Brown Convention Center and rejected a metro plan for a rail system.

### 1980s Lamar Students Speak Their Minds

In a January 1980 *Lancer* editorial, Andrew Milburn summarized a few inventions and phenomena from the 1970s: food processors, streaking, Watergate, mirrored sunglasses, and pocket computers. "What's Next?" Milburn asked. With a jab at the much-ballyhooed "1976" celebration, Milburn noted that America "manufactured bicentennial versions of all the above." He also took a jab at the "literary" publication, *I'm Ok, You're Ok*, along with technological advances and new folk heroes such as Willie Nelson, and noted that the 1980s was the first decade in which he and his fellow students would be mature enough to notice the world outside of Lamar High School.[308] Many of his classmates appeared to agree, as evidenced by the increase in student editorials in the *Lancer*. Serious essays addressed everything from mayoral and presidential debates to drugs, tobacco, terrorists, and the right to strike.

*Lamar's sensational fiftieth birthday celebration was held on October 17, 1987.*

During the 1980 presidential campaign, Lamar teachers noted that the Iran crisis "sparked student involvement as few current events ever had."[309] Lamar students participated in anti-Iranian demonstrations, sent letters to the hostages at Christmas, and aired their personal political views. Ronald Reagan, critical of President Jimmy Carter's handling of the hostage crisis, won a landslide victory, and the hostages were released minutes after his swearing-in ceremony.

Some Lamar students became concerned about Reagan's military policy that included more spending and a peacetime draft. A *Lancer* article outlined draft objectors' legal recourse, citing a warning issued by the Central Committee for Conscientious Objectors (CCCO) that the draft registration "increased the likelihood of an actual draft."[310] The following month, a *Lancer* poll showed 59 percent of the 380 seniors opposed a mandatory draft registration and would register only if required to do so. "Should women be required to register as well?" drew a 51-percent negative vote.[311]

A *Lancer* article, "Teens Work for Less," addressed the congressional debate excluding teens from $3.35-per-hour minimum wage requirements. Some students believed that working for less would make it easier for them to get jobs. Others, already working part-time minimum-wage jobs, opposed a teenage exemption, fearing salary cuts.[312]

Gordon Vaughan (Class of 1981), a National Merit Scholarship finalist, wrote a *Lancer* article about the national energy problems. Vaughan attended the student press reception sponsored by National Supply Company, the world's largest supplier of oilfield production equipment, and reported on the world energy problems and inadequate governmental policies he heard discussed.[313] The following year, he wrote an essay calling for legislation to resolve the problem of undocumented workers and the lack of public school education for their children.[314]

Charlie Earthman, *Lancer* staff member, responded to the Exxon Valdez oil spill by calling for a boycott of Exxon products. Outlining Exxon's "blunders," their refusal to accept help, and the time lag before they deployed emergency equipment, he vehemently ordered Lamar students not to support companies which displayed "such flagrant disregard for the environment."[315]

Close Up and SCALE (Student Congress and Legislative Enterprise) were popular after-school programs designed to give students firsthand knowledge of the federal government. Close Up was for students who prepared for an annual trip to Washington, D.C., by reviewing such topics as "the United States' domestic, foreign and defense policies." Government teacher Pam Young took a group of about twenty students to the Capitol, where they met with lobbyists and congressmen and attended seminars and workshops.[316]

*Close Up member Deidra Gasper (Class of 1981) remembers this trip to Washington, D.C., as an honor as well as an opportunity to experience the government "up close and personal."*

SCALE, led by Lamar teacher Trula Meglasson, taught students how federal bills were proposed and became law. Student delegates from five Houston high schools did exactly what the United States Congress does: they wrote bills, studied parliamentary procedure, and listened to political speakers. Bills submitted by Lamar High School delegates addressed the peacetime draft, energy conservation, welfare fraud, the death penalty, and regulation of immigration.[317]

Lamar students criticized historic House Bill 72, passed in 1984 by the 68th Texas Legislature. The bill was proposed by H. Ross Perot, tapped by newly elected governor Mark White, to strengthen secondary high school curriculum and to raise teachers' pay. Students objected to the "No Pass, No Play" provision, which required that a student pass all courses in order to participate in athletics or extracurricular activities. The bill was intended to stress the importance of academic courses and penalize those who neglected them, but the *Lancer* quoted the *Houston Post*, which charged the bill with "causing students to avoid courses that they might fail" in order not to jeopardize their extracurricular activities.[318] The bill also eliminated Senior Skip Day and senior exemptions from final exams. *Lancer* editor Liz Chadderdon complained that the Class of 1986 had lost "seniority those before us enjoyed."[319]

A front-page "In Memoriam" photograph and two pages of articles recorded Lamar students' sorrow over the explosion of the *Challenger* on January 28, 1986. Each of the seven astronauts was profiled, and the *Lancer* gave one student's reaction as, "Hearing about it left a lump in my throat."

Harry Susman (Class of 1970) reacted by writing an editorial, "We Must Explore: Reasons 7." He pleaded that the deaths of "these seven Americans [who] felt the manifestations of destiny" intensify the country's need to continue, rather than curtail, exploration. He called the continuation of space exploration the pursuit of "Manifest Destiny" and requested that Americans "not confine themselves to what they already know, but to seek the unknown."[320]

"Father Reagan and the Pride: Live From Capitol Hill," a *Lancer* article written by editor Liz Chadderdon (Class of 1986), made fun of what she considered to be unwarranted admiration for President Reagan's "simple answers" to complex problems. Chadderdon's editorial took issue with a magazine article that said, "America is coming alive again." She wondered if "alive" meant only that we have "jobs and food and money, and *The Cosby Show*." Citing the "crumbling farmers, homeless people, and a national deficit" along with "horribly extravagant defense spending," Chadderdon asked, "What pride? Where?"[321]

Chadderdon, who now makes her living writing about politics, gives Dr. June Smith, her Lamar English teacher, credit for her success and says that her entrance into their lives was "astounding." Wearing Birkenstocks and similar "mod" clothing, Smith neither looked nor acted like any teacher they had ever seen. The first day in class she burst out singing a Cole Porter tune, then tore up the curriculum for junior English and threw it on the floor.

She taught her students how to think by refusing to accept what they were accustomed to writing. The majority of the class received *C*'s at mid-semester and learned their teacher had created a "brand new ballgame." Smith would not accept any work that was not their best. When students produced work that met her high standards, Smith responded, "Thank God you finally got it."

She assigned Thoreau's *On Walden Pond*, but Chadderdon says they did not read it: they lived it, they dreamed it, and the book became part of their core knowledge. Dr. Carol Case, Chadderdon's next English teacher, displayed the "same level of intensity," also "cutting her students no slack." Chadderdon credits these two teachers with training her to take a complicated subject and reduce it to three sentences, a practice she now uses in her life's work.[322]

Chadderdon's liberal political views as expressed in *Lancer* editorials were the early writings of a woman who has spent her life working for the Democratic Party. After graduation from the University of Texas, she volunteered as a coordinator for Texas Governor Ann Richards, later working on campaigns for senatorial contests in North Carolina and Virginia.

She began a direct mail consultant business in 1999 and creates persuasion mail for presidential, congressional, and municipal political campaigns. Her success in twenty-five states has won her many awards and she has been a guest on television programs including *Larry King Live*, *CNN American Morning*, and *The O'Reilly Factor*. Chadderdon lives in Alexandria, Virginia, close to the U.S. political pulse, where, she says, she spends her free time "searching for decent Mexican food."[323]

*Principal Ray Reiner says despite the sixty-hour weeks he spent as principal of Lamar High School, this job was a high point in his career and notes that people seem to regard him differently once he mentions his Lamar credentials.*

## A New Administrator and a New Campus

Ray Reiner was appointed Lamar's seventh principal in 1984 and brought with him regulations from House Bill 72. The *Lancer*, introducing him in an article titled "Ray Reiner Plays By the Rules," noted that Reiner brought with him "a seemingly endless number of new rules." He was a direct appointment from HISD Superintendent Billy Reagan, who instructed him to get the Business Magnet and International Baccalaureate programs up and running. Reiner did just that, overseeing the expansion of both while supervising a $15-million bond fund to remodel and enlarge the building to "prepare Lamar for the next fifty years." Reiner cited the 600-to-700-member Parent Teacher Association (PTA) as an indication of the strong parental support he received at Lamar. Former governor Mark White served on Reiner's Magnet Executive Board.

Reiner said that after he hired Tommy Nolen as athletic director he never worried about the condition of the grounds or about students leaving class. All physical education teachers had fourth period free to eat their lunch and patrol the school's twenty-three acres. The PTA, under the leadership of Charlie Stubblefield, formed dozens of committees to look after every facet of life at Lamar and even had a "color committee" that decided the trim would be painted turquoise.

Reiner did not stay to see the remodeling project completed, leaving at mid-term 1988 to become superintendent of HISD District XIII. In his farewell letter to students, Reiner applauded the celebration of Lamar's fiftieth anniversary and called for students to maintain their traditions and academic excellence. He says that, even with sixty-hour weeks, being principal of Lamar was a high point in his career, and noted that people seemed to accord him special respect when he mentioned his Lamar credentials. He called Lamar a fish bowl; the most visible high school in HISD, the school always talked about and written about.[324]

Lamar's "reconstructive surgery" began in April 1986. All temporary buildings were taken away, and asbestos was removed from the chemistry building and the library. Construction added 115,700 square feet in a new library, ROTC facilities, a gym, vocational facilities, science labs, and new sidewalks. A mini-theater, a magnet school center, and several classrooms were built, and a two-story administration area was added at the back of the original building.

The renovation was done to "bring a Lamar future generations of Lamarians

*Completed in the 1990s, the remodeling of Lamar took two years longer than projected.*

can enjoy."[325] "The Nightmare on Westheimer," the 1989 *Orenda* spring essay, described the drastic alterations that caused the disorientation of "the entire student body and staff."[326] It was another year before renovations were completed, but school went on despite the mess.

Ronnie Veselka succeeded Ray Reiner as principal in 1989 and remained until mid-term 1991, dealing with the massive construction that dragged on while he shepherded Lamar's 2,700 students. But Veselka said that "being principal at Lamar High School was the best job I ever had." Like Reiner, he mentioned community support, especially when ending a beloved tradition: eating on the front lawn under the majestic oak trees. Littering, long a problem, had become untenable, and parents who came to clean up litter every day after lunch periods finally admitted defeat, causing Veselka to revoke the privilege in 1990.[327]

## STUDENT ACTIVITIES

In 1985, Lamar students revived the old Astronomy Club. Steven Booth was elected president, Laurel Ladwig vice-president, and Harry Susman treasurer. The new club lacked the amenities of its own off-campus planetarium and superior telescopes, but interest was similar to that of the earlier club. Members organized "Skywatch" trips to Brazos Bend State Park Museum, where four large telescopes were available to view deep-sky objects.[328] This high school pastime became a career for Ladwig, who served as manager of the Burke Baker Planetarium. Currently, she is developer of the planetarium at the New Mexico Museum of Natural History and Science.

The American Field Service (AFS) has had a long history at Lamar High School. Even before the school formed a chapter, many foreign students were housed by nearby families. The Lamar chapter was formed in 1970. AFS, an international organization, began during World War I as a private volunteer ambulance service and continued throughout World War II. After the war ended, members wanted to continue their tradition of working for "understanding between the people of the world." Today students, families, and volunteers in sixty countries work toward "stimulating an awareness of mankind's common humanity, a wider understanding of diverse cultures of the world, and a concern for global issues confronting society."[329] AFS is a private educational organization with no religious or political ties. In 1980, 3,000 foreign exchange students attended American high schools.[330]

Former Lamar student James DeGregori (Class of 1984), the school's first International Baccalaureate graduate, said that the value of the AFS program "cannot be overestimated." He credited the year he spent in Uruguay as "dramatically" shaping his entire outlook on life. In a letter to the 50th Anniversary Committee honoring him as a Distinguished Alumnus in 1987, DeGregori also acknowledged his debt to Lamar for its International Baccalaureate program, which provided the background he needed for academia. He praised Sylvia Bryant's math teaching, and said that Richard Millet instilled in him his love of chemistry and Carol Case enriched his life with literature and philosophy.

When he enrolled at the University of Texas in Austin, DeGregori received forty-eight hours of college credit. He earned his BA in Microbiology and received a full scholarship to MIT, where he received his PhD in Biology. After postdoctoral studies at Duke University, in 1997 he accepted a position as professor in the Department of Biochemistry and Molecular Genetics at the University of Colorado School of Medicine, where he focuses on new treatments for leukemia and lymphomas.[331]

### HOUSTON: A BUST TOWN, NOT A BOOM TOWN

Midway through President Reagan's second term, junk bonds, mergers, insider trading, and various activities on Wall Street caused a $500-billion crash on "Black Monday," October 19, 1987. Big and small investors lost, and many of Houston's residents crashed along with the rest of the world. The Port of Houston's shipments declined, building permits dropped, unprecedented numbers of property foreclosures and bankruptcies were recorded, and eleven banks closed as Houston fell to its knees.[332]

*Orenda* staff members Debbi Miller and Julie Doran responded to Houston's downturn in a 1988 essay, "Building for Tomorrow, Lamar and Houston Maintain Quality Growth." The two noted that, although Houston's economy's has taken "a turn for the worse," Lamar itself had originally opened its doors during an even more difficult time. They drew a parallel between the opening of the splendid new Lamar High School in 1937 at a time when the entire nation was still in the throes of Great Depression, and Lamar's elaborate fiftieth anniversary celebration in 1987.[333]

### LAMAR'S 50TH ANNIVERSARY CELEBRATION

Lamar's birthday celebration, "Fifty Years of Performing Arts at Lamar," took place two days before Black Monday and encompassed much more than the arts. Harris County District Attorney John B. Holmes (Class of 1959) was emcee. Former Texas governor Mark White (Class of 1958) presented a vacuum-sealed time capsule containing a 1987 Lamar brochure, issues of the *Lancer*, a 1987 *Orenda*, the Lamar Directory, a photo album called "A Day at Lamar," architectural designs for the remodeling, and other memorabilia. The capsule, its location marked by a large granite stone, was buried in the front lawn of the school. Former class presidents, valedictorians, Arrowhead members, *Orenda* and *Lancer* editors, former captains of team sports, May Fete Court members, and Homecoming Court members were introduced. The event concluded with a giant pep rally, the singing of the fight song and the alma mater led by former and current cheerleaders and band members.

The program noted Lamar's more recent changes—the admission of freshmen and the beginning of the International Baccalaureate program and the Magnet School of Business Education. Principal Ray Reiner was introduced as the "captain" of the new academic programs and the renovation that began in 1986. Enrollment was 2,474 students, and the racial makeup was 52 percent white, 29 percent black, and 19 percent Hispanic.

"How do you capture a moonbeam?" That was the question asked by the 1987–1988 *Orenda* staff as they struggled to blend the new with the old, respecting both the school's half-century history and recent additions which had so drastically changed Lamar. They spoke of their "commitment to quality," and their goal to produce the "best *Orenda* yet."

*The 1988* Orenda *staff paid homage to Lamar's fifty-year history with this impressive cover.*

# GOLDEN WARRIORS
# LAMAR HIGH SCHOOL'S
# 50TH ANNIVERSARY
# OCTOBER 1987

| | | | |
|---|---|---|---|
| SUZON LEPAT ADAM '49 | MARSHA ANN CUNNINGHAM '58 | BETTY SMITH JOSEY '48 | JOHN & KAREN TELLEPSON ROBINSON, LOREN, III, AND ELLEN KIRKPATRICK '56 '59 '87 '90 |
| DENE HOFHEINZ ANTON '60 | LEWIS WESLEY, JR. AND CATHY O'DONNELL CUTRER '49 '53 | JIMMY TOMPKINS KELLEY '55 | JO E. 'JED' SHAW, JR. '51 |
| MARY ELLEN AYDAM '59 | JOHN A. DAUGHERTY '62 | DR. WILLIAM H. KOLTER '45 | IN MEMORY OF KATHRYN LEWIS SPEARS '61 |
| RICHARD BURTON BALLANFANT AND ANDREA '65 '85 | HARRY R. DAWSON '40 | DONALD K. LEWIS '60 | JACK E. STALSBY '44 |
| THOMAS D. BARROW '41 | ANDREW MAURICE DUGGAN '41 | RICHARD B. MAYOR '51 | ROBERT STILLWELL '55 |
| RICHARD E. BEAN '62 | IN HONOR OF SARAH D. EARLE TEACHER | J. FRANK AND JANICE DOUGALL MELCHER '61 | WILLIAM J. AND WILLIAM M. STRADLEY AND LISA S. BERGEZ '58 '83 '82 |
| RAOUL BEASLEY '46 | DAVID ROSSLYN F. AND FRANKLIN FENNEKOHL '52 '54 '61 | BOYD B. MOORE '60 | GEORGE G. STUBBLEFIELD, III '54 |
| ALFRED AND ANNETTE CHEEK BISHOP '34 '39 | GARLAND W. FIELDER '51 | HARVIN C. JR. AND NANCY POWELL MOORE '55 '58 | HOWARD TELLEPSEN, JR. '62 |
| NORMAN BOYKER '61 | HOWARD H. GANO '46 | WILLIAM B. JR. AND NANCY BOWNE MORGAN '55 | RALPH B. THOMAS '62 |
| BLAKE W. BRENNAN '81 | ROSEMARY SCHNEIDER GARBETT '53 | STERLING B. AND MARIANNE OELAND McCALL '53 '55 | JOE REID THOMPSON '51 |
| BLANCHE R. BRENNAN '85 | DAVID K. GOFF '51 | THOMAS V., SUSAN SEARLS AND CATHERINE McMAHAN '55 '56 '84 | CRAIG W. AND ANTOINETTE ARNOLD WALLIN '82 |
| JACK R. BRENNAN '55 | RONALD W. HENRIKSEN '65 | COLETTA LAKE RAY McMILLIAN '47 | ROLAN W. WALTON '46 |
| ROBERT BLAKE BRYAN, JR. '86 | TRUDY HUTCHINGS HEROLZ '61 | DR. FABER F. McMULLEN, JR. '47 | RICHARD C. WEBB '51 |
| JAN STOCKARD CATO '63 | FRED HOFHEINZ '56 | JEANNETTE DANNENBAUM NAMEN '39 | BRADLEY WESTMORELAND '60 |
| REBECCA ANN SIMS CEMO '65 | BEVERLY BOND HOLMES '44 | PHILIP MALCOLM PETERSON '64 | WAYNE G. WICKMAN '55 |
| CLASS OF 1959 | E.G. 'BUDDY' HOOD '55 | MACEY AND BARRETT REASONER '55 '82 | WILLIAM DICKINSON YALE, JR. '63 |
| ANNE SERRING CONNER '65 | JAMES K. JENNINGS, JR. '39 | DAVID C. REDFORD '58 | |

## NOTEWORTHY ALUMS

Paul G. Bernhard (Class of 1981) continued the Lamar tradition of multigenerational graduates and followed in the footsteps of his father, Jim Bernhard (Class of 1955). At Lamar, both were involved in many school activities and won honors based on scholastics as well as popularity. Paul refers to his "ridiculous overachievement" in high school: Most Outstanding Junior Boy, Most Outstanding Senior (as his father had been), senior class president, cheerleader, and even runner-up for Most Attractive Boy. He was a National Merit Scholarship finalist, as was his father. He graduated magna cum laude with a mechanical engineering degree from Duke University. During his Navy stint following college, he served as a surface warfare officer. Recalled to active duty, he served as a United Nations liaison officer and retired from the Naval Reserve in 2004 as a commander.

Though he majored in mechanical engineering, the younger Bernard describes himself as a writer, producer, designer, and content specialist. He founded Paul Bernhard Exhibit Design and Consulting (PBE) and is comfortable discussing math, science, engineering, or fine arts. From 1996 to 2000, Bernhard wrote, produced, and appeared as "Doctor Howie Do-It," a nationally known television character he created for PBS. In 2011, he created the content and storyline for *Texas!*, an exhibition touring the state and featuring artifacts from Texas history.

Bernhard has designed museum exhibit halls in California, Dallas, and Houston, as well as projects overseas in Azerbaijan, China, Egypt, Kazakhstan, and Malaysia. Director of special projects for the Museum of Natural Science, Bernhard calls his job a "virtual" position in a life that's never dull. His advice to young people is to "be open to all kinds of randomness that might not necessarily be the 'norm' that you were expecting," and to "keep a sense of curiosity about the world."[334]

*Derrick Evans and Deidra Gasper (Class of 1981) were chosen as Most Representative Boy and Girl.*

Derrick Evans (Class of 1981) notes that he and Alan Wilson (Class of 1979) were part of the first generation of African Americans with significant career opportunities beyond teaching or the ministry. Evans says that Lamar "sparked his intellectual curiosity," and he believes that serving as president of the Key Club "rounded out his leadership skills." He praises Key Club sponsor D. C. Phillips, who mentored him and other club members.

Evans was admitted to Cornell University and received a BS in Electrical Engineering. He rose to vice-president of Wireless Global Semiconductor Sales with Motorola, his first employer. He has returned to Texas and is a part-time commercial pilot and flight instructor and partner in an Austin company that manufactures and sells natural hair products. Evans sits on several boards, notably for Huston-Tillotson University and the Zachary Scott Theatre.[335]

Mignon Guidry (Class of 1981) describes Lamar as a place where classmates, members of organizations, and participants in extracurricular activities, "white, black, brown, and yellow; wealthy, middle class, lower income, blurred lines, resulted in Lamar being a huge, fun, melting pot that has provided everlasting memories and friendships."

Nominated for a scholarship by one of her teachers, Guidry was able to attend a nearby college and graduated in three years with an accounting degree. She went to work the Monday after graduation, working for ten years as a financial analyst before migrating into marketing and eventually project management. Looking to open new doors, Guidry joined her husband in the video production business, producing safety films, a kids' television pilot, and several pro bono projects for various non-profit children's clubs and schools. Her next opportunity occurred when her husband was hired to work in Kuwait, where the two have worked together. Guidry says her eyes are "wide open now" to both the strife and the human trafficking in this tiny country. Her experiences with diversity at Lamar prepared her for similar experiences in her present life, although the scale is now global.[336]

*The David Fenwick White Memorial Cup was annually presented to the senior Most Representative Boy by Wichaka-Chums (Chums was the name of the original club formed in 1937). Recent recipients include Bill Dukes, Bill Savinoha, Paul Davidhizar, Alan Wilson, Russell Buchanan, Chris Abbott, Derrick Evans, and Derrick Wooden.*

*Mignon Guidry (Class of 1981) says her daily life in Kuwait is "an awesome eye-opening experience."*

Dr. Charles "Chip" Haynes (Class of 1981), another classmate of Bernhard, Evans, and Guidry, is an internationally known microbiologist. He earned his PhD from the University of California, Berkeley, and works in the Chemical and Biological Engineering Department of the Michael Smith Laboratories at the University of British Columbia, Canada, where his research focuses on the development of new instrumentation for "quantifying the delicate energetics of biological interactions and binding."[337]

Nat Moss (Class of 1982), an independent screenwriter for the Wildlife Conservation Society, majored in American Civilization at Brown University. After graduation, he became a speechwriter for U.S. Representative Ted Weiss (Dem.-NY) and later for the office of the New York City comptroller. Moss has written freelance articles for *Vanity Fair, Esquire, Glamour, House and Garden, Martha Stewart Living, Self,* and *This Old House.* His feature film *Adrift in Manhattan* was nominated for the

Grand Jury Prize at the 2007 Sundance Film Festival and won the Indianapolis International Film competition that year.[338]

Gretchen Sween (Class of 1982) left the fine arts world and, as she says, entered academia "through the back door." As a student at Lamar, Sween was all about drama, starring in numerous plays and winning awards for her performances. She received her BFA at the University of Texas, Dallas, and worked in theater for over two decades as a freelance writer, theater director, actor, and adjunct drama professor at several colleges. Her success as a coach for interscholastic moot court teams in the UT Law School's advocacy program altered her career path. She entered law school and earned a JD at the University of Texas, Austin. While in law school, Sween was associate editor for the *Texas Law Review*. She continues to win honors and accolades as a member of the legal profession and was named a "Rising Star" by *Texas Monthly* magazine beginning in 2006.[339]

Jessica Farrar (Class of 1984) was elected to represent District No. 148 in the Texas House of Representatives at age twenty-seven. She is now the longest-serving Hispanic female member from Harris County. At the beginning of each session, Farrar introduces a bill to abolish the death penalty. She is a strong supporter of women's issues and has worked hard to restore funding to programs which address women's health issues.

A brilliant dedicated scientist, Angela Belcher graduated from Lamar in 1985 and has devoted her life to "understanding and using the process by which nature makes materials in order to design applications as varied as... solar cells, batteries, medical diagnostics and basic single molecule interactions related to disease." Of the awards Belcher has won, only a handful are named here: the Wilson Prize in Chemistry, Harvard University (2001); the MacArthur Genius Award (2004); Four Star General Recognition Award, U.S. Army, (2004); Researcher of the Year, *Scientific American* (2006); and the Hero-Climate Change Award, *Time* Magazine (2007). At MIT, Belcher is a professor of energy in materials science and engineering and biological engineering and the university has created a "fun animated presentation of Prof. Belcher's life story," which describes her early life in Houston and the fact that she suffered from dyslexia. Angela Belcher is a graduate all Lamar alums should applaud.[340]

Dr. Jason Dworkin (Class of 1987) won first place in the Lamar Science Fair as a tenth-grader. He was a member of the National Honor Society and served on the Research Committee of the Astronomy Club. Dworkin earned his AB degree with distinction at Occidental College and his PhD in Biochemistry at the University of California, San Diego. He is chief of the Astrochemistry Laboratory in the Solar System Exploration Division at NASA's Goddard Space Flight Center. In 2007, as chief of the Astrochemistry Laboratory, he received the Goddard Exceptional Achievement Award and the Goddard IRAAD Innovator of the Year Award, then in 2009 received the Robert H. Goddard Leadership Award. He has written for many scientific journals and belongs to Alpha Chi Sigma, the Meteoritical Society, the American Chemical Society, and the International Society for the Study of the Origin of Life.[341]

*Jessica Farrar (Class of 1984) is the longest-serving Hispanic female member of the House of Representatives from Harris County.*

In the 1980s, Lamar High School continued its fine arts tradition by graduating in the same class two respected prima ballerinas. Martha Butler (Long) (Class of 1982) graduated from Lamar in three

*Martha Butler dances the part of the Swan Queen at Wortham Theater in Houston Ballet's production of* Swan Lake. *(Courtesy of Martha Butler Long)*

years, so that at age seventeen she could begin her ballet career. Two years later, she danced with Li Cunxin and was awarded the Silver Medal at the Tokyo International Ballet Competition as well as a dance fellowship from the Princess Grace Foundation. She won a Gold Medal at the Fourth USA International Ballet Competition in Jackson, Mississippi. A soloist in Houston Ballet, Butler was appointed principal dancer in 1990.

Butler left Houston to join American Ballet Theater in New York City, where she was appointed soloist in 1994 and danced leading roles in Twyla Tharp's *The Elements* and *Jump Start*. She retired from ballet in 1996. She praises Lamar for providing a solid academic foundation while enabling her to pursue her passion for ballet. Her husband, aunts, and uncles are also Lamar alumni, and she looks forward to the day her children attend Lamar High School.

Lamar's other prima ballerina, Lauren Anderson (Class of 1982), called "Ballet's Jackie Robinson" by *Houston Culture Map*, admits that she was a surprising choice for her first major role in Houston Ballet's production of *Alice in Wonderland*.[342] She was only thirteen, and although she had been sheltered from "the sting of racial animosity," she still knew that "Alice was really, really white," and "I was really, really brown."[343]

Anderson continued as a student at Houston Ballet, but admits that she never fit the standard white, pink, and frilly image of a ballerina; however, when legendary director Ben Stevenson suggested she might be better suited for musical theater, she replied that ballet was what she wanted. Stevenson

*Lauren Anderson danced the role of Jutting in Houston Ballet's* Don Quixote. *During her career she was on the covers of* People *and* Dance Magazine. *In 2006, she retired and became Houston Ballet's education ambassador. (Courtesy of Lauren Anderson)*

*A 2007 Distinguished Lamar Alumna, Lauren Anderson is pictured with her mentor, legendary choreographer Ben Stevenson.*

became her mentor and says Anderson's dancing became important to him because she gave him as much as he gave her.[344]

In 1990, Anderson's passion and hard work resulted in her becoming the first African American prima ballerina dancing in a major United States classical ballet company. She credits Stevenson for being a director "who had the guts to do it."[345] During her career, she was featured on the covers of *Dance Magazine* and *People*. Anderson summarizes her ballet success by saying, "All I did was dance. I got on a stage and did something I loved to do and got a check for it. And Houston let me do it."[346] After she hung up her dancing shoes at age forty-six, Anderson became an education ambassador for Houston Ballet. The Smithsonian Institution recently requested one of her costumes and the first contract she signed as prima ballerina for their Afro-American Fine Arts Collection. Lauren Anderson was honored as a Lamar Distinguished Alumna in 2007.

### Lamar Athletics in the 1980s

Known affectionately as "Coach," Sandy Carr began his nineteen-year career at Lamar when he was appointed assistant football coach in 1965. He was promoted to head football coach the following year and remained until his retirement from HISD in 1984, the same year House Bill 72 enacted the "No Pass, No Play" rule for athletics—a rule which Coach Carr had adopted years before.

Carr loved his job and the young men he coached loved him, as indicated at his funeral by testimonials of former players who spoke at his funeral. Mike Wolfe (Class of 1974) said, "Even if you were the worst player on the team, he still cared about you."[347] When Wolfe was knocked unconscious in a game, Coach Carr and his wife came to check on him in the hospital. Duane Hefley (Class of 1981) spoke of Carr as a "really good-hearted man" and a "personal friend to the players off the field" who inspired them to win out of respect for him.[348] Joe H. Martel (Class of 1977), now a football coach himself, described Carr as "the first white man I loved for the many things he taught me. He taught us to do our best regardless of any obstacles."[349] After Carr was diagnosed with cancer, he counseled others at M. D. Anderson Cancer Center. David L. Zipps (Class of 1974) remarked on the number of students for whom Sandy Carr made a difference: "It's really amazing that there are so many guys who feel inspired by him, not for football, but for how you grow up to live your life and be a man."³⁵⁰

Torrin Polk (Class of 1988) was an outstanding football player at Lamar, making All-District, All-Greater Houston Area, All-State, and the Touchdown Club, and was a finalist for Offensive Player of the Year. He played for LSU and then transferred to UH. Polk's quotes regarding his football days are widely circulated on the Internet. His most often-repeated quip refers to UH Head Coach John Jenkins: "He treats us like real men, he lets us wear earrings."

When Laura Ritchey (Class of 1989) won the girls' singles UIL state tennis competition in 1989, it had been forty years since Lamar's last state win in this category. Ritchey's father began teaching her the game when she was seven years old, and she entered Lamar having already made a name for herself in the world of tennis. At Lamar, in addition to winning the 5-A state title, she was named a Texas All-American Athlete. She turned pro immediately after graduation, but her professional tennis career was cut short by a torn rotator cuff. She entered college, received her RN, and has had a successful nursing career. Though she felt nursing had been a very rewarding career, Ritchey "could not shake her desire to return to tennis." Though she battled kidney problems, she continued playing, juggling tennis with twelve-to-fourteen-hour shifts at the hospital. She has played in the world tennis championship in Durban, South Africa, and was ranked No. 2 by the United States Tennis Association in the women's over-thirty age division. Despite how much she loves the game, Ritchey is quick to point out that she sees how people are affected by disease, which reminds her that "there's more to life than just tennis."³⁵¹

*Sandy Carr, head football coach at Lamar for eighteen years, was one of the last coaches to give up wearing a shirt and tie to the games. Note his Lamar Redskins tie. (Courtesy of Florine Carr)*

*Torrin Polk is remembered in collegiate football history as much for what he said as for his gridiron record.*

The 1980s brought Watergate and disillusionment, the government's first billion-dollar bailout bill, and the transformation of an economy based on defense spending to an economy based on microchips and floppy discs. But according to their yearbook, students at Lamar were still "reaching for the stars." Julie Doran, 1989 *Orenda* editor, called the student body the "LIFELINE" of Lamar High School, describing her classmates as "Loyal, Idealistic, Farsighted, Enthusiastic, Limitless, Individualistic, Nationalistic, and Exceptional!"³⁵²

During the eighties, Lamar students staunchly supported their alma mater, were concerned for the environment, tolerated the remodeling of their school building, cheered the athletic teams, approved of NASA's programs, and accepted responsibility for their personal growth. The Class of 1989 was proud to pass on the "new Lamar"³⁵³ and the structural changes that would make it ready to "take on the challenges of the next century."³⁵⁴

*The 1989* Orenda *called the Lamar girls' tennis team devastating to their opponents. Top row, left to right: Nancy Guyton, Suzanne Sklar, Abbey Pitner, Bethany Andell, Paige Ingebritson, and Jennifer Wise. Bottom row: Brandy Cramer, Julie Moore, Laura Ritchey, and Elizabeth Gerlach. "Once a tennis player, always a tennis player" seems to describe Laura Ritchey, who in 1999 returned to play professionally while still working as a nurse at Methodist Hospital.*

### THE 1990s AT LAMAR: A CHANGING OF THE GUARD

In 1990, for the fourth time in four years, Lamar's fall semester opened with a new principal. Walter Day, whose experience included administrative positions in Alaska and Africa as well as two HISD assignments—Bellaire High School and Burbank Elementary—said he was "very proud to be the new principal of the finest school in all of HISD."[355] Interviewed by *Lancer* staff reporter Richard Hannah, Day said he liked the diversity and the cosmopolitan vitality of Houston and expressed his intention to remain in Houston even if he was not at Lamar. He remained for five years.

When Walter Day resigned in 1995, HISD scrambled to find a replacement. Ms. Mary Chambers served as "acting principal" until mid-term, when the school board appointed Miss Charlotte Haynes as Lamar High School's first female principal. At HISD, Haynes had been a high school math teacher, a math supervisor, and principal of Roberts Elementary, but she stayed at Lamar only one year.

*The Class of 1989 was proud to pass on the "new Lamar," whose structural changes made it ready to "take on the challenges of the next century."*

## RICE UNIVERSITY HOSTS THE SIXTEENTH G7 SUMMIT

In July 1990, the City of Houston and Rice University hosted the Sixteenth G7 Summit, an event that brought worldwide attention. As senior Josh Jacobs proclaimed, "Houston has shed its oil capital stereotype. We are now an international city."[356]

Lamar High School began to embody Houston's new image. "Kaleidoscope," a prose poem by Cara Dougherty, appeared in the 1991 *Orenda* and reaffirmed Lamar students' positions on diversity, individualism, and their own brand of student unity.

Kaleidoscope—*anything that reflects a succession of changing colors, patterns, or phases*

Changing. Rearranging. Moving apart. Coming together to make new, colorful patterns. Like the kaleidoscope, students from diverse parts of Houston meld as a cohesive unit. Various cultures brought together, added a unique flavor to the student body. Students realized that they had similarities with unusual people, and that differences led to more exciting friendships. United, students created a stimulating environmentv to encourage both individuality and working together.

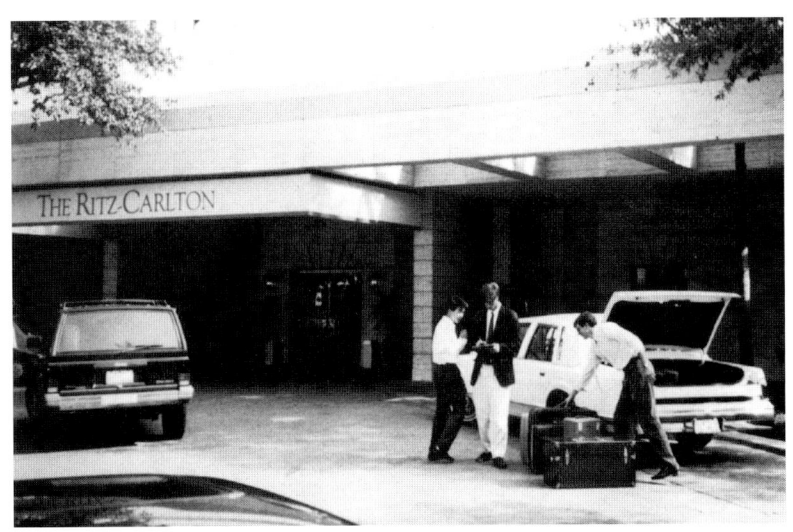

*Lamar's participation in any citywide event has become a given. Here the Key Clubbers are loading and unloading luggage for the delegates who came to Houston for the G7 Summit.*

Countless references in the yearbook referred to Lamar's diversity and to its students' changing priorities, interests, and ideas. Petrina Stultz quoted exchange student Samsa Lehtinen, who said, "The diversity that I found at Lamar made me think of America in a different manner."[357] Lamar High School somehow managed to combine diversity and individualism with a spirited sense of community and connectedness.

"Change the World: Attempt the Impossible" was the *Orenda* headline that appeared over staffer Cara Dougherty's essay and a list of the "Top 10 Ways" to effect change:[358]

10. Get dope off of the streets
9. Make everyone literate
8. Eliminate stereotypes
7. No superpowers
6. Stop gang violence

> 5. End world hunger
> 4. Create a stronger family structure
> 3. Place more emphasis on the United Nations
> 2. Mandatory recycling
> 1. No more wars—World Peace

In 1990, recycling was still a relatively new concept for Houstonians, but *Lancer* editorials indicated that, for Lamar students, this was a hot topic. The first *Lancer* issue of the 1990 fall semester contained a special section named "Concern for Our Earth." Another article, "Recycling in Houston," written by *Lancer* staff reporter Mark Haywood, cited two privately funded recycling programs: a "Bin Program" sponsored by Browning Ferris Industries, and a "blue bag program" sponsored by the Glad plastics company. Haywood directed interested parties to call a BFI Hotline for further information.[359]

Todd Rosson, junior *Lancer* staff reporter, wrote of "Five Simple Things You Can Do to Save the Earth." He began by pointing out that the 1990s were "bringing a new sense of global awareness to individuals that institutions alone could never solve." His solutions were as follows:

1. "Stop Junk Mail" provided a mailing address to request removal of your name from nationwide lists of organizations and businesses.
2. "Snip Six Pack Rings" cited the danger of these devices to marine animals and the 15,600 plastic six-pack rings found during a recent 300-mile Texas beach cleanup.
3. "Aerate Your Faucets" pointed to the 250 million gallons of water that would be saved daily if all Americans installed low-flow faucet aerators.
4. "New Ingredients" urged the use of ten fewer plastic bags per month, reusable containers instead of aluminum foil and plastic wrap, rags instead of paper towels, unbleached coffee filters, and biodegradable non-toxic garbage bags with an address for ordering these by mail.
5. "Don't Go with the Flow" suggested that you not leave the faucet running while you are brushing your teeth and use a sprayer when you wash your car.

Rosson also addressed the killing of dolphins in "When Will the Slaughter Stop?" and discussed the plight of 14,000 dolphins killed because they were swimming above schools of yellow fin tuna swept up annually in two-mile-long tuna nets. Rosson advised students to look for "dolphin-safe" tuna can labels and urged "congressional delegations to pass House Bill number 2926 and Senate Bill 2044."[360]

During the 1980s and 1990s, Lamar students became interested in volunteerism, as "volunteer rates among youth ages 16-19 soared."[361] In 1990, President George H. W. Bush signed the National Community Service Act providing $64 million in grants to encourage a variety of community service programs. President Clinton signed the National and Community Trust Act of 1993. These two bills allowed schools to apply for grant money to fund "service-learning curricula." According to members of Congress, for students who weren't interested in academics, volunteer work would provide a "safe and engaging outlet."[362]

The effect of this national movement was reflected in the 1991 *Orenda* article "United for a Cause, Students Reach Out." *Orenda* staffer Caldwell Kerr wrote, "Eager to share their time and resources, students worked together for the benefit of others." By 1996, *Orenda* staffer Zach Altneu noted that "any student with a passion for a specific cause" could find a club "made just for them." For Lamar organizations, service became the "lifeline," and projects ranged from the Key Club's "Adopt a Grandparent," which provided companionship for residents of the Hallmark Retirement Home, to the Keywanettes sorting food at the Food Bank.363 A club called Students for Social Responsibility (SSR) provided funds to adopt a whale or to help support a child in India.364 Organizations such as Saferides set up a base at a student's home on weekends to provide a ride for those unable to drive; PEACE (People Eager About Community Efforts), whose mission was "to help the world"; PRIDE (People Really Interested in a Drug-free Environment), which helped students make wise choices; and STEP (Students To End Prejudice), formed to "provide a prejudice-free environment."

*Barbie Ayesu said she felt privileged to come to Lamar High School as their first African AFS exchange student.*

Social clubs Desmoiselles and Gents raised funds by washing cars and selling mums and donated the proceeds to the United Negro College Fund. They also held food and clothing drives for the homeless.365 AFS helped handicapped students, distributed perishable food, and distributed toys at Christmas to underprivileged children.366 It is not known if Lamar High School received federal grant money for these activities.

The December 1993 *Lancer* gave full-page coverage to HISD's first AIDS Awareness Conference when Lamar was chosen to host the event. Representatives from service organizations all over the city came to speak to students and parents. The High School for the Performing and Visual Arts closed the day with a play entitled *The Age of Discretion*.367

Health awareness was another new topic for Lamar students. An article in the 1994 *Orenda*, "Healthy Habits: Students Turn Healthy and Physically Fit," contained photographs showing students who were taking care of their health, and pointed out that now "staying in shape and being fit became more important to everyone."368

*"Earth Alert" was used to describe the actions of the environmentally conscious Lamar volunteers who were cleaning the school's inner courtyard.*

Other *Lancer* editorials addressed the problem of violence in Houston, questioning whether the recently imposed curfew on all youths under eighteen would really solve the problem. The writer concluded that adults were doing much more damage than teenagers.

Another *Lancer* editorial called for a change in the mascot, pointing to St. John's School, which had just changed its mascot from Johnny Reb to the Mavericks: "If Lamar considers itself a truly diverse school, the school mascot should not discriminate against any ethnic group."[369]

### ONLY AT LAMAR?

Extraordinary opportunities continued to be offered to Lamar High School students during the 1990s. Novelist and screenwriter Sydney Sheldon spoke in September 1991, naming "Aspiring Youth his 'Big Secret' to Success." His advice: "Give more and do more, don't just do what is required." Sheldon urged students to recognize that "success is not being rich, but being the best you can be," and to get "the best education you can get," because "education is the building block of life." Sheldon's racial views were made clear with his comment, "Color doesn't matter one damn bit—it's what you are and who you are that counts."[370]

"We want books rather than crooks" were Senator Phil Gramm's words to Lamar students in 1991, promoting his new campaign against drugs and firearms on school campuses. An outgrowth of the Crime Control Act recently passed by the U.S. Congress, Gramm's campaign focused on eliminating the "dangerous distraction" of crime in schools. U.S. Attorney Ron Woods, U.S. Marshal Stu Baker, Harris County Sheriff Johnny Klevenhagen, and HISD Superintendent Frank Petruzielo accompanied Gramm to Lamar. Principal Walter Day praised the event.[371]

In April 1992, the Reverend Jesse Jackson came to speak to Lamar students about the "Challenges of our Age." According to the *Lancer* article, "Lamar students were very excited to have such a dignitary on campus." Jackson, who had made history as a worldwide activist addressing racial injustice and the plight of the voiceless, spoke about his concern that school budgets were being cut and jail budgets were being expanded. Delvin Gray, a Lamar student, said, "It always helps to have someone as important and special as Mr. Jackson." Jackson's message to the students was to "register to vote so they could elect leaders who are interested… in their futures."[372]

"Nabisco Awards Large Grant," a *Lancer* headline announced in the February 1992 issue. Twelfth-grade government and economics teacher Mrs. Ann Hoar was awarded $15,000 to produce a video to tie HISD's curriculum into the economic and political issues to be discussed at the Republican National Convention. The theme, "Put This in Your Platform," included student interviews of leaders in Houston's business and political community in order to formulate issues they would like to see included in the Republican platform. Hoar was commended for her "creative approach to making an important event come alive."

U.S. Secretary of State Madeleine Albright came to Lamar on February 7, 1996, spending thirty minutes with forty of the International Baccalaureate students. She discussed foreign policy, took questions that ranged from U.S. attitudes toward China to a concern about U.S. attitudes toward immigration, and urged the group to consider studying international affairs and relations in college. The *Lancer* article concluded with Lamar's pride in having "one of the most influential and honorable figures in the world" visit their school.

In the nineties, a crew of technicians, stage managers, and producers was at Lamar to film a commercial for Southwestern Bell. A *Lancer* reporter asked, "Is Lamar the next 90210?" referring to a popular television show featuring wealthy teenagers who attended West Beverly Hills High School. A Bell company official said Lamar was chosen for its "distinguishing look." Mrs. Malicote's room, located in Lamar's west wing, was the setting, but no students or faculty were in the commercial. The *Lancer* pointed out, "This was not the first time Lamar was used in video footage to be viewed nationwide."[373] In 1992, the movie *Sidekicks*, featuring karate expert Chuck Norris, was shot at Lamar, and several students performed as extras. Lamar was used again in 1998 for some of the scenes in Wes Anderson's film *Rushmore*.

## Notable Graduates from the 1990s

Three Lamar students who earned International Baccalaureate diplomas in 1991 illustrated the intellectual capacity and creativity fostered by this serious academic program. Thomas Yu spent his time at Lamar rigorously pursuing the prestigious diploma. A National Merit Scholarship finalist, Yu was chosen as the Outstanding Science Student and served as president of the Computer Club, but found time for the Asian Club and the drama honor society Kachina. These activities are reflected in his work today. After receiving his BS degree at MIT in Course XVI-Aeronautics/Astronautics, he remained in Cambridge, where he is a member of the MIT Kerberos Development Team, contributing to IETF security-related work and doing assorted work on computer and network security. He says he lives with five cats and a ferret, is a licensed radio amateur, tinkers with lasers and optics, rides two motorcycles, and works on graphic design and theatrical sound and lighting.[374]

In addition to being awarded an IB diploma at Lamar, Alex Avelallemant (Class of 1991) was a swimmer, a member of the Texaco Star Challenge Team, and a competitor in the Academic Decathlon as well as an Eagle Scout. He received his BA from Trinity University and headed to Philmont Scout Ranch, a 137,500-acre wilderness in the Rocky Mountains of northern New Mexico. He worked there for six summers and learned to play the guitar, recording the first Tabasco Donkeys album with some of his Philmont friends. Today, Avelallemant is a foreign service officer in the U.S. State Department officially assigned to the American Embassy in Kabul. He says it was a "wavy line that led from Houston to Bagram," but his interest in foreign affairs "began to sprout" when he attended Lamar. He credits history teacher Wendell Zartman for "cultivating my interest in things relating to both history and international affairs." His favorite class was World Area Studies, which he was taking when the Iron Curtain fell. He says they had T-shirts made up with a picture of Joseph Stalin that had "Farewell Tour" printed superimposed over a map of Eastern Europe. Mike Dorsey's government class influenced him as well because he sponsored Lamar's participation in an HISD Mock Congress which Avelallemant says stimulated his interest in government. His English teacher Ms. Ann Mahan's emphasis on mythology and the Homeric epics "served him well when he lived in Greece."[375]

Eric Sumner (Class of 1991) completed his IB diploma requirements and entered Princeton, earning a BSE in Chemical Engineering, magna cum laude. Sumner worked as an engineering consultant in New Orleans, but now lives in Minnesota, where he is a control engineer. He spends his spare time competing in running events, notably the 6K Mud Run and the Ortho Monster Dash.[376]

Megan Moir received an IB diploma in 1994 and entered Rice University, where she earned a BA in Latin American Studies with a minor in Biology. Her honors thesis, "Buffalo Bayou: Houston's Urban Stream," led to study for an MS in Water Resources at the University of Vermont.[377] Today she is a stormwater plangineer at the City of Burlington's Department of Public Works.

### Fine Arts at Lamar Embraces the New and the Old

By the early 1990s, Houston was the acknowledged Southern center of hip-hop music as those singers and promoters who had gradually moved here during the late 1980s now gained ascendancy in their profession. By 1999, Lamar's co-ed Dance Department offered hip-hop for beginning and advanced students. The classes introduced the culture of this dance style that incorporates loose but precise movements. According to the 2000 *Orenda*, students had an opportunity to "cross cultural barriers, stay in motion, and have fun."

Juxtaposed with this group was Houston's internationally acclaimed ballet center, Wortham Hall, where three Lamar graduates danced as soloists of Houston Ballet Company. Prima ballerina Marian Butler (Class of 1994) began at Houston Ballet Academy under Ben Stevenson's tutelage. The eighteen-year-old Marian joined the Houston Ballet Company upon graduation from Lamar but remained only six months before her older sister Martha persuaded her to come to New York. In an interview with journalist Gia Kourias, Marian says she called Stevenson and said, "I have an opportunity to dance at American Ballet Theater, and it's the best company and I am going to go."[378] Butler has been there ever since, but says that at age thirty-seven, she feels she will dance only a few more years. The Butler sisters and Lauren Anderson complete the trio of Lamar graduates who have reached stardom in professional ballet.[379]

*Right to left: Ashley Jones (Class of 1994) was honored in 2012 along with community volunteer Jonathan Day (Class of 1958), public health advocate Susan Cooley (Class of 1970), and Washington Redskins football player Brian Orakpo (Class of 2004).*

Television and movies have claimed Ashley Jones (Class of 1994), an actress who stays busy and "shows up in lots of unexpected places." She lives in California but still visits her family in Texas. While in high school, she began her television career with *Dr. Quinn, Medicine Woman* and the CBS mini-series *Fire Next Time*. In addition to working with Oscar award-winning actors and actresses in films and on television, Jones is seriously committed to community service. She has served as a Host Committee board member of the national non-profit Step-up Women's Network, a mentoring program that advances and connects underprivileged girls with professional women. She also works with the Alliance for Children's Rights and the City of Hope. She was a 2012 Distinguished Alum recipient and describes herself as "an avid animal lover and a tech geek."[380]

Catherine Frels (Class of 1998) was among the top ten students in the Magnet Business Program. An all-round star pupil, she was a cheerleader, vice-president of the National Honor Society, a member of Mu Alpha Theta and the Key Club, and played on the basketball and softball teams. After high school, Frels attended Duke University, where she earned a BA in International Comparative Studies, graduating magna cum laude. She is a graduate of the Honors Conservatory at the Theatre Lab School of Dramatic Arts in Washington, D.C., and received an MFA in Classical Acting from George Washington University's Shakespeare Theatre Company. Today she appears in *Thurston*, an online Western drama series. Frels was nominated for an Indie Soap as Best Actress in this popular series.[381]

## Lamar Athletics During the 1990s

"What has Eight Lanes and Two Diving Boards?" Lamar's new swimming pool, the Natatorium, opened in October 1993 after seven months of construction. The $2-million project had many asking, "How can a pool cost this much money?" The pool uses the finest diving boards and the best lane ropes, and includes an automatic filtration system that filters chlorine and other chemicals as needed without any manual labor, leaving the water sparkling clean. The pool's inaugural year was termed a "big success," as the Lamar swim team won both the 1993 District Championship and the Pasadena Invitational. One of the team members was Michael Mahlstedt, whose sister Allison won the UIL state medal for the fifty-yard freestyle competition six years later, in 1999–2000.[382]

*Allison Mahlstedt won the freestyle 1999–2000 UIL state title for Lamar by .003 seconds, what she calls "the length of a fingernail."*

The 1990s ended unhappily. Fire broke out in the copy room at the end of the administrative office area about 11:15 p.m. on Tuesday, October 13, 1998, destroying the administrative offices and delaying the school's opening for two days. The suspected cause was heavy use of the copier to prepare materials for Lamar's annual College Night. Lamar had only manually operated fire alarms and fire extinguishers. Fortunately, damage was "truly minimal considering the size and age of the sixty-one-year-old building."[383] The grandfather clock that had been in the office since the school opened in 1937 never missed a beat.

### THE 1980s AND THE 1990s: TWO DECADES THAT CHANGED LAMAR

Lamar students who graduated during these two decades were shaped by events very different from those their parents experienced. The *Challenger* space shuttle disaster, the end of the Cold War, Black Monday, the AIDS epidemic, the introduction of the personal computer, video games, cable television, and the Internet—all had a global impact on teenagers. High school students became committed to human rights and human dignity, to recycling, to their health, and were more interested in technology than were groups from previous decades.

The 1950s produced the most "uniform youth culture in living memory." William Strauss and Neil Howe, in *The Fourth Turning Point*, described them as the "silent" generation: "They married early, believed in 'sweet sentimentality' and eagerly climbed the corporate ladder." In contrast, the so-called Generation Xers of the 1980s and 1990s married late, possessed a "rock-hard reality," and preferred to be entrepreneurs or to work for non-profit companies.[384] Brittany Lewis described her classmates in the 1999 *Orenda*: "Although we do different things, the things we do reflect the lives we live; the way we see life provides the window to the soul."

Lamar teenagers realized military service was a possible part of their future as the 1990s brought Operations Desert Shield and Desert Storm. Many Houstonians felt sadness as the last Astros game was played in the Astrodome on October 9, 1999. The Oklahoma City bombing and school shootings combined with President Bill Clinton's impeachment trial to end the twentieth century with distressing headlines.

Chapter Seven: The 1980s and 1990s | 177

The 2012 Lamar Redskins football team was led by Head Coach Tim Nolen and Assistant Coaches Jerry Martinez, Ernie Saldivar, Lee Malowitz, Jerry VanDusen, Tyrone Green, Stephen Pinkney, Chad Scholz, Garry Johnson, Rene Glapion, Jeremy Davison, Demetrius Woods, Frank Romero, Ryan Holley, and Michael Lindsey. The players were, by jersey number: #1 Cedric Lancaster, #2 Derrick Carmouche, #3 Beau Wells, #4 John Bonney, #5 Holton Hill, #6 Nicholas Turner, #7 Darrell Colbert, #8 Darius Durall, #9 Cravon Rogers, #10 Jarrett Villery, #11 Nicholas Richardson, #12 Trevion Duncan, #14 Travi'ane Whiteing, #15 Ivy Smith, #16 Jordan Williams, #17 Dillon Payne, #20 Levy Whiteing, #21 Ronnie Wesley, #22 Scott Jacobs, #23 Darielle Smith, #24 James Williams, #25 Terrence Drew, #30 Bill Dang, #31 Daijon Druhet, #32 Tevin Weston, #33 Austin Fendley, #34 Regan Johnson, #35 Blake Smith, #36 Lee Duncan, #40 Jack Anderson, #41 Jesus Aguirre, #42 Gregory Gibson, #44 Cory Mitchell, #50 Frank Pecina, #51 Stephon Whitfield, #52 Travion Jones, #53 Noel Perez, #54 Reynaldo Garay, #55 Sergio Castillo, #56 Glenn Anderson, #57 Jesse Morales, #58 Dino Fernandez, #59 Kyran Mitchell, #61 Robert Meeker, #62 Celious Barner, #64 Xavier Flores, #65 Stephen Whitfield, #66 Norval Edwards, #67 Aaron Jones, #68 Jorge Rojas, #70 Braylon Hyder, #71 Charles Onyekwelu, #72 Marc Wilson, #73 Tim Ard, #74 Deon Ford, #75 Jonathan Beaudion, #76 Shaquille Gibson, #78 Ira Lewis, #79 Lee Stanton, #80 Alan Melgar, #81 Max Peddie, #82 Bradley Isensee, #83 Nathanael Rios, #84 Shelby Walker, #85 Tyler Speier, #87 Joshua Stewart, #89 Justin Hollie, #91 Brandon Martinez, #92 Zelt Minor, #94 Travon Elmer, #95 Phoenix Chukwu, #98 Abdul Ahmad, and #99 Evan Thomas.

# CHAPTER EIGHT
## The Years 2000 to 2012

Lamar sailed proudly into its sixty-third year at the turn of the twenty-first century. Few high schools in the nation could match its record for graduating alumni who embodied the school's motto, "Reach for the Stars." Just as the world changed during these six decades, so did Lamar. The school was no longer an enclave for students often categorized as "rich kids" or "tea sippers" by students at some rival schools as well as many Houstonians. Previously described as a "Camelot," the new Lamar instead became a melting pot. As Adrea Chow (Class of 2000) said, "Nothing portrays a melting pot more than the accumulation of Redskins that make up the Lamar Student Body."

In the 2000 *Orenda*, editor-in-chief Matt Robbins called Lamar's student body "dynamic" and described the school as a place where "faces, opinions, and hairstyles" did not remain the same for any length of time. "Constant motion, growth, and educational advancement" were what Robbins called the only certainties at Lamar, and he applauded the students who felt "absolutely at home" in this "maelstrom." Despite the ethnic diversity or perhaps because of it, a *Lancer* editorial, "Lamar Is First Choice for Many," described it as an "excellent school, academically, athletically, administratively, and socially." How has Lamar maintained its preeminence among Houston high schools?

In 1997, Dr. James McSwain became principal of Lamar, and his guidance has been an important influence in shaping the school as it exists today. A Fort Worth native, McSwain took his BA in History from the University of Texas at Arlington, his MEd from Tarleton State University, and his EdD degree at Texas Tech University with a specialization in Educational Leadership. After teaching history, English, and debate in Grapevine and Stephenville, Texas, for five years, he began his administrative career and first served as principal of the CAP High School in Coleman, Texas, a cooperative alternative high school serving students suffering from various severe disorders. Here McSwain developed a model program which he would expand during his next two

*Dr. James McSwain will soon become the longest-serving principal at Lamar. He says his goal is to produce the "largest number of students in the district who can achieve at the highest levels."*

appointments: principal of Colorado High School, Colorado, Texas, and Texas High School, Texarkana, Texas. His success at these high schools earned him the reputation of being an innovative principal who had the ability to improve test scores, academic offerings, and disciplinary problems by creating programs that were already serving as models for numerous other districts.

McSwain's outlook, which dovetailed that of Rod Paige (HISD superintendent from 1994 to 2000), is that "inner-city kids, many of them from very poor households, can and will learn." He has expanded Paige's vision of teaching these students rudimentary knowledge of what he calls an "expectation of excellence" at Lamar High School, a place where he says "failure is not allowed."[385]

Teaching tutorials, or what he refers to as "academic detention," are held daily for two hours after school at Lamar as a replacement for the punitive detention centers used elsewhere. He absolutely prohibits a "dumbing down" of the curriculum and fosters a "We are going to do this together" attitude, which he says ensures that the "most needy kids are given the most help."[386]

Soon to become Lamar's longest-serving principal, McSwain's goal is to produce the "largest number of students in the district who can achieve at the highest levels." Over 75 percent of Lamar's graduating seniors, regardless of their class standing, have taken at least one IB, AP, or Dual Credit class. The "Dual Credit" program brings Houston Community College instructors onto the Lamar campus to teach as members of the faculty. Students can earn college credit without leaving the campus or paying any tuition or fees. He calls all of this "giving the students opportunities"—giving them a future.

## Other Special Programs at Lamar

Lamar High School became an authorized IB school in 1982 with the implementation of the Diploma Programme. The Middle Years Programme was implemented in 2003. This worldwide program, which originated in Switzerland, is a globally standardized curriculum designed to develop well-rounded students who are knowledgeable thinkers and communicators, able to balance risk-taking with open-minded reflective caring. Students are required to complete one hundred hours of community service in addition to completing rigorous coursework. Teachers for this program undergo extensive subject-specific training and learn to work with colleagues to implement the interdisciplinary curriculum. The goal of the IB program is the development of the whole student: intellectually, emotionally, and ethically. Students who complete the Diploma Programme automatically receive a minimum of twenty-four hours of college credit at any public university in Texas, Colorado, California, and Florida. Lamar's IB graduates not only are admitted to the finest colleges in the United States, but also receive substantial scholarships.

Lamar is now the largest IB school in the State of Texas. During the middle years (ninth and tenth grade), all students at Lamar are required to take the IB curriculum. Usually about 350 students remain in the IB program and ninety or more annually receive IB diplomas. This interconnected program focuses on aims and values that produce motivated teachers and students better able to succeed in today's globalized world. Many students choose Lamar High School because of its strong IB program, and their achievements after graduation attest to the success of their completion of this curriculum. Lamar's long history of academic excellence, its strong AFS program, and its cultural diversity make it a natural partner for the IB Diploma Programme. As a result of McSwain's leadership as principal of Lamar, this HISD inner-city public high school has become the largest International Baccalaureate school in Texas and awards the highest number of IB diplomas in the state.

The Robotics program at Lamar is the result of the work of Judy Ley (Allen) (Class of 1957). In 2003, when a former classmate from Harvard Business School asked her to attend the FIRST (For Inspiration and Recognition of Science and Technology) Robotics Competition in Houston, Ley not only went to the contest, but also left convinced that this was a student activity that needed to be encouraged and amplified. Recognizing the value of FIRST's ability to encourage the student excitement that results from building and then competing with their own robots, Ley used her fundraising skills to provide financial support for the formation of additional Houston teams. In 2006, she approached Dr. McSwain about the need for Lamar High School to have a Robotics team. In 2008, the DiscoBots, as Lamar's team was named, entered the FIRST Robotics Competition and won two awards. Since then, the DiscoBots have won more than thirty awards, and a class is now offered which provides students with a brief introduction to robotics. Andrew Lynch, a professor at Rice University, sponsors the club and says his members spend from eight to twelve hours a week on their projects.

The Career and Technical Program enables students to enter the global workplace and provides opportunities to participate in internship and co-op programs and earn Microsoft Office and QuickBooks certification. Computer training in Lamar classrooms now ranges from basic keyboarding to webmastering. Classes in AutoCad and desktop publishing and Internet accessibility provide students with knowledge applicable to their modern world.

For seven years, Lamar High School has partnered with Communities in Schools (CIS), a national program that provides on-campus social services for students and their families. Trained social service workers counsel students, give them health information, and educate them about community resources. Students who deal with problems such as depression, abuse, anger management, and homelessness benefit greatly from the help of the CIS professional counseling staff. Their goal is to enable the students at Lamar to overcome problems that have the potential to prevent their graduation from high school. In addition, CIS partners with hospitals and law firms that provide summer internships for Lamar students who are interested in nursing or the legal profession. In 2012–2013, CIS provided nearly 5,000 hours of services to 500 Lamar students and their families. Lamar's CIS center has received national recognition from the U.S. Department of Education, one of the nine social service centers in the U.S. to be so commended.

Another rigorous choice for college-bound students is the Lamar Business Administration Magnet Program, which began in 1983 and has over 700 students who take courses in business support systems, management and multimedia, accounting, business law, economics, and banking and finance. Partnering with the students who enroll in this program are oil and gas, accounting, tax, legal, medical, advertising, financial, and insurance firms who provide work experience, intern programs, and tutelage.

FIRST, a national program, produces students who are significantly more likely to go to college, most of whom go on to major in science or engineering. Engineering companies strongly recommend that students participate in this program. The Lamar administration's strong support for this program attests to the school's commitment to helping students have successful careers. Students who are DiscoBot members have said they learned programming and CAD, as well as how to be a part of a design team. They have obtained scholarships as a result of their participation in FIRST.

## Lamar's Agricultural Program

No one in Houston considers Lamar a rural school, nor is the student body made up of those who are generally labeled "cowboys" or "rednecks," but for more than fifty years Lamar's Future Farmers of America (FFA) program has thrived in this city school located less than five miles from downtown. For fifty-two of these years, in the front yard of the school, at the intersection of Westheimer and River Oaks Boulevard, the Lamar FFA has pitched large tents and held an annual livestock show and live auction.

*The 2012 officers for the Future Farmers of America (FFA) were, from the left: Tevin Weston (far left); Leslie Morrow and Maynumbi Lozano (center foreground); Julianna Longoria, Katie Bogar, and Nhi Dinh (center background); and Vance Tillman and Kim Reiff (far right).*

FFA students work at remote HISD sites or leased farm sites west of town learning to care for, feed, and groom heifers, swine, goats, sheep, and rabbits. In 1992, the *Lancer* reported on the "dedicated FFA members' old-fashioned barn raising!" Using HISD property adjacent to farm sites occupied by Bellaire and Lee High Schools, Lamar's FFA students and Booster Club cleared the land, obtained donations of material and money, and constructed two barns and a road in less than three months.

The FFA program continues to grow and currently has almost one hundred members. One reason for its recent growth is the expansion of the program to include horticulture. Using a fully operational eighty-foot greenhouse provided by the Lamar Alumni Association, horticultural students are taught the art of creating Bonsais, growing air plants and plants from seeds and root cuttings, grafting plants, and making floral arrangements. They grow and market heirloom tomatoes, make herb and container gardens, and work on composting projects that will help them with horticultural classes in college. Floriculture classes provide them with training and career opportunities in floral design.

Lamar horticultural students contribute community service hours by volunteering at the Houston Bulb Mart and the Houston Food Bank. The agricultural students participate in the Harris County Fair, the Fort Worth and San Antonio livestock shows, and of course, the Houston Livestock Show and Calf Scramble.

FFA students profiled in a recent brochure attest to the caliber of the students who enroll in this program. In addition to raising farm animals or flowers, these students play varsity football, run track, are members of ROTC, and become cheerleaders. Many are honor students and winners of leadership awards, and most are dedicated church members. Some plan a career in agriculture or horticulture, but most choose FFA as an elective because, in accordance with the FFA Creed, they find this endeavor "pleasant and challenging." They say they learn dedication and responsibility along with having fun.

In addition, FFA students all seem to be personally committed to community involvement. They volunteer at their churches, local hospitals, soup kitchens, and the Children's Museum. They tutor elementary students and participate in the Galveston semi-annual beach cleanup and the AIDS walk.

*The eighty-foot-long greenhouse built for the Lamar Horticulture Department by the Alumni Association is used by the students to supply the local farmers' markets with heirloom tomatoes.*

What was previously known as the Home Economics Department is now an exciting culinary arts program focusing its training on all-important culinary skills as well as healthy eating. The students operate the Café M restaurant and offer a catering service. The Coffee Bar in the library is an extension of this program, and students can earn the National Restaurant Association's ServSafe food handling certification.

By 2005, Lamar's enrollment had grown to over 3,000, a far cry from the original 1,310 students who arrived at the new school in the fall of 1937. Of HISD's twenty-seven high schools, Lamar continues to have the second-highest enrollment in the district. For the past five years, Lamar has outscored both HISD and the state on TAKS tests in every subject at every grade level. Lamar's SAT scores are more than double those of the HISD average, almost one hundred points higher than the state average, and slightly above the national average. The Lamar faculty must be given a great deal of credit for these successes. All of the teachers have degrees; 35 percent have advanced degrees and 49 percent have eleven or more years of teaching experience.

When the enrollment continued to climb, McSwain took steps designed to bring about a more cohesive student body. Grade levels were clustered by floors to keep students near their peers, and in 2007 a school uniform was adopted. For the first time in the school's history, students, like their neighbors across the street, began wearing uniforms.

*Dorothy Polydoros, head of Lamar's popular culinary arts program, is lecturing to the students who operate the Café M restaurant. (Courtesy of Will LeBlanc)*

*Coach Tommy Nolen (left) is shown with Lamar's Most Valuable Player and All-District nose guard Eural Taylor (right) and a "top fan" they had "recruited."*

## LAMAR ATHLETICS

For twenty-eight years, Tom Nolen, who the *Houston Chronicle* says "has no peer among HISD coaches," has led Redskins football teams to a record fifteen district titles (tied for fifteenth place in UIL history and fifth place among active coaches) and twenty-six playoff trips (fifth in UIL history, second among active coaches), statistics that place him in an elite class among Texas' coaches.[387]

In 1985, when Principal Ray Reiner hired Nolen to be Lamar's football coach, it is doubtful anyone foresaw the level of strong leadership he would bring to the school's athletic program. In 2004, he was inducted into the HISD Hall of Honor and was named Class 5A Coach of the Year.[388]

Called an "old school" coach ("I don't care if you like it. We *will* line up and play hard-nosed football"), Nolen maintains "a solid blue-collar atmosphere in the shadow of Houston's tony River Oaks." His players, both current and former, say he demands perfection. Sixty-six-year-old Nolen, who doesn't care that he is past retirement age, grew up in Bellaire and went to Marian High School. A University of Houston graduate, he coached at Strake Jesuit, leading them to four private school titles from 1975 to 1981, before coming to Lamar.

As *Houston Chronicle* sports columnist David Barron said, Nolen "cherishes" Lamar as a microcosm of Houston, saying, "We are such a melting pot… we have kids from River Oaks and South Hampton and Fourth Ward." Principal McSwain and his head coach see eye-to-eye on how a school should be run, and both men believe "it's what the extracurriculars do for kids and not the other way around." Washington Redskins linebacker Brian Orakpo (Class of 2004), chosen as a Distinguished Alumnus in 2012, calls Nolen's leadership training invaluable, and remembers that "he treated us with such respect."

*Brandon LaFell's mother allowed him to play football only if he kept his grades up. Because of her guidance, he said he knew he had to concentrate on his studies.*

Over 200 of Nolen's athletes have gone on to play college football and four have played professional ball. One of his greatest success stories is a young man named Brandon LaFell (Class of 2005). When LaFell transferred to Lamar as a freshman, his mom would not let him play football until he had proven he could make good grades, so he entered the football program in the spring with her stipulation that she would take football away from him if his grades dropped. Because of her guidance, LaFell knew he had to concentrate on his studies.

His teachers at Lamar were of the same mind. He says they did not treat him like an athlete. While his best friends were skipping school, three of his teachers metaphorically "grabbed him by the collar" and were "really hard on me." They made no allowances for his long hours of practice and time spent on the playing field. They never let him leave class, they insisted he be in his seat before the first bell, and he was usually given a desk adjacent to the teacher's. LaFell felt they were making him understand that he needed an education. As a result, when he graduated from Lamar he got a football scholarship to LSU and graduated from college in 2009. He was picked in the third round of the NFL draft by the Carolina Panthers and has been in the starting lineup for them for three years.

LaFell credits his success to his excellent academic preparation at Lamar and the coaching staff who taught him "how to be a man." Coming to Lamar as a star athlete in middle school, LaFell thought he knew it all. His coaches, especially the basketball coach, Dennis Gillespie, "brought him down." If they felt his attitude was bad or he missed practice, they did not let him play. Tommy Nolen, Chad Muller, the quarterback coach, and Tyrone Green, the lineman coach, were always there if he needed a dollar for bus fare, to pick him up at 7 a.m. to bring him to school, or to take him home after a late game. This Lamar alum is filled with gratitude for what the school did for him, and because of that he holds a football camp at Lamar High School one weekend every April for underprivileged middle school and high school students who want to play football. He gathers his football buddies to help him spend time with these budding athletes and tries to make a difference in their lives as his mentors at Lamar did for him. He hopes to play professional football for twelve more years and then go into broadcasting or become a coach.[389]

*Sportswriters and players agree that Nolen is "grumpy" on game days, and in 2012 he had a lot of extra game days as Lamar entered its first state playoff since 1953.*

But sportswriters and players agree: Nolen is "grumpy" on game days, and in 2012, Nolen had a lot of extra game days as Lamar entered its first state playoff since 1953. Sports commentator Jerome Solomon, quoted in the December 12, 2012 *Houston Chronicle*, compared their odds of winning the state title to the odds of the Mayans predicting the world's end, but praised Lamar for "carrying the torch for all of HISD's teams." In today's world of football, it is supposedly impossible for an HISD school with "their smaller rosters, fewer coaches, and less equipment" to win a state championship. Suburban schools generally have state-of-the-art facilities and equipment and large coaching staffs.

Typical of these suburban schools was Lamar's opponent for the 2012 state championship title. Allen High School, located north of Dallas in Allen, Texas, had already won a state championship in 2010. With Allen's enrollment of 5,000, an 848-member band which is the largest in the nation, and a brand new $60-million football stadium, it was not surprising that Lamar, the first HISD school to play for the state title in twenty years, was a "huge underdog." Lamar's chief assets were Nolen, his excellent coaching staff—three of whom (Jerry Martinez, Lee Malowitz, and Ernie Saldivar) have been with him for more than twenty years—and a football team that, Nolen says, gave "everything they had."[390]

*Coach Nolen and Jerry Martinez, assistant football coach, are photographed in Lamar's weight room with David Munoz, assistant baseball coach.*

*Below: Lamar coach Tom Nolen served as a bat boy for the Abbot Stansell Shorthorns, named after the UT freshman team. His father, John "Chubby" Nolen, was the coach. Tommy Nolen is the youngster holding the bats in the bottom row. Two Lamar graduates were also on the team: Fritz "Buzzy" Shubert (Class of 1958) and Jim Brock (Class of 1957). (Courtesy of Nancy Brock)*

The final score, Allen 35, Lamar 21, doesn't tell the whole story. The statistics clearly record Lamar's dominance in first downs, rushing yards, and passing yards, but it was, unfortunately, the big plays that won this game. Although the Lamar players and coaches were disappointed in the end result, Tom Nolen said, "I don't think I have ever been prouder of a football team." The sportswriters had predicted that Allen would "blow Lamar off the field" in the game played on December 22, 2012, at Cowboys Stadium in Arlington, Texas, but the Redskins played hard, never gave up, and "put on a show" before a huge crowd. Jeff Jenkins quoted HISD Athletic Director Marmion Dambrino, who expressed the feelings of Houstonians, the Lamar alums who flew in to watch the game, the football players, the coaches, and the students when she said, "It didn't end like we all wanted, but it was still a great ride!"[391]

*Coach Robert Collett's track stars in 2011 were, left to right: Mayorca Young, now at UH; Tyneisha McCoy, now at Rice; Gabriella Handy, now at Huston-Tillotson; and Kelsey Alexander, now at Prairie View A&M University. Young, who comes from a family of outstanding athletes, won the Class 5A-Region III in the 400-meter dash and competed unsuccessfully for the UIL State Championship. The* Houston Chronicle *calls Lamar's successful female track team "a Redskins tradition."*

Aside from the outstanding football record, Lamar's male and female track stars have accumulated a total of five UIL state titles during the first decade of the twenty-first century: Zenobia Reed won the 100-meter dash in 2000 and again in 2001, when she also won the 800-meter relay. In 2003, Brandon Dixon won the 800-meter run, and Lamar won the overall team championship in 2001. Tyneisha McCoy (Class of 2008) won the 1,600-meter relay in 2009 and 2010. McCoy, a National Honor Society graduate of Lamar, is attending Rice on a track scholarship and is still setting records.

*Zach Holmes (Class of 2009), Lamar's All-State and All-American swimmer, was the national champion in the 4-by-100 free relay and competed in the 2008 Olympic trials. Currently, Holmes attends Ohio State University on a swimming scholarship.*

Sophomore Lamar swim team member Haley McGregory won the UIL State Championship in the 100-yard freestyle competition. She moved to Austin, where she graduated from high school. She set records at the University of Texas and won the 100-meter and the 200-meter backstroke competition at the U.S. Nationals and then transferred to the University of Southern California.[392]

Several fine baseball players from Lamar have gone on to careers in the Major League. Jeff Niemann (Class of 2001), a six-foot, nine-inch player who pitched for Lamar and Rice University before turning professional, is now a starting pitcher for the Tampa Bay Rays. His classmate Vincent Blue (Class of 2001) was selected as the Lamar baseball team's Most Valuable Player in 2000. Following his graduation from Lamar, at age eighteen he was drafted by the Detroit Tigers in the tenth round. Blue has played ten seasons of professional baseball for the Tigers, and the baseball cards, autograph cards, game-used bats, and jersey memorabilia available on the Internet attest to his popularity with baseball fans.

Joe Savery (Class of 2004), a four-year letterman for the Lamar Redskins under Coach Jorge Garza, was zoned to Bellaire High School but transferred to Lamar because he wanted to play all sports, and Bellaire forced students to choose just one.[393] He calls it a "great decision," saying some do not realize the advantages of going to a school that has Lamar's diversity, and decries the "bad rap" public schools get—especially inner-city schools.

*Baseball player Joe Savery is a starting pitcher for the Philadelphia Phillies.*

At Lamar, Savery was chosen for the All-State high school team, was a three-time All-District 18-5A honoree, and was voted Most Valuable Player in the District in 2004. As a senior, he was also named the Proline Player of the Year after he achieved a .556 batting record with seven home runs and forty runs batted in. Under his leadership, the Redskins team was nationally ranked by three different polls.

Savery talked about the academic challenges at Lamar and particularly of Dennis Phillips' biology class, which provided an "awakening" for him. Jorge Garza and David Munoz, Lamar's baseball coaches, helped make his dream of becoming a Major League player come true. He praises the Lamar coaches for guiding their athletes into realistic college choices, making sure the underprivileged students are fed, and providing all of the team with a positive environment.

Savery went on to play for Rice University for three years before turning professional, selected in the first round draft in 2007. He currently is a starting pitcher for the Philadelphia Phillies and is taking online courses to finish his degree.

Anthony Rendon (Class of 2008) excelled in academics as well as baseball. Transferring to Lamar as a senior, Rendon was selected All-State shortstop, and when he graduated was drafted by the Atlanta Braves. He turned them down to play for Wayne Graham at Rice University, where he distinguished himself by winning honors such as the Dick Howser Trophy in 2010. Houston's Mayor Annise Parker declared June 29, 2010 "Anthony Rendon Day in Houston." Rendon was drafted in 2011 to play for the Washington Nationals.

During this decade, Lamar expanded its athletic offerings to include girls' field hockey and boys' wrestling, the world's oldest sport, which became Lamar's youngest sport. Club sports now include a Frisbee team, ice hockey, and bowling. The boys' lacrosse team is part of the Texas Lacrosse top division, competing against St. John's, Kinkaid, Episcopal, The Woodlands, and Kingwood, and hopes to add to the two state championships Lamar won in 1989 and 1995. In 2001, the Lamar girls' lacrosse team led by Coach Anthony Petrucciani was ranked No. 5 in the Texas High School Lacrosse League.

## Lamar Music

Though Lamar athletes have made headlines more often than other graduates in the twenty-first century, there have been other types of champions. In 2000 and 2001, Kate Phillips won the UIL State Outstanding Performer award in the strings competition. Violinist Chelsey Green also won state in 2000 and has gone on to be a professional symphonic violinist. The daughter of an HISD band director, Green says she was born into a family of jazz and "funk" musicians and started playing at the age of five. She has performed at the 2012 NAACP National Convention, the White House Correspondence Dinner Reception, the Mid-Atlantic Jazz Festival, the John F. Kennedy Center, and many other venues. Green, who is passionate about community service and recycling, is known as "The Green Violinist."[394]

*"Anthony Rendon Day in Houston" occurred on June 29, 2010, when Mayor Annise Parker honored him only two years after his graduation from Lamar.*

## Lamar's Exemplary Infrastructure

Benjamin Griffith taught Spanish at Lamar High School for twenty-four years. One of the most recognized teachers in HISD, Griffith was Teacher of the Year at Lamar in 2001, the Rotary Club's Outstanding Community Leader Educator in 2003, Huesped Distinguide de la Ciudad de Cuernavaca, Mexico, in 2004, a finalist for the 2008 National School Conference Award for International Youth Exchange, and the winner of Lamar's Lee Keding Award for Teaching Excellence in 2009.

Griffith sponsored the American Field Service program, started a soccer team, and traveled with student groups throughout Latin America, Europe, and Asia. Lamar lost a gifted and beloved teacher when he died of cancer on May 16, 2012. His dear friend and colleague Sandy Vera mentions his eccentricities such his abhorrence for the sound of ballpoint pens clicking, his need at all times for three pens—red, blue, and black—and his insistence on students keeping grammar notebooks containing all the points he taught—notebooks that usually followed

*Coach Benjamin Griffith is pictured with the 1991–1992 Championship trophy won by his soccer team.*

them to college because they found them so useful. Vera describes him as an adored teacher who knew how to bring out the best in his students, like other Lamar teachers who have left their mark on this school.

Ann Southwell has become almost a fixture at Lamar. For thirty-five years she has taught Distributive Education courses and for twenty-two years has sponsored the cheerleaders, a job which she says keeps her young![395]

The sparkling floors and carefully maintained classrooms, cafeteria, and administrative offices at Lamar are no accident, but rather the result of two custodians who have made the infrastructure of this school their life's work. Ricardo Garza, the head custodian, has been at Lamar for twenty-five years and still loves his job. He cares about what he does and is proud that this school was his first assignment and, he hopes, his last. Dr. McSwain's support and recognition of the importance of a well-maintained building, the faculty's respect for his conscientious work, and the reliance of everyone on his ability to handle all obstacles make Garza's job rewarding.[396]

*Ricardo Garza and Ida Amstead are in charge of keeping Lamar shiny and operating smoothly. They are also staunch supporters of the students, alumni, and faculty.*

Custodian Ida Lazard Amstead came to Lamar thirty-seven years ago and, while the school is much different now than in 1976, she still loves the school. In the old days, she says, kids did not wear uniforms, did not curse in front of teachers or janitors, and did not destroy school property. When female students were dropped off by their parents, they headed for the bathrooms to apply makeup, and in the afternoon they were there again to wash it off. The food in the cafeteria was wonderful, and the appetizing aromas greeted anyone who entered. Though the kitchens were only cooled by large fans, the workers daily baked melt-in-your-mouth yeast rolls.

Today, the cafeteria is a food court and students no longer eat on the lawn. Amstead remembers the telephone calls they got from people passing by who complained about trash on the campus. When alumni come to Lamar, they still remember how Amstead helped them stay out of trouble! She is proud that McSwain has created an English as a Second Language Class for custodians to help improve their communication skills. Amstead has been at Lamar longer than any principal or teacher, and feels her employment is much more than a custodial job. She says, "Lamar is part of me."[397]

*Fran Callahan (left), energetic, knowledgeable, and enthusiastic, is Lamar's most respected booster. She is pictured at the 2006 Distinguished Alumni Luncheon with DeAnn Englert (center) and Linda Ittner (right).*

### THE LAMAR HIGH SCHOOL ALUMNI ASSOCIATION

The Lamar High School Alumni Association, formed by Fran Callahan and a small group of parents and alumni in 1996, began by seeking to raise money for remodeling Lamar's bathrooms, but soon became an important factor in the schools' commitment to excellence. Callahan, an involved parent, read the book written for the 50th Anniversary event and learned about the many famous and successful alumni. She suggested to Principal Walter Day that these graduates might be interested in supporting their alma mater. They collected a donation of $505 from fifteen people and got the ball rolling. They planned a dinner and sent invitations to all known alumni. Guests ate at tables set up on the stage and were served by students. Callahan had tapped into a tremendous network already existing among Lamar graduates, many of whom had remained lifetime friends. As a result of this unique connection between Lamar alumni and their high school, an association was formed, with Bracewell & Patterson Law Firm providing pro bono 501(c)3 legal documentation. In 1997–1998, student workers were hired to research the names and addresses of graduates in order to produce a current directory of alumni.

*Left to right: Penny Hess (Butler) (Class of 1957), pictured with Judy Ley (Allen), is one of the many volunteers who has provided invaluable assistance and advice to Fran Callahan and the Lamar Alumni Association.*

The first alumni newsletter was published in September 1998. An early Alumni Association member who contributed to his alma mater was Michael T. Willis (Class of 1963). After talking with Principal McSwain about Lamar's woeful lack of computer technology, Willis, who is an information technology expert, gave funds to bring Lamar's computers up to date.

*Jimmy Brill (Class of 1951) is pictured with his granddaughter Kathryn Brill (Class of 2007). Brill, who is a 2010 Distinguished Alum honoree, is the keeper of the records for the Class of 1951 and a staunch supporter of his alma mater.*

Lamar's alumni group, which has few peers in the United States, contributed over $2 million for its first major project: the renovation of the original auditorium into the Ned S. Holmes Performance Hall complete with modern lighting, a sound system, the new Ruth Denney Stage, curtains, carpet, 1,000 upholstered seats, and a nine-foot Steinway grand piano once belonging to Harry Connick, Jr. The auditorium is named for Holmes (Class of 1963), who was the major donor.

*Left to right: Lamar supporters Mickey Norton and Jan Cato from the Class of 1963 are pictured at the Distinguished Alumni Luncheon.*

Other Association contributions during its sixteen-year history are the monument sign at the corner of Eastside Street and Westheimer Road, the wrought-iron fencing encircling the school that replaced the rusted cyclone fence, funding for the Robotics team, the Lamar Cable Television group, the girls' softball team, and other student and teacher needs. All available football films of past Lamar games have been converted to DVDs through Association funding and made available to those for whom Lamar's football history is so important. They also sponsor the "all-school" class reunions.

The Association has created the HOPE (Having the Opportunity for Post-secondary Education) Scholarship program and has given over $75,000 to its cause. Thirty students have received

*Left to right: David Redford (Class of 1958) is shown with Kimberly Lopez and Trang Nguyen, the first two recipients of the HOPE Scholarship.*

*The construction of the new west side entrance gates was graciously underwritten by Phoebe and Bobby Tudor, parents of three Lamar graduates.*

*Six of Lamar's 1940s graduates are lined up, left to right: Tom Whitehead, Allen Lewis, Micky Carmichael, Billy Mize, George Butler, and an unidentified sixth gentleman.*

scholarships, eight have graduated, and the rest are currently enrolled except for one. It also hosts the annual Dick Elledge Memorial Golf Tournament, which raises funds to support Lamar's golf program and provide scholarships. The Association publishes a hardback directory every five years, and in 2010 they developed a new Lamar Alumni Association website. Working in conjunction with the PTO, the Association also provides school tours, student assistance, and support for parents.

In October 2012, the Alumni Association hosted a 75th Birthday Party for the student body and graduates. The cheerleaders, the band, and volunteers welcomed the alumni who came to enjoy the festivities. Former governor Mark White (Class of 1958) spoke, along with Peter Roussel (Class of 1961) and former principal Ray Reiner.

*At right is Lieutenant Governor David Dewhurst (Class of 1963), Distinguished Alumni Luncheon honoree, standing with Master of Ceremonies Peter Roussel (Class of 1961).*

*Lamar ROTC cadets assist at all of the Distinguished Alumni Luncheons. Left to right: Kathy Casares, Jenifer Muench, Jenna Pressley, Norma Torres, and Yesinia Flores.*

*The banner announces to Westheimer Road that Lamar High School is celebrating another birthday.*

*In the school's inner courtyard, Lamar's cheerleaders show off their gymnastic talents. The Lamar Band is lined up on the balcony waiting for their turn to perform.*

*Lamar's Choralettes take to the stage during the 75th Anniversary celebration, organized and led by Betty Conrad (Adams). The pianist is Marshall Maxwell and also shown is Gary Patterson (Class of 1963), Lamar's fine arts director.*

## Conclusion

The 1937 Kampus Kamera Klub and the Radio Guild have been transformed into the Lamar Cable Television Club, which provides students with the facilities to film, edit, and broadcast a daily news program. The Hiking Club has changed to the Biking Club, the Typing Club is now the Industrial Technology Club, the Choralettes are now called the Concert Women's Choir, and the original Safety Patrol Club would seem archaic on today's campus with its security guards who cover the grounds in their golf carts. Gone is the annual May Fete, as well as the choosing of beauties, and the election of only a few cheerleaders, but these are simply a reflection of the changing world. Lamar has been such a major part of Houston's history; it is not surprising that it now mirrors the globalization of this city.

In an October 1961 article, former *Lancer* editor Jim Bernhard (Class of 1955) visited with Louise Fuller's journalism class. He acknowledged the impact of radio and television news coverage but said, "I feel confident the newspaper business will never die."[398] Bernhard, who had been editor of Rice University's school newspaper, *The Thresher*, was then working as a copy editor at the *Houston Press*. Fifty years ago, Bernhard, like most people, could not have fathomed a world without newspapers, but the *Lamar Lancer* has joined the ranks of the *Houston Press* and *Houston Post*, which have been gone for years. Its loss presents obvious problems in writing about Lamar High School's current and future history. Unfortunately, the content of yearbooks no longer provides an historical record of a school's

*Lamar Cable Television "broke through the airways" in 2002. Jim "Mattress Mac" McIngvale generously donated an entire set to the department. These broadcast journalism students tackle many community and world issues and keep the student body up to date. The department now has state-of-the-art equipment and a brand new studio.*

students or events. The younger generation prefers social networking. Whereas previous generations had film cameras, scrapbooks, and paper notebooks, all of which were used to chronicle this history of Lamar High School, these reference tools have been replaced by Facebook, Instagram, and Twitter. This is, of course, a national/worldwide trend, and it is up to historians to determine new means of piecing together the history of our daily lives for posterity.

When Lamar opened in 1937, William J. Moyes was appointed principal and provided strong guidance for sixteen years. Today the school is fortunate to have another strong principal. In 2014, Dr. James McSwain will be the only principal in the history of the school to have served longer than Moyes. McSwain's commendable leadership is providing a firm foundation and a sure hand to propel Lamar into the uncharted territories of this new century.

Despite myriad changes during Lamar's seventy-five-year history, one enduring truth is the legacy of the graduates' love of and pride in their school. The words "tradition" and "legacy" frequently appear in the *Orenda*, especially those of the last fifteen years, indicating that students and alumni are conscious of Lamar's history and revel in its preeminence.

The second strength of Lamar is its commitment to excellence, a commitment that is reflected in the accomplishments of its alumni. "Reach for the Stars" is surely one of the most beloved of any high school motto; chosen so long ago, the often-repeated motto has almost become a mantra. Students, teachers, principals, and alumni seem to have been guided by these words for seventy-five years, and there is every sign that this will continue.

In 2012, history almost repeated itself as Lamar's football team competed valiantly for the state football championship previously won in 1953. Although Lamar lost the game, the importance of their even making a playoff and entering the sports arena where suburban schools rule shone a new spotlight on Lamar and its successes during its seventy-five-year history. Sportswriter Jerome Solomon called attention to the rebuilding of Lamar thanks to the passage of the most recent bond issue and commended the school for not letting "its championship dreams die."[399]

Solomon refers, of course, to Lamar's athletic prowess, which in itself is notable, but the words can just as easily refer to all of the successes of the school, a school that has produced state, national, and world leaders, scientists, businesspeople, actors and actresses, dancers, artists, musicians, and writers. How did one public high school produce the most acclaimed science fiction writer and the most acclaimed literary mystery writer, two men who have been compared to Shakespeare, Dickens, and Faulkner? The youngest Nobel Prize winner? The nation's first African American prima ballerina?

To repeat the question with which this book began: How did Lamar happen? The answer is best described as a complex combination of location, demographics, administrators and faculty, and a mysterious driving force at a school that for seventy-five years has graduated eighteen-year-olds who want to do something with their lives. The alumni of Lamar High School, whether consciously or subconsciously, have always and will still "Reach for the Stars."

# APPENDICES

## Lamar High School Principals

| | | | |
|---|---|---|---|
| 1938–1953 | William J. Moyes | 1984–1988 | Ray Reiner |
| 1954–1957 | J. H. Wright | 1989–1990 | Ronald F. Veselka |
| 1958–1962 | Dr. Woodrow Watts | 1991–1995 | Walter Day |
| 1963–1976 | Harold K. Costlow | 1996–1997 | Charlotte Haynes |
| 1976–1978 | Dr. John Brandstetter | 1997– | Dr. James A. McSwain |
| 1979–1984 | Herbert Smith | | |

## Lamar High School Class Officers, 1938–2000

| | | | |
|---|---|---|---|
| June 1938 | President | Fenwick White |
| June 1938 | Vice President | William Spaw |
| June 1938 | Secretary | Betty Finnegan |
| June 1938 | Treasurer | Ben Hancock |
| June 1939 | President | Tom Hardy |
| June 1939 | Vice President | Ralph Anderson |
| June 1939 | Secretary | Elma Landram |
| June 1939 | Treasurer | Margie McEnnis |
| June 1940 | President | David Embry |
| June 1940 | Vice President | Bob Gay |
| June 1940 | Secretary | Carolyn Knapp |
| June 1940 | Treasurer | Bob Bell |
| June 1941 | President | William Fox |
| June 1941 | Vice President | Alice Picton |
| June 1941 | Secretary | Sadie Gwin Allen |
| June 1941 | Treasurer | Carolyn Wilson |
| June 1942 | President | George Gartner |
| June 1942 | Vice President | Ellen Picton |
| June 1942 | Secretary | Lois Holmes |
| June 1942 | Treasurer | Lucy Gray |
| June 1943 | President | Bob Nunn |
| June 1943 | Vice President | Margee Scott |
| June 1943 | Secretary | Ann Japhet |
| June 1943 | Treasurer | Evelyn Burke |
| January 1944 | President | Frank Bryan |
| January 1944 | Vice President | Mickie Purcell |
| January 1944 | Secretary | Sara Meredith |
| January 1944 | Treasurer | Jane Farnsworth |
| June 1944 | President | Bobby Howard |
| June 1944 | Vice President | Hally Beth Walker |
| June 1944 | Secretary | Bettye Phillips |
| June 1944 | Treasurer | Fritz Seyfarth |
| January 1945 | President | Richard Davenport |
| January 1945 | Vice President | Alice Filley Johns |
| January 1945 | Secretary | Betsy Cottingham |
| January 1945 | Treasurer | Hamilton Dixie |
| June 1945 | President | J. D. Sugg |
| June 1945 | Vice President | Jetta Schumacher |
| June 1945 | Secretary | Martha Hodson |
| June 1945 | Treasurer | Charlie Tighe |
| January 1946 | President | J. S. Binford |
| January 1946 | Vice President | Carolyn Croom |
| January 1946 | Secretary | Beverly Hollingsworth |
| January 1946 | Treasurer | Richard Rauch |
| June 1946 | President | Bobby Norris |
| June 1946 | Vice President | Betty Jo Joplin |
| June 1946 | Secretary | Eugenia Harris |
| June 1946 | Treasurer | Bill Cooley |
| January 1947 | President | Walter Clemons |
| January 1947 | Vice President | Gordon White |
| January 1947 | Secretary | Don Nowlin |
| January 1947 | Treasurer | Wade Ridley |
| January 1948 | President | Bill Davis |
| January 1948 | Vice President | Emily Thompson |
| January 1948 | Secretary | Mary Sue Sheffield |
| January 1948 | Treasurer | Allan King |
| June 1948 | President | Sam Croom |
| June 1948 | Vice President | Carolyn Douglas |
| June 1948 | Secretary | Lee Duggan |
| June 1948 | Treasurer | Ray Winters |
| January 1949 | President | Dick Bintliff |
| January 1949 | Vice President | Shirley Lockwood |
| January 1949 | Secretary | Mary Gene Johnson |
| January 1949 | Treasurer | Martin Scheid |
| June 1949 | President | Robert Clemons |
| June 1949 | Vice President | Bill Munnerlyn |
| June 1949 | Secretary | Beverly Kemp |
| June 1949 | Treasurer | Beverly Ward |
| January 1950 | President | Jim Street |
| January 1950 | Vice President | Kendall Mower |
| January 1950 | Secretary | Libby Herndon |
| January 1950 | Treasurer | Bob Barton |

| | | | | | | | | |
|---|---|---|---|---|---|---|---|---|
| June | 1950 | President | Claude Hooton | | June | 1956 | President | Richard Royds |
| June | 1950 | Vice President | Barbara Lee Brown | | June | 1956 | Vice President | Bill Moore |
| June | 1950 | Secretary | Marilyn Graves | | June | 1956 | Secretary | Joan Baker |
| June | 1950 | Treasurer | Diane Lehman | | June | 1956 | Treasurer | David Abright |
| January | 1951 | President | Ben Brewer | | January | 1957 | President | Russel Jacobe |
| January | 1951 | Vice President | Kenneth Horton | | January | 1957 | Vice President | Linda Lackner |
| January | 1951 | Secretary | Joy Nicolai | | January | 1957 | Secretary | Mac Hail |
| January | 1951 | Treasurer | Glenna McCarthy | | January | 1957 | Treasurer | Edna Rogers |
| June | 1951 | President | Richard Webb | | June | 1957 | President | Jimmy Bertrand |
| June | 1951 | Vice President | Dick Mayor | | June | 1957 | Vice President | Chuck Caldwell |
| June | 1951 | Secretary | Mary Coy | | June | 1957 | Secretary | Ann Milton |
| June | 1951 | Treasurer | Barbara Jean Cook | | June | 1957 | Treasurer | Homer Luther |
| January | 1952 | President | John Brunson | | January | 1958 | President | Jay Harris |
| January | 1952 | Vice President | Philip Kidd | | January | 1958 | Vice President | Norma Adams |
| January | 1952 | Secretary | Ann Spears | | January | 1958 | Secretary | Barbara Mangum |
| January | 1952 | Treasurer | John Brokaw | | January | 1958 | Treasurer | Bill Stradley |
| June | 1952 | President | Murray Finer | | June | 1958 | President | Ronnie Woliver |
| June | 1952 | Vice President | Donald Stewart | | June | 1958 | Vice President | Mary Sue Sparks |
| June | 1952 | Secretary | Marialice Binford | | June | 1958 | Secretary | Kathy Sangster |
| June | 1952 | Treasurer | Vic Morris | | June | 1958 | Treasurer | Chris Brown |
| January | 1953 | President | Bonner Herren | | January | 1959 | President | Ronnie Jacobe |
| January | 1953 | Vice President | Bruce Durrenberger | | January | 1959 | Vice President | Betty Knauth |
| January | 1953 | Secretary | Janie Morris | | January | 1959 | Secretary | Sharon Stremmel |
| January | 1953 | Treasurer | Frank Webber | | January | 1959 | Treasurer | Marty Bradt |
| June | 1953 | President | Jimmy McBride | | June | 1959 | President | Bill Conner |
| June | 1953 | Vice President | Dale Miller | | June | 1959 | Vice President | Larry Hitt |
| June | 1953 | Secretary | Patricia Pennington | | June | 1959 | Secretary | Ann Knickerbocker |
| June | 1953 | Treasurer | Rex Martin | | June | 1959 | Treasurer | Letitia Kinzbach |
| January | 1954 | President | Jack Spinks | | January | 1960 | President | Bill Brizzolara |
| January | 1954 | Vice President | Jimmy Strawn | | January | 1960 | Vice President | Barry Bryson |
| January | 1954 | Secretary | Celia Posey | | January | 1960 | Secretary | Judi Gudger |
| January | 1954 | Treasurer | Lynn Elliott | | January | 1960 | Treasurer | John Knowles |
| June | 1954 | President | Allen Lingo | | June | 1960 | President | Bob Ball |
| June | 1954 | Vice President | Edith Elliott | | June | 1960 | Vice President | Don Lewis |
| June | 1954 | Secretary | Carol Whitehurst | | June | 1960 | Secretary | Becky Marshall |
| June | 1954 | Treasurer | Ben Orman | | June | 1960 | Treasurer | Don Longcope |
| January | 1955 | President | Lionel Hallonquist | | January | 1961 | President | Jim Patterson |
| January | 1955 | Vice President | Jim Smelley | | January | 1961 | Vice President | Andy Carothers |
| January | 1955 | Secretary | Eddie Shipe | | January | 1961 | Secretary | Kathy Koberlina |
| January | 1955 | Treasurer | Buddy Hood | | January | 1961 | Treasurer | Kathryn Lewis |
| June | 1955 | President | Harvin Moore | | June | 1961 | President | David Hedges |
| June | 1955 | Vice President | Steven Oaks | | June | 1961 | Vice President | Bill McGee |
| June | 1955 | Secretary | Diane Doherty | | June | 1961 | Secretary | Nellie Thomas |
| June | 1955 | Treasurer | Johnny Brown | | June | 1961 | Treasurer | Phyllis Santamaria |
| January | 1956 | President | Billy Armer | | January | 1962 | President | Mark Belton |
| January | 1956 | Vice President | Jackson Arnold | | January | 1962 | Vice President | Charlie Moore |
| January | 1956 | Secretary | Jen Tomlinson | | January | 1962 | Secretary | Carol Spaw |
| January | 1956 | Treasurer | Jack Douglas | | January | 1962 | Treasurer | Tom Sartwelle |

| | | | | | | | |
|---|---|---|---|---|---|---|---|
| June | 1962 | President | Andy Rembert | June | 1968 | President | Kelly Faloon |
| June | 1962 | Vice President | Elizabeth Mendell | June | 1968 | Vice President | Walter Bissex |
| June | 1962 | Secretary | Judy Robinson | June | 1968 | Secretary | Pat Barnes |
| June | 1962 | Treasurer | Parker Gregg | June | 1968 | Treasurer | Sharon Johnson |
| January | 1963 | President | Shannon Matthews | January | 1969 | President | Sharon Fredrick |
| January | 1963 | Vice President | Betty Jones | January | 1969 | Vice President | Tina Brown |
| January | 1963 | Secretary | Peggy Young | January | 1969 | Secretary-Treasurer | Linda Levens |
| January | 1963 | Treasurer | Mary Margaret Murff | June | 1969 | President | Steve Word |
| June | 1963 | President | Ned Holmes | June | 1969 | Vice President | Bill Chilivetis |
| June | 1963 | Vice President | Dana Crowley | June | 1969 | Secretary | Robbie Harvey |
| June | 1963 | Secretary | LaNeil Gregory | June | 1969 | Treasurer | Susan Mims |
| June | 1963 | Treasurer | Dick Post | January | 1970 | President | Mary Cain |
| January | 1964 | President | Steve Cummings | January | 1970 | Vice President | Collie Constantatos |
| January | 1964 | Vice President | Barry Wallace | January | 1970 | Secretary | Janice Larson |
| January | 1964 | Secretary | Chris Williams | January | 1970 | Treasurer | Kelly McFarland |
| January | 1964 | Treasurer | Kathleen Greengrass | June | 1970 | President | Chris Ransom |
| June | 1964 | President | Dan Hedges | June | 1970 | Vice President | Parker Ransom |
| June | 1964 | Vice President | Ashley Smith | June | 1970 | Secretary | Claudia Talley |
| June | 1964 | Secretary | Gavin Smith | June | 1970 | Treasurer | Emily Fourmy |
| June | 1964 | Treasurer | Corless Beasley | June | 1971 | President | Peter Waldron |
| January | 1965 | President | Charlene Tomfohrde | June | 1971 | Vice President | Jay Johnson |
| January | 1965 | Vice President | Pam Smith | June | 1971 | Secretary | Jay Kolb |
| January | 1965 | Secretary | Barbara Skaggs | June | 1971 | Treasurer | Camille Simpson |
| January | 1965 | Treasurer | Nance Hines | June | 1972 | President | Buster Courreges |
| June | 1965 | President | David Price | June | 1972 | Vice President | Tom Clement |
| June | 1965 | Vice President | Johnny Brock | June | 1972 | Secretary | Karl Doerner III |
| June | 1965 | Secretary | Susan Jewell | June | 1972 | Treasurer | Peter Johnston |
| June | 1965 | Treasurer | Jeff Suttles | June | 1973 | President | Mike Bellmont |
| January | 1966 | President | Alice Fisher | June | 1973 | Vice President | Charlie Hensen |
| January | 1966 | Vice President | Brenda Dean | June | 1973 | Secretary | Susan Smith |
| January | 1966 | Secretary | Paula Fenoglil | June | 1973 | Treasurer | Claire Wilson |
| January | 1966 | Treasurer | Laura Sanders | June | 1974 | President | Mike Longoria |
| June | 1966 | President | Bill Hamill | June | 1974 | Vice President | Reginald Stewart |
| June | 1966 | Vice President | Anne Taylor | June | 1974 | Secretary | Sheri Malick |
| June | 1966 | Secretary | Lynn Ferguson | June | 1974 | Treasurer | Lynn Blunt |
| June | 1966 | Treasurer | Barbara Mendell | June | 1975 | President | Janet Thompson |
| January | 1967 | President | Ted Huddle | June | 1975 | Vice President | Denise Hinds Cartwright |
| January | 1967 | Vice President | Dana Dumas | June | 1975 | Secretary | Sharon Ames |
| January | 1967 | Secretary | Susan Woodhouse | June | 1975 | Treasurer | Anita Webber |
| January | 1967 | Treasurer | Susan Heard | June | 1976 | President | John Moore |
| June | 1967 | President | Doug Keats | June | 1976 | Vice President | Debbie Sashaw |
| June | 1967 | Vice President | Cad Simpson | June | 1976 | Secretary | T. Lancaster |
| June | 1967 | Secretary | Gay Whitley | June | 1976 | Treasurer | Harry Holmes |
| June | 1967 | Treasurer | Bob Schoenvogel | June | 1977 | President | Basil MacDonald |
| January | 1968 | President | Mike Vaughn | June | 1977 | Vice President | Grantham Coleman |
| January | 1968 | Vice President | John Lav | June | 1977 | Secretary | Honornell Harris |
| January | 1968 | Secretary | Martha Trammel | June | 1977 | Treasurer | Suzanne FitzGerrell |
| January | 1968 | Treasurer | Betsy Redding | June | 1978 | President | Marty Schafer |

| | | | | | | | | |
|---|---|---|---|---|---|---|---|---|
| June | 1978 | Vice President | Cynthia Burns | | June | 1989 | Secretary | Cynthia Brown |
| June | 1978 | Secretary | Cathy Ryan | | June | 1989 | Treasurer | Cedric Devereaux |
| June | 1978 | Treasurer | Julie Arbuthnot | | June | 1990 | President | Cean Cotton |
| June | 1979 | President | John David Browder | | June | 1990 | Vice President | Derrick Barnes |
| June | 1979 | Vice President | Dawn Brown | | June | 1990 | Secretary | Russell Sharman |
| June | 1979 | Secretary | Elaine Bell | | June | 1990 | Treasurer | Mark Ybarra |
| June | 1979 | Treasurer | Angela Jackson | | June | 1991 | President | Jennie Dollinger |
| June | 1980 | President | Debbie Herb | | June | 1991 | Vice President | Shawna Herbert |
| June | 1980 | Vice President | Karen Baker | | June | 1991 | Secretary | Christian Herbert |
| June | 1980 | Secretary | Gillette Burns | | June | 1991 | Treasurer | Delvin Burton |
| June | 1980 | Treasurer | Darryl White | | June | 1992 | President | Cella Butler |
| June | 1981 | President | Paul Bernhard | | June | 1992 | Vice President | Malene Jackson |
| June | 1981 | Vice President | Andrew Jefferson | | June | 1992 | Secretary | Nickie Landry |
| June | 1981 | Secretary | Deidra Gasper | | June | 1992 | Treasurer | Thomas Ufer |
| June | 1981 | Treasurer | Gigi Sacaris | | June | 1993 | President | Melanie Porche |
| June | 1982 | President | Terrence Gee | | June | 1993 | Vice President | Unknown |
| June | 1982 | Vice President | Marie Lawson | | June | 1993 | Secretary | Nichelle Taylor |
| June | 1982 | Secretary | Kathy Herb | | June | 1993 | Treasurer | Kevin Simmons |
| June | 1982 | Treasurer | Kim Davis | | June | 1994 | President | John Cruz |
| June | 1983 | President | Bill Stradley | | June | 1994 | Vice President | Shani Jackson |
| June | 1983 | Vice President | Brenda Clay | | June | 1994 | Secretary | Phoenix Baca |
| June | 1983 | Secretary | Theresa Guillory | | June | 1994 | Treasurer | Dina Chambers |
| June | 1983 | Treasurer | Katie Brock | | June | 1995 | President | Thomas Harris |
| June | 1984 | President | Mark Mitchell | | June | 1995 | Vice President | Rachelle Mason |
| June | 1984 | Vice President | George Davis | | June | 1995 | Secretary | Cynthia Rojas |
| June | 1984 | Secretary | Kim Anderson | | June | 1995 | Treasurer | Margaret Medina |
| June | 1984 | Treasurer | Kelly Whitby | | June | 1996 | President | Alec Sevy |
| June | 1985 | President | Douglas Burns | | June | 1996 | Vice President | Elizabeth Watkins |
| June | 1985 | Vice President | Cara Wallin | | June | 1996 | Secretary | Warren Ellsworth |
| June | 1985 | Secretary | Alisa Manning | | June | 1997 | President | Christina Yanascavage |
| June | 1985 | Treasurer | Tricia Carter | | June | 1997 | Vice President | Jonathan Toombs |
| June | 1986 | President | Cedric Smith | | June | 1997 | Secretary | John Singleton |
| June | 1986 | Vice President | Steve Marcontell | | June | 1997 | Treasurer | Nekima Williams |
| June | 1986 | Secretary | Karri Bradley | | June | 1998 | President | Brandi Robinson |
| June | 1986 | Treasurer | Raquel Brown | | June | 1998 | Vice President | Carl Harleaux |
| June | 1987 | President | Henry Gasper | | June | 1998 | Secretary | Catherine Frels |
| June | 1987 | Vice President | Stacey Batiste | | June | 1998 | Treasurer | Sinit Lob |
| June | 1987 | Secretary | Jennifer Day | | June | 1999 | President | Mindy Willeford |
| June | 1987 | Treasurer | Shawn Hutchison | | June | 1999 | Vice President | Allison Seeman |
| June | 1988 | President | Hazel Cebrun | | June | 1999 | Secretary | Orly Sulami |
| June | 1988 | Vice President | Rosalyn Grimes | | June | 1999 | Treasurer | Patra Brannon |
| June | 1988 | Secretary | Hailey Etheridge | | June | 2000 | President | Emily Young |
| June | 1988 | Treasurer | Cortny Jackson | | June | 2000 | Vice President | C. J. Webster |
| June | 1989 | President | Brinell Anderson | | June | 2000 | Secretary | John Michael Raborn |
| June | 1989 | Vice President | Tony Nguyen | | June | 2000 | Treasurer | Susan Kelly |

*After 2000 there were no more elected class officers, the Student Council members took over those responsibilities.*

## Lamar High School International Baccalaureate Graduates

**1984**
James DeGregori

**1985**
Monica Poss

**1986**
Alexandra King
Eva Portius
Eric Voegler

**1987**
Deborah Dalton
Margaret Hill

**1988**
Chelo Carter
Frank Lau
Ann Ong
Amy Wheeler

**1990**
Robert Harvey
Jennifer White

**1991**
Eric Barrett
Kimberly Freedman

**1992**
Christine Carlisle
Renny Talianchich

**1993**
Juan Alban
Cara Honzak
Justin Nelson
Isaac Pesin
Roger Stephens
Jason Stevens
Ryan Townsend
Basil Umari
Raymond Witt

**1994**
Amanda Clark
Christopher DiPaolo
Geji Mathew
Elizabeth McCormick
Megan Moir
Katarzyna Mucha
John Pfaffenberger
Britta Riley
Sunday Riley
Daniel Wyatt

**1995**
Nicholas Collins
Jay Crossley
Lisa Davis
Sarah Ebaugh
Mindy Haynes
Betty Law
Catherine Matusow
Amanda Moulder
David Nachtigall
Julia Rothstein
Micheal Sanchez
Kathryn Stone
Jocylin Williams
Jennifer Zhou

**1996**
Richard DeLaveaga
John Horne
Ivonne McLean
Jillian Pesin
Matthew Shaddock
Kelley Whitmer

**1997**
Gary Bland
Rachel Callahan
Magdalene Conner
Alden Doyle
Bryan Dunagan
Timothy Edwards
Colin Harrington
Travis Meyer
Gregory Moy
Andrew Nelson
Katie Stone
Christina Yanascavage

**1998**
Stefan Beck
Stefanie Beckner
Scott Chait
Travis Combs
Marina Cruz
Graham Davis
Daniel Devinney
Daniel DiPaolo
Courtney Hurst
Brian Izard
Patricia Lew
Sarah Moorhead
Zachary Moser
Carrie Price
Jason Stalinsky
Kenyon Weaver
Tyler Whitmer
Jonathan Wolfe

**1999**
Margaret Anadu
Kathryn Ban
Jessica Beard
Sasha Buchanan
Erick Calderon
Hwanjoon Choi
Ian Hogue
John Kellogg
Scott Moorhead
Erin Murdock
Jessica Pentz
Marcel Poisot
Andreana Reeves
James Schleicher
Jun Wei
Mindy Willeford

**2000**
Mary Air
Ntiense Akpan
Bridgit Antwi
Rebecca Barnett
Laurel Barrett
Christina Chambers
Jacquelin Debien
Luis Hernandez
Lauren Johns
Benjamin Lehrer
Jason Methner
Stephanie Oddo
Alexis Ortiz
Lauren Patterson
John Raborn
Matthew Robbins
Elizabeth Swift
Tony Tai
Rebecca Wiener
Tessa Wilkin
Brice Wilson
Aimee Wu

**2001**
Gobind Anand
Jennifer Ban
Barbara Biehl
Patrick Callahan
Nicholas Chan
Christoph Chavez
Mary Crowley
Caroline Dubinsky
Megan Edwards
Alison Erzinger
Christopher Foley
Jakub Lukomski
Fritha Morrison
Thuy Nguyen
Robin Rahe
Alexander Rapp
Daniel Rodriguez
Thomas Rodriguez
Lauren Schultz

Yanyan Shi
Carolyn Sylvan
Kathryn Turner
Sahil Warsi
Daniel Wieser
Lauren Wiggins

**2002**
Rishi Aggarwal
Cristina Bagos
Virginia Baird
De'Awn Barkers
Melissa Danaczko
Patrick Eberle
Meaghan Ehni
Samuel Heller
Melita Igbokewe
Dmitry Khabashesku
Lauren Kohlhoff
Ingrid Mantor
Amy McMahan
Margaret Melton
Ashley Monteil
Nicholas Moser
Laura Noel
Samuel Petner
Mor Regev
Meredith Steele
John Szentirmay
Michael Taska
Ashley Thanos
Amy Thompson
Christopher Transier
Mia Wilkin
Yan Xu
Mathew Zalk

**2003**
Alexandra Aurisch
Carson Baker
Joi Bartholomew Dru
Andrew Boling
Maresha Clark
Kirstin Doyle-Cooney

Erica Farber
Julia Fleckman
Sarah Foltz
Jennifer Hau
Sarah Hawkins
Erin Hazel
Anna Johnson
Lindsay Kohlhoff
Ian Levy
Sarah Lowes
Annie McBride
Nathan Meeks
Candice Olund
Erin Patten
Eric Rachlin
Philip Rajan
Jamil Shah
Sonya Tamarchenko
Lourdes Valdes
Erin Wiggins
Victoria Williams
Yamanda Wright

**2004**
Margo Aaron
Christopher Albin
Judith Boggess
Bennett Boyd
Helen Caudle
Stephanie Erzinger
Rachel Kaufman
Isabel Kerr
Che Knight
Christine Langlois
John McNeely
John Kyle Mesko
Jessica Meyer
David Monroe
William Musgrove
Kelly Nash
Laura Nash
Callon Nichols
Abigail Noebels
Patrick Nugent

Veronica Parker
Katherine Powell
Grace Rogers
Amelia Ross
Skyler Schawe
Lauren Scott
Katherine Slimp
Neil Stockbridge
Claire Thielke
Patrick Thielke
Jade Thomas
Steven Thomson
Carol Tyger
Jennifer Walls
Alexandra Ward
Michael Wei
James Weiss
Diana Whitney
Nicole Yeroshalmi

**2005**
Marcus Aguilar
Lauren Allen
Julia Avery
Katherine Beck
Lisa Beckner
Sarah Cancelmo
Diana Caperton
Lauren Chinault
Hannah Citron
Chelsea Coburn
Tyrus Cukavec
Elizabeth Curo
Anastasia Eriksson
Sarah Fleckman
Daniel Hochman
Cathryn Homier
Ashley Kempenski
Melissa LaMond
Lawrence Lander
Hilary Lane
Dylan Leach
LaTrenda Leonard
Diana Ling

Robert Long
David Lugo
Lauren Lytle
Lindsey Mellon
Jordann Milbauer
John Miller
Nicholas Reiland
Corinne Snow
Charles Tanenbaum
Kwelina Thompson
Elissa Venable
Michael Voss
Chelsea Wade
Marina Willis
Joseph Zaragoza

**2006**
Eden Amerson
Chidiogo Anyigbo
Irma Ayala
Alane Blakely
Roseanne Bodin
Megan Bogany
Christopher Boling
Thomas Browder
Sarah Bryan
Carter Cole
Mickenzie Cross
Mary Cuclis
Zachary Cuyler
William Davidson
Kathryne DeLeon
Sean Donahue
Dione Drew
Maria Dusenbury
Caroline Echols
Brandon Englert
Samira Irani
Alyx Jones
Matthew Kelly
Anastasia Kirages
Justin Kizer
Christopher Lindee
Matthew Lowes

Nathan Miller
Annelise Musgrove
Vanessa Ng
Kathleen Nguyen
John Pavlick
Cameron Prather
Jeffrey Rachlin
Baily Rankin
John Rassenfoss
Thomas Roinesdal
Lauren Rosin
Christopher Rouxel
Flavio Salinas
Emily Sanders
Sarah Sparker
Laura Suttles
Elizabeth Temple
Monica Tseng
Stephanie Wehrung
Logan Wexler
Juliana Wilking
Magdalena Wistuba
Brook Woldemariam
Dinara Yangirova
Jennifer Young
Zachary Zeidman

**2007**
Lindsay Aldrich
Jacqueline Arevalo
Blane Barker
Lauren Baughman
Emily Brents
Asasia Carter
William Collie
Ross Couvillon
Melaine Cruthirds
Christina Culotta
Cassady Davidson
Grace Fletcher
Joe Franco
Christopher Gilliard
Michael Hurta
Lauren Ibarra
Ali Irani
Courtney Jay
Andrew Kennedy
Jan-Dirk Kieback
Jordan Kincaid
Christopher Lange
Sian Leach
Zachary Lebovitz
Alexander Levy
Erica Lokken
Rebecca Long
Axia Lopez
Juan Macias
Devin Nath
Hoa Nguyen
Nancy Nguyen
Robyn Nguyen
Grant Niccum
Christopher Nunu
Antonio Quintanilla
Sonja Radovancevic
Joel Rajan
Leah Robbins
Samantha Roe
Isabelle Rowdon
Dulce Salazar
Jackson Sanders
Raphaela Sapire
James Sayre
Sawyer Sellers
Daisy Soriano
Gregory Story-Lindstro
Mariam Tejeda
Jacob Tice
Marianne Tiutan
Frederick Tuthill
Zachary VanBrunt
Cassie Walker
Zihe Wang
Rebecca Young

**2008**
Eva Agoulnik
Cameron Albin
Alyson Almaguer
Sarah Atkins
David Barron
Melissa Beasley
Steven Bhutra
Fredy Bonilla
Shelby Bottoms
Matthew Bourda
Dana Bowman
Erica Butler
Kyle Caid-Loos
Kate Cancelmo
Chelsey Carothers
Claudia Casbarian
Grant Chandler
Taylor Chen
Alena Chinault
David Cisneros
Nicole Clements
Nicolas DeLacey
Arundhati Desai
Dominic Dorsey
Thomas Downs
Leila El Murr
Sarah Elkins
Auria Fellows
Carlye Ferrill
Amy Fontenot
Andrew Frierson
Kelli Fyke
Christopher Gardner
Randall Gay
Rachel Globe
Vivian Graves
Morgan Haenchen
Sarah Holland
Kaitlyn Howard
Anne Jones
Simi Joseph
Sloane Kaminski-Ditzel
Amara Keller
Krishna Kulkarni
Stephen Liu
Sara Llansa
Matthew Long
Jose Lopez
Lorri Marlow
Travis Marshall
Antonia McCasker
Sofia Medina
David Moore
Kathy Mostajeran
Camille Moughon
Rafael Mujica
Jackson Murrey-Ittmann
Katherine Muth
Robert Oliver
Sieda Omar
Andrew Osterhus
Anne Palmer
Priyank Pillai
Layne Piper
Ethan Pollard
Stephanie Presenti
Sarah Rattan
Ashley Reed
Samuel Roberts
Candice Rodriguez
Artur Safin
Ryan Sanchez
Ashley Savage
Lea Sorret
Patrick Squier
John Stavinoha
Joseph Steed
Erica Stivison
Jena Tavormina
Lauren Taylor
Melanie Teater
Jasmine Thomas
Caroline Tudor
Kathryn Turnham
Robert Tysor
Gabriela Villareal
D'arcy Wainwright
Daniel Wicoff
Christopher Widdowson

**2009**
Richard Alanis
Basel Al-Barghouthi
Jackson Allen
Charles Alumbaugh
Nicole Andrews
Alton Avery
Amy Ballanfant
Ananias Barrios
Brian Biekman
Sydney Bottoms
Theodora Browne

Jose Bueno
William Burns
Melissa Cameron
Eric Chao
Nivriti Chowdhry
Andrew Clarage
Brian Cohen
Elizabeth Culotta
Luis De las Cueva
Ezekiel DeLeon
Neal Dennis
Victoria Edrington
Jamie Englert
Ellen Farber
Nicholas Feronti
Rebecca Flowers
Keila Fong
Christopher Fruge
Luis Gallegos
Mallory Gammage
Thomas Gray
Sparkle Grueso
Molly Hamill
Caitlin Harris
Sarah Hartzell
Helen Hau
Gregory Henson
Elizabeth Hill
Gabriella Hulet
Bonnie Hunold
Rehana Jamal
Lori Johnson
Matthew Killary
Charles Lander
Ryan Lindee
Ioanniss Liras
Daniella Llinas
Angela Lloyd
Catherine Lowe
Daniel Macias
Elisa Marshall
Samuel Mayer
Ellen McCloskey
Mary McCloskey
Katherine Miller
Daniel Myerson
Blake Niccum

Samantha Olafson
Martha Pacheco
Sonia Pena
Martin Pham
Jena Presley
Andrew Rachlin
Scott Ravyts
Myrna Reyes
Alice Romero
Megan Ruthven
Melissa Samano
Katherine Sandhop
Benjamin Scheiner
Rebecca Searle
Christine Snyder

**2010**
Zuhdi Abdo
Michelle Aldrich
Jose Arrazolo
Ashley Augustino
Elizabeth Beasley
Evan Bernard
Paul Bunch
Lauren Butler
Keefer Caid-Loos
Beatriz Carboni
Alexandra Castro
Hunil Cha
Pavel Chaguine
Julie Chen
Yaribey Clavel-Lobaina
Shannon Copley
Carrie Cornelius
Brittany Currier-Martin
Akash Dewnani
Allison Dietert
Elena Douglass
Jessica Easter
David Elkin
Yesenia Flores
Helen Frierson
Jorge Galicia
Brianna Garcia
Sarah George
Gabriella Hauser
Allison Heinrich

Arseniy Kolonin
Brian Kovacs
Vishnu Kumar
Emily Laird
Stefan Levy
Bradley Livengood
Morgan Machiorlette
Amanda Macune
Hannah Mann-Hiscock
William Marshak
Andrew Martin
Mai Ling Mattewa
Reilly McClellan
Clay Mealy
Ross Michie-Derrick
Ruth Morales
Catherine Moreno
Lehlohonolo Mosola
Grace Murphy
Jacob Muth
Tonhu Nguyen
Mary Norman
Patrick Oathout
Benjamin Oliver
Eric Olszewki
Kristeen Onyirioha
Eleanor Pellegrin
Rachel Pennington-Hill
Evan Pun
Irene Rodriguez
Liliana Ruiz
Refugio Ruiz
Rachael Samano
Erika Sanabria
Paige Shugart
Sidney Simpson
Charles Sims
Samantha Smith
Jordyn Stanek
Sean Stone-Ashe
Kelley Sullivan
Austin Taghavi
Courtney Thevenot
Naomi Tice
Gregory Tuthill
Elena Vann
Kylie Wade

Rachel Wells
Tiana Zdravic

**2011**
Johanna Acosta
Fady Al
Katheryne Angel
Niru Anya
Emily Arnold
Amanda Augustino
Sarah Beck
Zachary Bednorz
Marc Benitez
Donovan Berens
Victoria Brown
Isabel Browne
Jennifer Bui
Nathan Burchard
Brit Byrd
Marie Chatfield
Nelson Chen
Kirby Cornelius
Ryan Cranfield
Emma Culotta
Diana Dang
Kelsey Davenport
Erica Davies
Danielle Dewhirst
Shelton Elwood
Lucelli Enriquez
Linda Garrison
Muttahir Gire
Haley Goble
Brenda Gonzalez
Elizabeth Gonzalez
Haley Gratzer
Alyssa Hansen
Alexander Hardee
Harriette Harrison
Jeremy Hasson
Barbara Hector
Leah Hoffpauir
Michael Holmes
Alexander Hoyer
Ryan Huiszoon
Vikram Iyer
Taylor Jackson

Daniel Krause
Madison Kuhner
Vesta Kuntz
Jacqueline Laguarta
John LaMond
Alexandra Larsson
Nathaniel Leeds
Katherine Lewis
Christopher Licato
Karsten Lutz
Veronica Maes
Safa Maharsi
Stephanie Mills
Marcus Mitchell
Katherine Morgan
Clarissa Murra
Morgan Murrey-Ittmann
Ana Navarrete
Estelle Nguyen
Thu-Mai Nguyen
Kyle Nielsen
Alexander Nunu
Katherine Opila
Bennett Ostdiek
Viet Pham
Emily Pun
Leo Putnam
Kornel Rady
Anne Ratnoff
Daniel Rauch
Kimberly Reiff
Maxwell Roark
Emma Roberts
Daniel Rocha
Rebecca Rosenfield
Lauren Rothwell
India Rucker
Marina Schneider
Lucy Schofield
Austin Seewald
Sarah Shepherd
Alexander Shulyak
Charlotte Simons
Treasure Stone
John Strauss
Leslie Sullivan

Seyed Tabatabai
Abby Thevenot
Jessica Thomas
Sara Thomas-Martinez
Victoria Thompson
Vance Tillman
Kristen Valenzuela
Lydia Velasquez
Duyen Vo
James Wadman
Erin Wainwright
Stephanie Wang
Zachary Ward
Alex West
Claudia Willis

**2012**

Hayder Ali
Dara Anya
Benito Apreza
Benito Aranda-Comer
Stephen Armstrong
Davis Atkins
Evelin Benitez
Radhika Bhakta
Kendall Bousquet
Noah Brace
Alexander Brown
Mariah Caid-Loos
Jennifer Chavez
Raymond Clarage
Kimberlyn Cruz-Herrera
Kendall Currier
Wesley Draper
Tiffany Duong
Audrey Dupuis
Amy Durand
Carolina English
Melanie Franco
David Frazier
Reid Geissen
Chardonae Givens
Samuel Gonzales-Luna
Adriana Gonzalez
Elizabeth Goodell
Andrea Guerra-Marin

Juliana Gutierrez
Jackson Haenchen
Christopher Hamad
Nicholas Harris
Emma Heitmann
Ann Henson
Kieara Hooey
Elisabeth Hoyer
Farhana Jamal
Margaret Kelly
Selina Khwaja
Layne Kinney
Hannah Lange
Christopher Lanham
Ron Lastimosa
Alyssa Lehmann
Meredith Lerner
David Lindsay
Jennifer Lloyd
Ericka Mabrie
Brette Machiorlette
Louisa Mayer
Anna McGhee
Leslie Mejia
Meredith Mejia
Martin Mengesha
Gabriel Moreira
Noah Morrison
Hannah Mortazavi
Jennifer Mueller
Carmin Munoz-Lavanderos
Grace Newick
Lily Nguyen
William Nixon
Adam Nixon-Torres
Rebecca Nunu
Grace Oathout
Christian Ordaz
Dhaval Patel
Khortlan Patterson
Emily Puig
Deana Radovancevic
Hanna Read
Samuel Reid
Emily Rice
Amelia Roskar

Kevin Roy
Daniela Sanabria
Elana Saynay
Amel Sengal
Michelle Sheena
Robert Spratlin
Mikhaela Stavrinou
Emily Stivison
Lavanya Sunder
Raquel Torres
Margaret Tysor
Imogen Van der Werff
Alexander Wheeler
Andrea Wistuba

## LAMAR HIGH SCHOOL CHEERLEADERS, 1938–2013

| Year | Name | Year | Name | Year | Name | Year | Name |
|---|---|---|---|---|---|---|---|
| 1938 | Mary Ann Anderson | 1946 | Fred Rogers | 1954 | Fairfax Crow | 1961 | Susann Horton |
| 1938 | Joe Gilmore | 1946 | Marilyn Skipwith | 1954 | Nancy Crow | 1961 | Dave Roemer |
| 1938 | Howard Settlemyre | 1946 | McClure Smith | 1954 | Kathleen Kimbro | 1961 | Jamie Wright |
| 1938 | Hester Stewart | 1947 | Martha Eubank | 1954 | Jimmy Lindsey | 1961 | Ken Wynne |
| 1938 | Betty Jo Tomfohrde | 1947 | Kitty Fox | 1954 | Dick McKeever | 1962 | Fred Boone |
| 1938 | Jimmy Whitehurst | 1947 | Jimmy Jamison | 1954 | Barbara Nash | 1962 | Carolyn Dudley |
| 1939 | LaVern Pass | 1947 | Allan King | 1954 | Taylor Smith | 1962 | Anne Holland |
| 1939 | Grace Picton | 1947 | Mary Knoblesdorf | 1954 | Ronnie Waldie | 1962 | Toey Russell |
| 1939 | Bob Shepherd | 1947 | Eddie Shaw | 1955 | Johnny Brown | 1962 | Howard Tellepsen |
| 1939 | Hester Stewart | 1948 | Earl Bellamy | 1955 | Fran Marye | 1962 | Sam Winkelman |
| 1939 | Maurice Thomason | 1948 | Joyce Brawner | 1955 | Harvin Moore | 1963 | Glenn Graham |
| 1939 | Betty Jo Tomfohrde | 1948 | Hickman Corley | 1955 | Garrett Tucker | 1963 | Ronnie Hankamer |
| 1940 | Bobby Abercrombie | 1948 | Carolyn Douglas | 1955 | Fay Veyon | 1963 | Randy House |
| 1940 | Betty Amsler | 1948 | Shirley Edwards | 1955 | Shirley Zapp | 1963 | Margie Mallet |
| 1940 | H. L. Haberlie | 1948 | Al Hildreth | 1956 | David Abright | 1963 | David Roark |
| 1940 | June Jones | 1948 | Joe Hitchcock | 1956 | Barbara Bayer | 1963 | Linda Sokolosky |
| 1940 | Gloria Powell | 1949 | Bobby Carsey | 1956 | Kay Jester | 1963 | Jan Stockard |
| 1940 | Betty Jo Tomfohrde | 1949 | Dale Fooshee | 1956 | Tinsley Jones | 1964 | Roy Collins |
| 1941 | Nadine Guthrie | 1949 | Mavis Hardy | 1956 | Charlene Markle | 1964 | Jerry Converse |
| 1941 | Margretta Herod | 1949 | Sue Hastings | 1956 | Don Robinson | 1964 | Doug Craig |
| 1941 | Lois Holmes | 1949 | Al Hildreth | 1957 | Light Bailey | 1964 | Joan Frensley |
| 1941 | Bill (Unknown) | 1949 | Clare Williams | 1957 | Glenn House | 1964 | Sharon Haralson |
| 1941 | Jack (Unknown) | 1950 | Barbara Lee Brown | 1957 | Judy Ley | 1964 | Bobby Hellbusch |
| 1942 | Lawrence Blieden | 1950 | Shari Collins | 1957 | Amel Rodriguez | 1964 | Barbara Krause |
| 1942 | Pat Dougherty | 1950 | Ed Grubbs | 1957 | Joanne Sweet | 1965 | Jerry Goff |
| 1942 | Lois Holmes | 1950 | Ben Kostial | 1957 | Richard Tinsley | 1965 | Charlene Lusk |
| 1942 | Marjorie Lawry | 1950 | Glenna McCarthy | 1958 | Anne Allen | 1965 | Steve Mims |
| 1942 | Joe Moss | 1950 | Pat Whitworth | 1958 | Chris Brown | 1965 | Susan Murray |
| 1942 | Trebie Perry | 1951 | Sue Eckhardt | 1958 | Gus Comiskey | 1965 | Larry Rodgers |
| 1943 | Betty Blades | 1951 | Georgie Leland | 1958 | Ann Craig | 1965 | Stephanie Sokolosky |
| 1943 | Beverlye Brown | 1951 | Charlie Pace | 1958 | Charles Giraud | 1966 | Mace Brindley |
| 1944 | Roy Bandy | 1951 | Newton Rayzor | 1958 | Mary Sue Hanks | 1966 | Charles Comiskey |
| 1944 | Molly Barnes | 1951 | Sally Schmucker | 1959 | Mike Hattwick | 1966 | Bill Hamill |
| 1944 | Miles Croom | 1951 | Bill Van Wart | 1959 | Tom Herren | 1966 | Biff Kennedy |
| 1944 | Iris Herral | 1952 | Gus Brann | 1959 | Betty Knauth | 1966 | Barbara Mendell |
| 1944 | Bubba Morrison | 1952 | Lou Hardy | 1959 | Pat Shannon | 1966 | Susan Terry |
| 1944 | Wookie Sinclair | 1952 | Margie Laughlin | 1959 | Patsy Smith | 1966 | Candy Tovar |
| 1945 | Bob Dawson | 1952 | Jane Ryba | 1959 | Jere Wicker | 1967 | Bob Borden |
| 1945 | Ben Hammond IV | 1952 | Larry Schmucker | 1960 | Corry Adams | 1967 | Bob Edens |
| 1945 | Doug Pitcock | 1952 | Ronnie Tynes | 1960 | Frank Comiskey | 1967 | Terri Geaccone |
| 1945 | Patsy Smith | 1953 | Celia Buchan | 1960 | Jessica Darling | 1967 | Sis George |
| 1945 | Ruth Smith | 1953 | Billy Jamail | 1960 | Dene Hofheinz | 1967 | Vivian Kleiderer |
| 1945 | Pat (Unknown) | 1953 | Neill Masterson | 1960 | Liz Mobley | 1967 | Keith Rabe |
| 1946 | Cletus Brown | 1953 | Carol Roberts | 1960 | Bob Wynne | 1968 | Susie Alexander |
| 1946 | Kitty Fox | 1953 | Connie Roberts | 1961 | Ray Hankamer | 1968 | Mike Biggs |
| 1946 | Gloria Neuhaus | 1953 | Carlton Wilde | 1961 | Prissy Hester | 1968 | Kelly Faloon |

| Year | Name | Year | Name | Year | Name | Year | Name |
|---|---|---|---|---|---|---|---|
| 1968 | Tommy Holmes | 1975 | Mark Power | 1980 | Kevin Mazeika | 1985 | Katrina Cashaw |
| 1968 | David Kerbow | 1975 | Marilee Roach | 1980 | Donna Murphy | 1985 | Paul Curry |
| 1968 | Nancy Martin | 1975 | Margie Santamaria | 1980 | Maude Robbins | 1985 | Ellen Drushel |
| 1968 | Barbara Powell | 1975 | Mark Soper | 1980 | Paul Sharkey | 1985 | Scott Finley |
| 1969 | Jim Bowen | 1975 | Bill Stavinoha | 1980 | Don Tomasco | 1985 | Marcus Lewis |
| 1969 | Frances Council | 1975 | Faith Stone | 1980 | Jennifer Wilde | 1985 | Alisa Manning |
| 1969 | Beth Edens | 1975 | Kenny Waldt | 1981 | Paul Bernhard | 1985 | Laura Modesett |
| 1969 | Tony Meyer | 1976 | John Eppright | 1981 | Marc Ellison | 1985 | Randy Stallworth |
| 1969 | Albert Shannon | 1976 | Katie Kelley | 1981 | Derrick Evans | 1985 | Jon Tucker |
| 1969 | Mindy Stamey | 1976 | T. Lancaster | 1981 | Deidra Gasper | 1985 | Tiffany Turner |
| 1970 | Kristen Foster | 1976 | Susan Lunn | 1981 | Glenn Hartzell | 1986 | Jennifer Bailey |
| 1970 | Barbara Frank | 1976 | John Maldonodo | 1981 | John Rappazzo | 1986 | Karri Bradley |
| 1970 | Jim Giles | 1976 | John Moore | 1981 | Linda Smith | 1986 | Clare Carpenter |
| 1970 | Jon Levy | 1976 | Mark Schwartz | 1981 | Emily Stewart | 1986 | Jeanne Hansen |
| 1970 | Parker Ransom | 1976 | Scott Wallace | 1981 | Terrilyn Tarlton | 1986 | Sam Hansen |
| 1970 | Adele Taylor | 1976 | Marcella Whiting | 1981 | Anne Thomas | 1986 | Katherine Knolle |
| 1970 | Chip Wells | 1977 | Eric Booth | 1982 | Cindy Benson | 1986 | Jos Milton |
| 1971 | Sherri Collins | 1977 | Eric Britton | 1982 | David Deal | 1986 | Jennifer Pye |
| 1971 | Danny Hoffman | 1977 | Georgeanne Cissel | 1982 | Dude Hall | 1986 | Mike Singleton |
| 1971 | Don Holloway | 1977 | Mitch Craft | 1982 | Susanna Heard | 1986 | Cedric Smith |
| 1971 | Laura Holmes | 1977 | Suzanne FitzGerrell | 1982 | Kathy Herb | 1986 | Peter Steinfeld |
| 1971 | Jackson Hooper | 1977 | Joe Garcia | 1982 | Raymond Kerprta | 1986 | Alec Urquhart |
| 1971 | Lisa Kerbow | 1977 | Kathy Mohnke | 1982 | Marie Lawson | 1986 | Kendra Weber |
| 1972 | Jack Campbell | 1977 | John Moretti | 1982 | Chris Reynolds | 1987 | Sophia Andoh |
| 1972 | Victor Conrad | 1977 | David Sessum | 1982 | Amy Silver | 1987 | Debi Burris |
| 1972 | Jody Fehr | 1978 | Mike Krause | 1983 | John Bevil | 1987 | Bentley Craft |
| 1972 | Scott Gamble | 1978 | Martha Mazeika | 1983 | Katie Brock | 1987 | Kevin Farrel |
| 1972 | Paul Vita | 1978 | Jim Ray | 1983 | Shelley Doran | 1987 | George Gibson |
| 1972 | Jackie Wilson | 1978 | Kenny Robberts | 1983 | Phyllis Dunn | 1987 | Argola Jennings |
| 1973 | Kate Constantatos | 1978 | David Robertson | 1983 | Kevin Lyons | 1987 | Mark Jones |
| 1973 | Jimmy Fourmy | 1978 | Lisa Sanders | 1983 | Bill Stradley | 1987 | Brian Kapiloff |
| 1973 | Greg Goodman | 1978 | Marty Schafer | 1983 | Michelle Tyson | 1987 | Marcus Lewis |
| 1973 | Charlie Hensen | 1978 | Camille Spreen | 1983 | Toby Whitby | 1987 | Meredith Steinfeld |
| 1973 | David Jones | 1978 | Sherry Woodard | 1984 | Kris Able | 1987 | Peter Steinfeld |
| 1973 | Deborah Parker | 1979 | Brad Alexander | 1984 | Margret Ann Arias | 1987 | Kirk Tomasco |
| 1973 | Susan Smith | 1979 | Dawn Brown | 1984 | Brad Caldwell | 1987 | Ann Wukash |
| 1974 | Bill Dukes | 1979 | Darrell Carrow | 1984 | Ellen Chernosky | 1988 | Victor Arias |
| 1974 | Amy Dunn | 1979 | Tom Dartez | 1984 | Daniel Davidson | 1988 | Kelly Caughlin |
| 1974 | Steve Edwards | 1979 | John Draper | 1984 | Felicia Kennerson | 1988 | Natalie Dickson |
| 1974 | Julie Fekete | 1979 | Paul Macias | 1984 | Jim Kennet | 1988 | Shannon Dunlap |
| 1974 | Suzanne McCurley | 1979 | Cindy Migliore | 1984 | Pat Pettit | 1988 | Jon Richardson |
| 1974 | Chris Reinhart | 1979 | Missy Roach | 1984 | Heather Ryan | 1989 | Oliver Butler |
| 1974 | Carl Schmidt | 1979 | Lisa Wallace | 1984 | Rick Singleton | 1989 | Taamika Conway |
| 1974 | David Skaggs | 1980 | Gillette Burns | 1984 | Tim Taite | 1989 | Andrew Craft |
| 1974 | Jill Thompson | 1980 | Lolly Dazey | 1984 | Kelly Whitby | 1989 | David Dollinger |
| 1975 | Peter Atkins | 1980 | Lev Fisher | 1985 | David Ambrose | 1989 | Trice Donatto |
| 1975 | Phyllis Lee | 1980 | Debbie Herb | 1985 | Debi Burris | 1989 | Erin Furr |

| | | | | | | | |
|---|---|---|---|---|---|---|---|
| 1989 | Heather Handel | 1992 | Nickie Landry | 1996 | Vaughn Crawford |
| 1989 | Harris Lamkin | 1992 | Nikki Love | 1996 | McKenzie Davis |
| 1989 | Schulanda Manning | 1992 | Collin Rose | 1996 | Erika Fulenwinder |
| 1989 | Mica Parks | 1992 | Catherine Urquhart | 1996 | Meg Garrett |
| 1989 | Jon Richardson | 1993 | Kim Bennet | 1996 | Hayley Gough |
| 1989 | Martin Rubio | 1993 | Dina Chambers | 1996 | Bill Hart |
| 1989 | Joel Smith | 1993 | Rolanda Cotton | 1996 | Collen Kelly |
| 1989 | Peter Taffe | 1993 | Christian Cutler | 1996 | Shawn Porter |
| 1989 | Ruthie Thompson | 1993 | Derek Digrepont | 1996 | Kelly Rieth |
| 1990 | Tanisha Cherry | 1993 | Shelby Holman | 1996 | Abby Sims |
| 1990 | Cathie Coatsworth | 1993 | Cori Jones | 1996 | Matt Spalding |
| 1990 | Dave Davis | 1993 | Alicia Kerr | 1996 | Brad Steinfeld |
| 1990 | Marisol Espinoza | 1993 | Lanecia McKenzie | 1996 | Carrie Van DeWeile |
| 1990 | Jimmitria Ford | 1993 | Jeff Peterson | 1996 | Elizabeth Watkins |
| 1990 | Jimmy Giacona | 1993 | Dylan Schrader | 1996 | Ray Younkin |
| 1990 | Monica Goosby | 1993 | Ellen Thomason | 1997 | Jennie Gibson |
| 1990 | Nikita Harris | 1993 | Becky Urquhart | 1997 | Angela Gobert |
| 1990 | John Harrison | 1994 | Chris Carlise | 1997 | Brad Steinfeld |
| 1990 | Jamie Holman | 1994 | Sonia Davis | 1998 | Elizabeth Pinson |
| 1990 | Katina Johnson | 1994 | Cara Donatto | 1998 | Sara Schoenfield |
| 1990 | Trey Lozes | 1994 | Victor Garza | 1999 | Katey Blakely |
| 1990 | Nicola Mayhorn | 1994 | Katharine Karnaky | 1999 | Destiny Brown |
| 1990 | Nicole Nelms | 1994 | Jaletta McHenry | 1999 | Sheri Byrd |
| 1990 | Natalie Nicholson | 1994 | Margaret Medina | 1999 | Chris Cardinas |
| 1990 | La Chanda Nowlin | 1994 | Molly Mitchell | 1999 | Ivanna Colan |
| 1990 | Randy Philips | 1994 | Tikisha Mosley | 1999 | Brooklyn Guillory |
| 1990 | Sonji Robinson | 1994 | Michele Rutherford | 1999 | Maria Hadjialexiou |
| 1990 | Gary White | 1994 | Alysia Simmons | 1999 | Michele Housley |
| 1991 | Tanisha Cherry | 1994 | Jeanie White | 1999 | Annie Larkin |
| 1991 | Jennie Dollinger | 1995 | Andrea Blackley | 1999 | Courtney Lee |
| 1991 | Jimmy Giacona | 1995 | Cara Donata | 1999 | Antoinette Mahoney |
| 1991 | Monica Goosby | 1995 | Erika Fulenwinder | 1999 | Ashley Marsh |
| 1991 | Shawna Herbert | 1995 | Meg Garrett | 1999 | Charann McNeil |
| 1991 | Shelby Holman | 1995 | Victor Garza | 1999 | Courtney Rammelt |
| 1991 | Michael Meagher | 1995 | Hayley Goughs | 1999 | Amanda Reese |
| 1991 | Natalie Nicholson | 1995 | Denise Guerra | 1999 | Jody Schmal |
| 1991 | Joel Smith | 1995 | Collen Kelly | 1999 | Leah Simms |
| 1992 | Vahid Brignoni | 1995 | Zelma Lee | 1999 | Yashanda Stafford |
| 1992 | Cella Butler | 1995 | Lyntrecia Lunnon | 1999 | Mindy Willeford |
| 1992 | Christian Cutler | 1995 | Rachelle Mason | 1999 | Kejuanna Wright |
| 1992 | Holly Day | 1995 | Margaret Medina | 2000 | Bridgit Antwi |
| 1992 | Adam Delange | 1995 | Tammi Owens | 2000 | Melissa Barrerra |
| 1992 | Jimmitria Ford | 1995 | Jennifer Reyna | 2000 | Laurel Barrett |
| 1992 | Lucy Gonzalez | 1996 | Nadirah Al'Uqdah | 2000 | Mariama Barrie |
| 1992 | Jamyce Harper | 1996 | Kendra Batiste | 2000 | Ashley Coleman |
| 1992 | Jennifer Herolz | 1996 | Sarah Blissard | 2000 | Asia Diggs |
| 1992 | Malene Jackson | 1996 | Ebony Butler | 2000 | Courtney Duncan |

| Year | Name | Year | Name | Year | Name | Year | Name |
|---|---|---|---|---|---|---|---|
| 2000 | Mary Elizondo | 2002 | Rachel Crockett | 2005 | Chelsea Coburn | 2007 | Rebecca Ide |
| 2000 | Melanie Frogozo | 2002 | Christine Fallon | 2005 | Aubrey Cook | 2007 | Jasmine Imran |
| 2000 | Selam Iob | 2002 | Mariann Hablinski | 2005 | Renitra Fisher | 2007 | Jasmine Johnson |
| 2000 | Susan Kelly | 2002 | Theresa Hernandez | 2005 | Katrina Glenn | 2007 | Khala Jones |
| 2000 | Judy Mommani | 2002 | Kelby Lynch | 2005 | Mayia Guidry | 2007 | Kasey Keller |
| 2000 | Lamonica Orr | 2002 | Jessica Meyerson | 2005 | Katy Hale | 2007 | Brooke Kelley |
| 2000 | Kisha Perter | 2002 | Mercedes Mosby | 2005 | Rena Iglehart | 2007 | Keneshia Lane |
| 2000 | Kathryn Sawyer | 2002 | Andrea Newsome | 2005 | Stephanie Martinez | 2007 | Stacy Lenoir |
| 2000 | Natalie Senkel | 2002 | Amber Pickens | 2005 | Erin Robinson | 2007 | Jessica Macklin |
| 2000 | Kimberly Smith | 2002 | Leigh Sanders | 2005 | Sarah Sanchez | 2007 | Hailey McCleskey |
| 2000 | Cori Smith | 2002 | Summer Terry | 2005 | Ashlynn Sanders | 2007 | Cassandra Meeks |
| 2000 | Ashley Sparks | 2002 | Kerri Thompson | 2005 | Britney Santellana | 2007 | Laura Obando |
| 2000 | Catherine Stiles | 2002 | Cindy Trevino | 2005 | Chelsea Sonpon | 2007 | Shetoi Pierre |
| 2000 | Joanna Stone | 2002 | Katie Wilcox | 2005 | Jessica Texada | 2007 | Destiney Pratt |
| 2000 | Christina Tan | 2002 | Lauren Yambra | 2005 | Kwelina Thompson | 2007 | Sarah Rattan |
| 2001 | Iris Abrego | 2003 | Kristi Abraham | 2005 | Brittany Wingate | 2007 | Christi Rodriguez |
| 2001 | Jade Alexander | 2003 | Meagan Ash | 2006 | Lyndsey Alexander | 2007 | Kinishia Smith |
| 2001 | Jennifer Ban | 2003 | Angelle Bacon | 2006 | Maleka Broussard | 2007 | Domineq Strothers |
| 2001 | Lauren Beamon | 2003 | Monica Barrera | 2006 | Etalvia Cashin | 2007 | Lauren Taylor |
| 2001 | Kristan Bettis | 2003 | Kristin Bellamy-Lloyd | 2006 | Aubrey Cook | 2007 | Courtney Teagle |
| 2001 | Rachel Blacklock |  |  | 2006 | Meredith Crockett | 2009 | Shaunte Bouie |
| 2001 | Kiana Cousin | 2003 | Brianna Belvin | 2006 | Brittney Ewing | 2009 | Lauren Butler |
| 2001 | Asia Diggs | 2003 | Starr Broussard | 2006 | Renitra Fisher | 2009 | Melissa Cameron |
| 2001 | Mariann Hablinski | 2003 | Autumn Caldwell | 2006 | Robyn Ford | 2009 | Jasmine Chandler |
| 2001 | Sarah Jansey | 2003 | Ashley Crayton | 2006 | Katrina Glenn | 2009 | Ashley Clenny |
| 2001 | Katie Keenan | 2003 | Amanda Espinosa | 2006 | Samantha Huang | 2009 | Damita Denton |
| 2001 | Andrea Marks | 2003 | Christine Fallon | 2006 | Rena Iglehart | 2009 | D'Ann Dickson |
| 2001 | Judy Mommani | 2003 | Emma Goodman | 2006 | Carissa Jones | 2009 | Demara Gonzales |
| 2001 | Heather O'Conner | 2003 | Crystal Hemphill | 2006 | Hallie Kerrigan | 2009 | Giana Gray |
| 2001 | Lamonica Orr | 2003 | Angelica Hernandez | 2006 | Lindsay Longshore | 2009 | Raquel Grosman |
| 2001 | Amber Pickens | 2003 | Lizzie Hill | 2006 | Cassandra Meeks | 2009 | Eve Grow |
| 2001 | Samantha Schatte | 2003 | Emily McCoin | 2006 | Ashlynn Sanders | 2009 | Arianna Guidry |
| 2001 | Natalie Senkel | 2003 | Brandy Monk | 2006 | Ashley Sorrels | 2009 | D'Angela Guillory |
| 2001 | Cori Smith | 2003 | Sharon Noel | 2006 | Karen Springer | 2009 | Gabriella Hauser |
| 2001 | Ashley Sparks | 2003 | Leigh Sanders | 2006 | Annie Wolpert | 2009 | Taylor Henderson |
| 2001 | Kerri Thompson | 2003 | Rebecca Sanders | 2006 | Hope Wuertz | 2009 | Secret Hunter |
| 2001 | Cindy Trevino | 2003 | Danielle Sweeney | 2007 | Lyndsey Alexander | 2009 | Raveen Johnson |
| 2001 | Carrie Turner | 2003 | LaQuinta Sykes | 2007 | Lauren Bell | 2009 | Raven King |
| 2002 | Lindsay Amos | 2003 | Jessica Taylor | 2007 | Gabrielle Brigham | 2009 | J'Vonne Lowe |
| 2002 | Meagan Ash | 2003 | Katie Wilcox | 2007 | Sydney Burgoyne | 2009 | Mailing Matthews |
| 2002 | Monica Barrera | 2003 | Amanda Zabodyn | 2007 | Erica Butler | 2009 | Alexys Price |
| 2002 | Lauren Beamon | 2005 | Roya Bailey | 2007 | Joseph Chargois | 2009 | Jessica Randle |
| 2002 | Rachel Blacklock | 2005 | Melissa Baldwin | 2007 | Jazmin Dow | 2009 | Jaeci Roberts |
| 2002 | Dominique Bradford | 2005 | Mary Katherine Butler | 2007 | Sydney Feece | 2009 | Kacie Rogers |
| 2002 | Autumn Caldwell |  |  | 2007 | Morgan Haenchen | 2009 | Lauren Scott |
| 2002 | Nereyda Castillo | 2005 | Savannah Carter | 2007 | Ashley Hines | 2009 | Kara Smith |
| 2002 | Kiana Cousin | 2005 | Ashley Chilivetis | 2007 | Samantha Huang | 2009 | Alana Smith |

| | | | | | | | |
|---|---|---|---|---|---|---|---|
| 2009 | Katherine Smith | 2011 | Alexus Davis | 2012 | Maia Harvey | 2013 | Sydney Stanek |
| 2009 | Hannah Tysor | 2011 | Crystal Davis | 2012 | Megan Hildreth | 2013 | Elizabeth Tan |
| 2010 | Taylor Ashley | 2011 | Amy Durand | 2012 | Chelsey Izegbu | 2013 | Paris Taylor |
| 2010 | Amanda Augustino | 2011 | Iman Eli | 2012 | Sarah Knop | 2013 | Arthur Thompson |
| 2010 | Raven Bradley | 2011 | Shelton Elwood | 2012 | Madison Koogler | 2013 | Cecilia Torres |
| 2010 | Adreanna Broussard | 2011 | Rita Fernandez | 2012 | Brianna Lilly | 2013 | Marisa Valente |
| 2010 | Lauren Butler | 2011 | Bria Finley | 2012 | Victoria Mackert | 2013 | Rebecca Wolpert |
| 2010 | Camilla Caicedo | 2011 | Roman Galmiche | 2012 | Chasity McFarland | 2013 | Shira Yoram |
| 2010 | Lindsey Cameron | 2011 | De'Angela Giles | 2012 | Alexandra Miertschin | | |
| 2010 | Ashley Clenny | 2011 | Kyle Girard | 2012 | Leslie Morrow | | |
| 2010 | Brittany Coleman | 2011 | Amber Hamilton | 2012 | Emily Puig | | |
| 2010 | Erica Davies | 2011 | Raigan Harris | 2012 | Moriah Sells | | |
| 2010 | Bria Finley | 2011 | Mallory Henderson | 2012 | Sydney Stanek | | |
| 2010 | DeAngela Guillory | 2011 | Maria Hill | 2012 | Arthur Thompson | | |
| 2010 | Amber Hamilton | 2011 | Hannah Johannes | 2012 | Raquel Torres | | |
| 2010 | Gabriella Hauser | 2011 | Bethany Kelm | 2012 | Kathryn Widdowson | | |
| 2010 | Drew Hedgebeth | 2011 | Eboni Lewis | 2012 | Rachel Yee | | |
| 2010 | Mallory Henderson | 2011 | Heather Meeks | 2012 | Shira Yoram | | |
| 2010 | Meghan Hitchens | 2011 | Alexandra Miertschin | 2013 | Jordan Azcue | | |
| 2010 | Secret Hunter | 2011 | KeAna Moutra | 2013 | Charlotte Blakemore | | |
| 2010 | Bethany Kelm | 2011 | Meghan Murchison | 2013 | Sydney Brown | | |
| 2010 | Raven King | 2011 | Tyonte Norwood | 2013 | Haley Chilivetis | | |
| 2010 | Eboni Lewis | 2011 | Jamiscia Nunn | 2013 | Courtney Davis | | |
| 2010 | Amber Lilly | 2011 | Victoria O'Neill | 2013 | Sally Durand | | |
| 2010 | Rachel Mackert | 2011 | Emily Puig | 2013 | Katie Froehlich | | |
| 2010 | Chassidy McAfee | 2011 | Payton Reed | 2013 | Ariella Hauser | | |
| 2010 | Heather Meeks | 2011 | Ainsley Roark | 2013 | Audrey Hawkins | | |
| 2010 | Meghan Murchison | 2011 | Rebecca Rosenfield | 2013 | Payton Hernandez | | |
| 2010 | Tyonte Norwood | 2011 | India Rucker | 2013 | Chelsey Izegbu | | |
| 2010 | Jamiscia Nunn | 2011 | Austin Seewald | 2013 | Erica Johnson | | |
| 2010 | Alexys Price | 2011 | Victoria Thompson | 2013 | Katherine Kaitson | | |
| 2010 | Ainsley Roark | 2011 | Raquel Torres | 2013 | Caroline Kelly | | |
| 2010 | Kacie Rodgers | 2011 | Priscilla Villareal | 2013 | Ashley Lewis | | |
| 2010 | Rebecca Rosenfield | 2011 | Elizabeth Wheeler | 2013 | Kierra Lewis | | |
| 2010 | Stephanie Salazar | 2011 | Kathryn Widdowson | 2013 | Brianna Lilly | | |
| 2010 | Lauren Scott | 2011 | Taryne Williams | 2013 | Julian Malone | | |
| 2010 | Alana Smith | 2011 | Rachel Yee | 2013 | Sunday Martinez | | |
| 2010 | Victoria Thompson | 2012 | Ivory Adams | 2013 | Lauren Morgan | | |
| 2010 | Priscilla Villareal | 2012 | Jordan Azcue | 2013 | Anna Morris | | |
| 2010 | Demetria White | 2012 | Charlotte Blakemore | 2013 | Jacoya Neloms | | |
| 2011 | Taylor Ashley | 2012 | Sydney Brown | 2013 | Nadirah Perkins | | |
| 2011 | Amanda Augustino | 2012 | Leah Catley | 2013 | Kailah Pink | | |
| 2011 | Victoria Bowman | 2012 | Brianna Colbert | 2013 | Mattison Pittman | | |
| 2011 | Raven Bradley | 2012 | Alexus Davis | 2013 | Brittnay Posey | | |
| 2011 | Alexis Coates | 2012 | Chrystal Davis | 2013 | Tamiah Robertson | | |
| 2011 | Yevonne Connor | 2012 | Amy Durand | 2013 | Amanda Rosenfield | | |
| 2011 | Erica Davies | 2012 | Sally Durand | 2013 | Kaitlyn Ross | | |

## Lamar High School PTA and PTO Presidents

| | | | |
|---|---|---|---|
| 1937–1938 | C. S. Simons | 1976–1977 | Monroe Talley |
| 1938–1939 | Carl M. Knapp | 1977–1978 | Marlene Schmidt |
| 1939–1940 | R. J. Slagle | 1978–1979 | Marlene Schmidt |
| 1940–1941 | H. M. Stevenson | 1979–1980 | Fab Wallace |
| 1941–1942 | Mrs. A. Blieden | 1980–1981 | Pleas Doyle |
| 1942–1943 | Walter C. Burer | 1981–1982 | Nancy Mafrige |
| 1943–1944 | Walter C. Burer | 1982–1983 | Emmalee Stradley |
| 1944–1945 | Mrs. J. Frank Jungman | 1983–1984 | Elizabeth Aubry |
| 1945–1946 | Mrs. Harry Ferguson | 1984–1985 | Nancy Brock |
| 1946–1947 | Mrs. D. H. L. Donoho | 1985–1986 | Nancy Haywood |
| 1947–1948 | Cameron Fairchild | 1986–1987 | Nancy Haywood |
| 1948–1949 | Walter C. Clemons | 1987–1988 | Clyde Peterson |
| 1949–1950 | Mrs. Arthur V. Pace | 1988–1989 | Kathy Lord |
| 1950–1951 | Harry D. Duckett | 1989–1990 | Linda Sumner |
| 1951–1952 | O. Strother Simpson | 1990–1991 | Marianne Renner |
| 1952–1953 | Frank Sharp | 1991–1992 | Sharron Strang |
| 1953–1954 | Mrs. Guy E. Knolle | 1992–1993 | Mary Lynn Rushing |
| 1954–1955 | Mrs. Brady Cole | 1993–1994 | Lana Short |
| 1955–1956 | Mrs. Willis B. Davis | 1994–1995 | Johnita Lebow |
| 1956–1957 | Mrs. David J. Bratton | 1995–1996 | Malla Brandenburger |
| 1957–1958 | Mrs. Harvin Moore | 1996–1997 | Anne Young French |
| 1958–1959 | Mrs. J. M. Cook | 1997–1998 | Dee Haggard |
| 1959–1960 | Mrs. Mark Storm | 1998–1999 | Pat Rosenberg |
| 1960–1961 | Mrs. John G. Holland | 1999–2000 | Fran Callahan |
| 1961–1962 | W. O. Swift | 2000–2001 | Jan Kellogg |
| 1962–1963 | Mrs. C. F. Niebuhr | 2001–2002 | Sherry O'Connor |
| 1963–1964 | Mrs. P. E. Werlein | 2002–2003 | Kathy Johnson |
| 1964–1965 | Mrs. Sam Winkelmann | 2003–2004 | Sheryl Androphy |
| 1965–1966 | Sherman Glass | 2004–2005 | Vicki Lange |
| 1966–1967 | Dr. D. Y. Oldham | 2005–2006 | Carleta Sandeen |
| 1967–1968 | Judge Wendell Odom | 2006–2007 | Leslie King |
| 1968–1969 | J. Wiley Caldwell | 2007–2008 | DeAnn Englert |
| 1969–1970 | Cecilia Talley | 2008–2009 | Cynthia Lange |
| 1970–1971 | Cecilia Talley | 2009–2010 | Lynnette Mafrige |
| 1971–1972 | Carolyn Hudson | 2010–2011 | Heather Koogler |
| 1972–1973 | Jean Morris | 2011–2012 | Bonnie Clements |
| 1973–1974 | Jean Morris | 2012–2013 | Mary Lynn Khater |
| 1974–1975 | Carolyn Stout | | |
| 1975–1976 | Fran Schoenvogel | | |

## Lamar High School Alumni Association Distinguished Alumni

**2000**
Elizabeth Dennis Rockwell (Class of 1938)
Carolyn Burton Hamilton (Class of 1957)
Carlos Hamilton (Class of 1957)
Peter Roussel (Class of 1961)
John Daugherty (Class of 1962)
Ned Holmes (Class of 1963)
Mike Willis (Class of 1963)
Sherry Spradley Holmes (Class of 1964)
Anita Webber Smith (Class of 1975)

**2001**
Jeannette Clift George (Class of 1942)
Elsa Roberts Rosborough (Class of 1942)
Walter Fondren III (Class of 1954)
Corbin Robertson, Jr. (Class of 1965)
Sherry Woodard Williams (Class of 1978)

**2002**
Mark White (Class of 1958)
Mac Dunwoody (Class of 1963)
Cynthia Potter (Class of 1968)
Alvis Prince, Jr. (Class of 1976)

**2003**
Carol Vance (Class of 1951)
Johnny Holmes, Jr. (Class of 1959)
Chuck Rosenthal (Class of 1963)

**2004**
(No Luncheon)

**2005**
Thomas Barrow (Class of 1941)
Robbin Parish (Class of 1961)
Lee Hogan (Class of 1962)
Ernie Cockrell (Class of 1963)
Kathy Ruiz (Class of 1975)

**2006**
Charles Duncan (Class of 1943)
Robert Whilden (Class of 1953)
Louise Strong (Class of 1962)
Francie Mendenhall (Class of 1969)

**2007**
Doug Pitcock, Jr. (Class of 1945)
Eugenie Mygdal (Class of 1957)
Randy House (Class of 1963)
Bill Poland (Class of 1963)
Lauren Anderson (Class of 1982)

**2008**
John Lindsey (Class of 1940)
Joanne King Herring (Class of 1945)
David Dewhurst (Class of 1963)

**2009**
Leila Gadbois (Class of 1943)
Henri Gadbois (Class of 1948)
Donald Haragan (Class of 1954)
Joe Santamaria (Class of 1957)
Phillip Santamaria (Class of 1958)
Vincent Santamaria (Class of 1960)
Phyllis Santamaria (Class of 1961)
Dorothy Knox Houghton (Class of 1962)
Jane Santamaria Gnazzo (Class of 1963)
Richard Santamaria (Class of 1964)
Lillian Santamaria (Class of 1967)
John Santamaria (Class of 1968)
George Santamaria (Class of 1969)
Michael Longoria (Class of 1974)

**2010**
Bruce Belin (Class of 1944)
Jimmy Brill (Class of 1951)
Tommy Tune (Class of 1957)
Scott Caven (Class of 1960)
Jan Redford (Class of 1960)

**2011**
Conrad Bering (Class of 1939)
Joyce Pounds Hardy (Class of 1942)
Judy Ley Allen (Class of 1957)
Robert Foxworth (Class of 1960)

**2012**
Jonathan Day (Class of 1958)
Susan Cooley (Class of 1970)
Ashley Jones (Class of 1994)
Brian Orakpo (Class of 2004)

**2013**
Ray Alborn (Class of 1957)
Jaclyn Smith (Class of 1964)
Margo Sappington (Class of 1965)
Dominic Walsh (Class of 1989)

## LAMAR HIGH SCHOOL ALUMNI ASSOCIATION BOARD MEMBERS

| | | | | |
|---|---|---|---|---|
| 1966 | George Adams | | 1960 | Marilyn Ralls Johnson |
| 1970 | John Adkins | | 1989 | Delia Wolf Johnson |
| 1965 | Burt Ballanfant | | 1969 | Jan Clark Kellogg |
| 1961 | Bill Bammel | | 1999 | Allison Seeman Kellogg |
| 1978 | Gil Baumgarten | | 2005 | Dustin Landry |
| 1978 | Alison Ayres Bell | | 1994 | Sarah Jones Lane |
| 1969 | Mindy Stamey Benefield | | 1961 | Jay Loucks |
| 1966 | Joel Berry | | 1984 | Allison Howell Malone |
| 1942 | Katherine Hackney Bertelsen | | 1981 | Itze Soliz Matthews |
| 1957 | Nancy Nunnery Brock | | 1969 | Helen Holmes Maxson |
| 1989 | Maury Bronstein | | 2000 | Amy Kugali McWilliams |
| 1957 | Nancy Thornall Burch | | Parent | Eunice Meyer |
| 1957 | Penny Hess Butler | | 1969 | Nancy Eversole Moncrief |
| 1989 | Christopher Byrd | | 1973 | George Morris III |
| Parent | Fran Farrell Callahan | | 1980 | Debbie Herb Pedrick |
| 1996 | Aaron Cohan | | 1962 | Larry Penney |
| 1968 | Marianne Nevill Crain | | 1985 | Alisa Manning Peppers |
| 1970 | Rebecca Dawson Cubberly | | 1976 | Alvis Prince |
| 1969 | Charles Dabney | | 1962 | Daisy Whitridge Quayle |
| 1989 | David Dollinger | | 1953 | Carolyn Schill Rappazo |
| 1971 | Sandy Crowder Eckles | | 1958 | David Redford |
| 1944 | Thomas Erwin | | 1939 | Elizabeth Dennis Rockwell |
| 1959 | Arlen Ferguson | | 1955 | Joe Rogers |
| 1994 | Jonathan Frels | | 1999 | Gerome Sapp |
| 1973 | Theresa Moore Frierson | | 1959 | Lee Chatham Seureau |
| 1973 | Ray Frierson | | 1964 | Roland Sledge |
| 1958 | Charles Giraud III | | 1967 | Mark Stamey |
| 1963 | Harry Glauser | | 1965 | Bill Stewart |
| 1961 | Suzan Clark Glickman | | 1974 | Amy Dunn Taylor |
| Parent | Tim Gorham | | 1977 | Tina Prevost Thompson |
| 1953 | Charles Gregg | | 1963 | Dick Walters |
| 1945 | Benjamin Hammond | | 1958 | Ronald Woliver |
| 1961 | Ray Hankamer | | 1969 | Lois Hamilton Wright |
| 1958 | Ellen Dillingham Heemer | | 1959 | Lynn Zarr |
| 1963 | Melton Henry | | 1974 | Jill Thompson Zivley |
| 1977 | Jill Kerbow Imhoff | | | |
| 1974 | Steve Jenkins | | | |
| 1945 | Marjorie Bintliff Johnson | | | |

## Lamar High School Alumni Association Presidents

| | |
|---|---|
| 1998–2002 | Fran Callahan |
| 2002–2003 | John Adkins |
| 2003–2004 | Jan Kellogg |
| 2004–2005 | David Redford |
| 2005–2007 | Harry Glauser |
| 2007–2009 | George C. Morris III |
| 2009–2010 | Dick Walters |
| 2010–2012 | Roland Sledge |
| 2012–Present | Aaron Cohan |

# ENDNOTES

1 Betty Chapman, "Dr. Ray Kay Daily: Standing Firm in the Face of Controversy," p. 11. Paper presented at the Texas State Historical Association Meeting, August 2004.
2 Kenneth Franzheim has been credited as the major designer for Lamar High School, probably because of his partnership with John Staub, but his name was never brought up in the 1935 Houston Independent School District Board Minutes. Franzheim was, however, chosen to design the 1949 addition.
3 Jim Parsons and David Bush. *Houston Deco: Modernistic Architecture of the Texas Coast*. Albany, Texas: Bright Sky Press, 2008.
4 Ibid.
5 Jim Parsons, "A City Builds Its Identity: Houston's Deco Era," Rice University Continuing Studies, Session 3, Neighborhood Deco, March 17, 2012.
6 Houston Architectural Survey, Vol. 3, 1980.
7 Houston Independent School District Board Minutes, January 18, 1936.
8 HISD Board Minutes, September 13, 1937.
9 *Houston Chronicle*, March 6, 1937.
10 HISD Board Minutes, December 13, 1937.
11 *The Lamar Lancer*, November 23, 1937.
12 *Houston Chronicle*, August 2, 1937.
13 Ibid.
14 *Houston Press*, January 15, 1936.
15 *Houston Post*, September 8, 1937.
16 *Houston Chronicle*, August 17, 1937.
17 *Houston Press*, August 6, 1937.
18 Brochure in River Oaks Property Owners Association Archives.
19 HISD Board Minutes, August 16, 1937.
20 *Houston Press*, August 23, 1937.
21 *Houston Press*, September 12, 1937.
22 *Houston Press*, September 8, 1937.
23 *Houston Post*, September 23, 1937.
24 During World War II, the same problem occurred at the Kinkaid School. Because of gas rationing, the students needed to ride on buses rather than in their parents' cars. Mrs. Kinkaid, who operated this private school, could quickly agree to change the school hours (Susan H. Santangelo, *Kinkaid and Houston: 75 Years*, p. 49).
25 *Lancer*, Vol. 7, No. 11.
26 National Annenberg Election Survey, "Most Indians Say Name of Washington 'Redskins' Is Acceptable While 9 Percent Call It Offensive, Annenberg Data Show," September 24, 2004.
27 *Lancer*, Vol. 24, No. 3.
28 Lamar Directory, 1938.
29 *Lancer*, Vol. 1, No. 3.
30 Senior Class Minutes, February 10, 1938.
31 Ibid.
32 Senior Cabinet Minutes, February 10, 1938.
33 Lamar Students, 1937–1953.
34 *Austin Statesman*, n.d.
35 Obituary of Jess B. Bessinger, Jr., *The New York Times*, June 28, 1994.
36 WorldCat Identities, Jess B. Bessinger.
37 Diana J. Kleiner, "Anderson, Ralph Alexander, Jr.," Handbook of Texas Online, accessed December 3, 2012. Published by the Texas State Historical Association.
38 *Orenda*, 1938.
39 *Orenda*, 1939.
40 *Lancer*, Vol. 1, No. 8.
41 *Orenda*, 1939.
42 *Orenda*, 1938.
43 *Orenda*, 1940.
44 *Lancer*, Vol. 1, No. 1.
45 *Orenda*, 1938.
46 *Lancer*, Vol. 1, No. 10.
47 *Lancer*, Vol. 2, No. 12.
48 *Houston Chronicle*, September 17, 1937.
49 *Lancer*, Vol. 1, No. 1.
50 Conrad Bering, author interview, February 2012.
51 Pamphlet, Lamar High School Alumni Association Distinguished Alumni Luncheon, 2011.
52 *Lancer*, Vol. 1, No. 1.
53 *Lancer*, November 5, 1937.
54 *Lancer*, Vol. 3, No. 2.
55 *Lancer*, Vol. 1, No. 5.
56 *Orenda*, 1939.
57 *Lancer*, Vol. 1, No. 12.
58 *Lancer*, Vol. 2, No. 12.
59 *Lancer*, Vol. 3.
60 *Dallas Morning News*, March 12, 1940.
61 *The Houston Review*, Vol. 4, No. 1.
62 Ibid.
63 Lamar Directory, 1940.
64 Lamar Directory, 1944.
65 *Houston Post*, n.d.
66 Pamphlet, Distinguished Alumni Luncheon, 2011.
67 Obituary, *Houston Chronicle*, January 7, 2010.
68 Ibid.
69 *Lancer*, Vol. 7, No. 5.
70 *Houston Magazine*, November 1942.
71 Pamphlet, Distinguished Alumni Luncheon, 2006.
72 See Chapter Two, p. 24, for more on Fenwick White.
73 Lamar Directory, 1943.
74 *Orenda*, 1942.
75 Gillian Griffin, quoted in the *Houston Chronicle*, September 5, 1996.
76 Ibid.
77 Ibid.
78 Pamphlet, Distinguished Alumni Luncheon, 2001.
79 Nomination Form, Texas A&M University Distinguished Alumnus Award, 2008.
80 Pamphlet, Distinguished Alumni Luncheon, 2011.
81 Senior Cabinet Minutes, March 16, 1943.
82 Vassar Miller, unsigned letter, October 9, 1987.
83 Obituary of Vassar Miller, *The New York Times*, accessed May 6, 2012.
84 Obituary of Donald Barthelme, *The New York Times*, accessed July 17, 2012.
85 Ty Hardin personal website, www.tyhardin.net/AllAboutTyHardin.htm, accessed September 8, 2012.
86 Pamphlet, Distinguished Alumni Luncheon, 2011.
87 Dr. R. Norris Keeler, biography sent to the author via email, November 1, 2012.
88 Office of Historian, Department History, People, Samuel Winfield Lewis, accessed August 29, 2012.
89 Pamphlet, Distinguished Alumni Luncheon, 2011.
90 Celia Morris. *Finding Celia's Place*. College Station: Texas A&M University Press, 2000, p. 42.
91 Morris, *Finding Celia's Place*, p. 41.
92 Morris, *Finding Celia's Place*, p. 42.
93 Ibid.
94 *Orenda*, 1959.
95 Marguerite Johnston. *Houston: The Unknown City, 1836–1946*. College Station: Texas A&M University Press, 1991, p. 228.
96 George Fuermann, *Houston Deplored*, No. 4 in a series of 6, limited to an edition of 1,000 copies, 1968.

97 Marvin Hurley. *Decisive Years for Houston*. Houston: Houston Chamber of Commerce, 1966, p. 155.
98 Hurley, *Decisive Years for Houston*, p. 126.
99 Hurley, *Decisive Years for Houston*, p. 121.
100 Hurley, *Decisive Years for Houston*, p. 120.
101 Fuermann, *Houston Deplored*.
102 Hurley, *Decisive Years for Houston*, p. 156.
103 David G. McComb. *Houston: A History.* Austin: University of Texas Press, 1981, p. 117.
104 Ibid.
105 Betty Chapman. *Historic Houston: An Illustrated History and Resource Guide.* San Antonio: Lammert Publishing, 1997, pp. 90–91.
106 HISD Board Minutes, May 9, 1949.
107 School Board Minutes, January 8, 1951.
108 References to the *Houston Press*, except where indicated otherwise, refer to the original newspaper, which ceased publication in 1964.
109 John Cramer, email essay and author interview, July 2012.
110 *Houston Post*, November 22, 1951.
111 Lamar Students, 1937–1953.
112 *Orenda*, 1951.
113 *Houston Post*, December 19, 1953.
114 Ibid.
115 Ibid.
116 *Sports Illustrated*, September 3, 1962.
117 Clem Barrere, author interview and email, July 2012.
118 Ibid.
119 Clem Barrere, email, "ROTC questions," July 15, 2012.
120 *Lancer*, Vo. 16, No. 17.
121 *Lancer*, April 20, 1953.
122 *Houston Chronicle*, newspaper clipping, n.d.
123 Ralph O'Leary, "Titled Texans," *Houston Post*, n.d.
124 Obituary, *Houston Post*, July 2, 1959.
125 *Lancer*, Vol. 17, No. 14.
126 *Time* Magazine, October 21, 1957.
127 Morris, *Finding Celia's Place*, p. 42.
128 Morris, *Finding Celia's Place*, p. 46.
129 The Golden Age of Science Education, 1950–1977, http://artofteachingscience.org.
130 Tom Green. *Bright Boys, 1938–1958: Two Decades That Changed Everything.* Natick, Massachusetts: A. K. Peters, 2012, p. 1.
131 Green, *Bright Boys*, p. 25.
132 Robert Woodrow Wilson, Autobiography, The Official Website of the Nobel Prize, www.nobelprize.org, May 2012.
133 Ibid.
134 John Cramer, email, September 2012.
135 John G. Cramer, Jr., essay "Lamar Memories" sent to the author, p. 1.
136 Ibid.
137 Cramer, Jr., "Lamar Memories," p. 2.
138 John G. Cramer, "BOOMERanG and the Sound of the Big Bang," from "The Alternate View," *Analog: Science Fiction & Fact Magazine*, January 2001.
139 Obituary of William H. "Hank" Carter, *Washington Post*, April 17, 2009.
140 Wendell Mendell, "Memories of Lamar," Class of 1957 website.
141 *Orenda*, 1957.
142 Thomas M. Biggs: The Main Hero, www.b-med.ru/biggs/index_en.html, accessed June 2012.
143 http://www.informed-llc.com/pubsite/about/bios/mhattwick/aspx, accessed August 2012.
144 Program, Distinguished Alumni Luncheon, 2011.
145 J. Hofheinz, Profile, Forbes, http://www.forbes.com/profile/f-hofheinz, accessed June 2012.
146 Judge Lynn N. Hughes, Biography, http://www.txs.uscourts.gov/district/judges/lnh/biography.htm, accessed June 2012.
147 Pamphlet, Distinguished Alumni Luncheon, 2009.
148 Catharine and David Hamilton, New York Social Diary, www.newyorksocialdiary.com, accessed May 2012.
149 Ibid.
150 American Friends of Versailles, New York Cool, www.newyorkcool.com, November-December 2011.
151 "2011 Reach for the Stars," Pamphlet, Lamar High School Alumni Association.
152 Joan Ryba Gillis, author interview, December 11, 2012.
153 Joan Ryba Gillis. "Rice Cheerleaders to Las Vegas Showgirls: The Odyssey of Joan and Jane Ryba," *Newsletter of the Rice Historical Society*, Vol. 14, No. 1, Spring 2009.
154 "Reach for the Stars: Honoring Ruth Denney," Taped interview with Paula Prentiss, February 12, 2004.
155 *Lancer*, May 14, 1958.
156 Ibid.
157 *LIFE* Magazine, December 22, 1958.
158 *Lancer*, January 15, 1958.
159 *Lancer*, May 14, 1958.
160 "Reach for the Stars: Honoring Ruth Denney," February 12, 2004.
161 *Orenda*, 1956.
162 *Orenda*, 1955.
163 Ned Battista, author interview, September 2012.
164 Josef Helfenstein and Max Neuhaus, oral interview, File Info: mp4 (191MB) TRT: 00:58:44, October 18, 2006.
165 *Lancer*, January 15, 1958.
166 Battista interview, September 2012.
167 Tommy Tune, author telephone interview, September 2012.
168 Biography, The Official Tommy Tune Website, www.tommytune.com, accessed June 2012.
169 Tune interview, September 2012.
170 "Reach for the Stars: Honoring Ruth Denney," February 12, 2004.
171 Jim Bernhard, http://www.doollee.com/PlaywrightsB/bernhard-jim.html, accessed June 2012.
172 Jim Bernhard biography, Amazon, www.amazon.com/Jim-Bernhard/e/B001JSBA8S, accessed June 2012.
173 "Reach for the Stars: Honoring Ruth Denney," February 12, 2004.
174 Tommy Overstreet Press Biography, Dejavu Records, included in "Lamar High School Fiftieth Anniversary, 1937–1987," privately printed history.
175 Carol Williams, author interview, September 12, 2012.
176 *Houston Post*, April 16, 1976.
177 *Lancer*, March 27, 1957.
178 *Lancer*, October 3, 1974.
179 *Post*, December 19, 1953.
180 Robin Parrish, Pamphlet, Distinguished Alumni Luncheon, 2005.
181 Ibid.
182 R. Reese Fuller, "The Man Behind Dave Robichaux, www.reesefuller.com/articles/the-man-behind-dave-robicheaux, accessed July 2012.
183 Kamrath Mygdal, author telephone interview, May 2012.
184 Pamphlet, Distinguished Alumni Luncheon, 2007.
185 *Orenda*, 1957.
186 Tom Brokaw. *Boom! Talking About the Sixties: What Happened, How It Shaped Today, Lessons for Tomorrow.* New York: Random House Publishing, 2007, p. xv.
187 John F. Kennedy, Inaugural Address, January 20, 1961.
188 Stanley Siegel. *Houston: A Chronicle of the Supercity on Buffalo Bayou*, Aurora, Illinois: Windsor Publishing, 1983, p. 192.
189 Hurley, *Decisive Years for Houston*, p. 201
190 Hurley, *Decisive Years for Houston*, p. 208.
191 McComb, *Houston: A History*, p. 140.
192 Hurley, *Decisive Years for Houston*, p. 234.
193 Edgar W. Ray. *The Grand Huckster, Houston's Judge Roy Hofheinz, Genius of the Astrodome.* Memphis, Tennessee: Memphis State University Press, 1980, p. 231.
194 Ray, *The Grand Huckster*, Appendix A.

195 Ray, *The Grand Huckster*, p. 305.
196 Ray, *The Grand Huckster*, p. 192.
197 D. Hofheinz, author email interview, August 2012.
198 Melanie Saxton, *Houston Lifestyles & Homes*, November 2012, pp. 36–38.
199 Robert Foxworth, author telephone interview, August 3, 2012.
200 *Lancer*, Vol. 23, No. 2.
201 Rembert, email to the author, August 13, 2012.
202 *Lancer*, Vol. 23, No. 16.
203 Tommy Tune, author telephone interview, August 21, 2012.
204 *Lancer*, n.d.
205 *Lancer*, Vol. 23, No. 15.
206 *Lancer*, Vol. 25, No. 12.
207 *Lancer*, Vol. 24, No. 7.
208 *Lancer*, Vol. 27, No. 8.
209 Lee Hogan: Executive Profile & Biography, *Businessweek*, www.investing.businessweek.com, accessed October 22, 2012; Pamphlet, Distinguished Alumni Luncheon, 2005.
210 Leaders' Quest Case Study: Lee Hogan, February 2010; Lee Hogan, author interview, October 22, 2012.
211 S. E. Buttrill, telephone interview, September 18, 2012.
212 E. Linn Draper, Jr., Reference for Business, Encyclopedia of Business, www.referenceforbusiness.com/biography/A-E/, accessed August 29, 2012.
213 Pamphlet, Distinguished Alumni Luncheon, 2010.
214 Pamphlet, Distinguished Alumni Luncheon, 2008.
215 Pamphlet, Distinguished Alumni Luncheon, 2008.
216 Pamphlet, Distinguished Alumni Luncheon, 2000.
217 W. McComb Dunwoody, Brief Biography, www.reuters.com, accessed January 19, 2013.
218 Pamphlet, Distinguished Alumni Luncheon, 2000.
219 Email to the author from Lamar Roemer, January 2012.
220 Pamphlet, Distinguished Alumni Luncheon, 2007.
221 Pamphlet, Distinguished Alumni Luncheon, 2002.
222 *Lancer*, Vol. 25, No. 9.
223 Requirements for Graduation, *Reaganite 1958–59*, Reagan High School Directory, p. 21.
224 *Orenda*, 1961, p. 66.
225 *Lancer*, single sheet, n.d.
226 Hamilton Beazley, internet interview, 2006, www.authorinsider.com, accessed August 12, 2012.
227 *Lancer*, Vol. 22, No. 16.
228 *Orenda*, 1965, p. 111.
229 *Orenda*, 1963, p. 68.
230 *Lancer*, Vol. 24, No. 5.
231 Margo Sappington Biography, MTV, www.mtv.com/artists/margo-sappington/biography.
232 Obituary of Jay Wallace Colvin, Jr., *Houston Chronicle*, November 12, 2008.
233 Susan H. Santangelo. *Kinkaid and Houston: 75 Years*. Houston: Gulf Publishing, 1981, p. 95, p. 103.
234 Ibid.
235 *Lancer*, Vol. 23, No. 1.
236 *Lancer*, Vol. 24, No. 14.
237 *Lancer*, February 20, 1969.
238 *Lancer*, Vol. 22, No. 9.
239 *Lancer*, Vol. 22, No. 2.
240 *Lancer*, Vol. 24, No. 7.
241 *Lancer*, Vol. 28, No. 15.
242 *Lancer*, Vol. 24, No. 15.
243 *Lancer*, Vol. 26, No. 9.
244 *Lancer*, Vol. 25, No. 10.
245 *Lancer*, Vol. 28, No. 7.
246 Ibid.
247 *Lancer* (no volume number available).
248 *Lancer*, Vol. 28, No. 7.
249 *Lancer*, Vol. 27, No. 8.
250 Alan Pike, email essay, n.d.
251 Linda Ellerbee, *River Oaks Monthly*, November 1997.
252 *Orenda*, 1960.
253 *Lancer*, Vol. 24, No. 2.
254 *Lancer*, Vol. 26, No. 15.
255 *Lancer*, Vol. 24, No. 1.
256 *Lancer*, Vol. 29, No. 10.
257 *Lancer*, Vol. 27, No. 8.
258 *Lancer*, Vol. 29, No. 10.
259 "Limelight," *Orenda*, 1969, p. 58.
260 Gregory Curtis, *Texas Monthly*, December 1974, p. 54.
261 Santangelo, *Kinkaid and Houston: 75 Years*, p. 103.
262 *Orenda*, 1970, p. 135.
263 *Orenda*, 1970, p. 121.
264 *Lancer*, Vol. 32, No. 2.
265 Ibid.
266 Clifton Daniel, ed., *Chronicle of America*. Mount Kisco, New York: Ecam Publishing, 1993, p. 828.
267 William Henry Kellar. *Make Haste Slowly: Moderates, Conservatives, and School Desegregation in Houston*. College Station: Texas A&M University Press, 1999, p. 3.
268 Kellar, *Make Haste Slowly*, p. 158.
269 Kellar, *Make Haste Slowly*, p. 159.
270 Ibid.
271 Kellar, *Make Haste Slowly*, p. 160.
272 Ibid.
273 Kellar, *Make Haste Slowly*, p. 161.
274 Kellar, *Make Haste Slowly*, p. 162.
275 Kellar, *Make Haste Slowly*, p. 165.
276 *Orenda*, 1971, p. 4.
277 *Lancer*, Vol. 33, No. 9.
278 *Lancer*, Vol. 32, No. 10.
279 Curtis, *Texas Monthly*, December 1974, p. 57.
280 *Lancer*, Vol. 38, No. 10.
281 *Lancer*, Vol. 36, No. 8.
282 *Orenda*, 1976, p. 64.
283 Sherry Evans, email to the author, September 4, 2012.
284 *Lancer*, Vol. 36, No. 12.
285 Inventory of the Lisa Tuttle Collection: ca. 1975–2004, Biographical Note, www.lib.utexas.edu/taro/tamucush/00162/tamu-00162.html, Texas Archival Resources Online, Cushing Memorial Library, Texas A&M University, College Station, TX 77843-5000.
286 Brandon Smith, author interview, February 10, 2013.
287 Christopher Calnan, "Austin, Aggies and Innovation: Jamie Rhodes sniffs out 'next big thing' at A&M," *Austin Business Journal*, April 6, 2012.
288 Mike Godwin Biography, The MIT Press, http://mitpress.mit.edu/authors/mike-godwin.
289 Mike Godwin, "Meme, Counter-meme," *Wired*, www.wired.com/wired/archive/2.10/godwin.if_pr.html, accessed February 1, 2013.
290 John Culberson Biography, www.culberson.house.gov/biography, accessed February 1, 2013.
291 Vanderbilt University Center for Biomedical Ethics & Society, "Who We Are," www.medicineandpublichealth.vanderbilt.edu.
292 "Dr. Emily Cutrer named president of Texas A&M University-Texarkana," The Texas A&M University System News, January 9, 2013.
293 "About Dr. Samuel I. Miller," Samuel Miller Laboratory, University of Washington, Seattle, www.miller-lab.net/MillerLab, accessed August 25, 2012.
294 *Lancer*, 1972, n.d.
295 Video, Distinguished Alumni Luncheon, 2009.
296 *Lancer*, Vol. 33, No. 16.

297 Gregory M. Senofsky Biography, www.newstjohns.org/Gregory_M_Senofsky,_MD.aspx, accessed September 4, 2012.
298 Great Chef Kathy Ruiz, www.greatchefs.com/great-chefs/kathy-ruiz/, accessed January 30, 2013.
299 Sherry Williams Biography, www.khou.com/community/bios/67784697.html, accessed February 24, 2013.
300 *Orenda*, 1975, p. 6.
301 Juana Gregory Bernard, email to the author, August 26, 2012.
302 *Orenda*, 1977, p. 12.
303 *Orenda*, 1979, p. 231.
304 *Orenda*, 1979, p. 3.
305 *Orenda*, 1979, p. 46.
306 *Lancer*, Vol. 6, No. 7.
307 Chapman, *Historic Houston*, p. 102.
308 *Lancer*, Vol. 41, No. 5.
309 *Orenda*, 1980.
310 *Lancer*, Vol. 42, No. 2.
311 *Lancer*, Vol. 42, No. 3.
312 *Lancer*, Vol. 43, No. 1.
313 *Lancer*, Vol. 42, No. 4.
314 *Lancer*, Vol. 42, No. 1.
315 *Lancer*, April 1989.
316 Deidra Gasper, email to the author, October 22, 2012.
317 *Lancer*, Vol. 41, No. 5.
318 *Lancer*, Vol. 47, No. 3.
319 Lancer, Vol. 47, No. 4.
320 *Lancer*, Vol. 47, No. 3.
321 *Lancer*, February 1986.
322 Liz Chadderdon, author telephone interview, October 10, 2012.
323 The Chadderdon Group's Official Website, www.chadderdongroupagecom/about-us/liz-chadderdon.
324 Ray Reiner, interview with the author, November 14, 2012.
325 *Lancer*, April 1986.
326 *Orenda*, 1989, p. 2.
327 Ron Veselka, interview with the author, November 14, 2012.
328 *Lancer*, October 1985.
329 Lamar Directory, 1986.
330 *Lancer*, 1980, n.d.
331 James DeGregori, Colorado Café Scientifique, http://cafescicolorado.org/DeGregori.htm, accessed September 8, 2012.
332 Chapman, *Historic Houston*, p. 105.
333 *Orenda*, 1988, p. 11.
334 Paul Bernhard, private papers shared with the author.
335 Derrick Evans, email to the author, November 1, 2012.
336 Mignon Guidry, email to the author, February 11, 2013.
337 Charles Haynes Biography, www.msl.ubc.ca/faculty/haynes, accessed November 6, 2012.
338 Nat Moss, LinkedIn Profile, www.linkedin.com/in/natmoss, accessed October 19, 2012.
339 School of Law, The University of Texas at Austin, www.utexas.edu/law/faculty/sweengs, accessed October 10, 2012.
340 Angela Belcher, http://www.web.mit.edu/be/people/belcher.html, accessed March 2013.
341 Jason Dworkin, CV, http://astrobiology.gsfc.nasa.gov/analytical/dworkinCV.html, accessed September 23, 2012.
342 "Ballet's Jackie Robinson: The story of the first African-American ballerina in H-Town," Culture Map Houston, May 3, 2012.
343 *Houston Chronicle*, n.d.
344 Ben Stevenson, video interview, Lamar High School Alumni Association, 2007.
345 Gia Kourlas, "Where Are All the Black Swans?" *The New York Times*, May 6, 2007.
346 Aimee L'Heureaux, *Houston History Magazine*, Vol. 7, No. 2, pp. 22–23.
347 Obituary of Sandy Carr, *Houston Chronicle*, November 17, 2007.
348 Ibid.
349 Ibid.
350 Ibid.
351 Sylvia Coleman, "Life as RN and Pro Tennis Player Makes This Nurse Happy," NurseZone.com, 2006.
352 *Orenda*, 1989.
353 Julie Doran, *Orenda*, 1989.
354 Debbie Miller, *Orenda*, 1989.
355 *Orenda*, 1991.
356 *Orenda*, 1991, p. 14.
357 *Orenda*, 1991.
358 *Orenda*, 1993.
359 *Lancer*, Vol. 53, No. 4.
360 Ibid.
361 Diana Ryan, "Required Community Service in High Schools and Civic Engagement," May 3, 2012, from a course website, Educ 300: Education Reform, Past and Present.
362 Ibid.
363 *Orenda*, 1991, p. 10.
364 Ibid.
365 *Orenda*, 1996, p. 145.
366 *Orenda*, 1996, p. 157.
367 *Lancer*, December 1993.
368 *Orenda*, 1994, p. 30.
369 *Lancer*, February 13, 1992.
370 *Lancer*, September 12, 1991.
371 *Lancer*, n.d.
372 Orenda, 1992.
373 *Lancer*, n.d.
374 Thomas Yu, personal website, http://web.mit.edu/tlyu/bio.html, accessed October 12, 2012.
375 Alex Avelallemant, email to the author, February 20, 2013, sent from a "shipping container in Eastern Pakistan."
376 Eric Sumner Biography, Meet the Team, Cargill website, www.cpo.cargill.com/people/sumner.shtml.
377 Megan Moir, LinkedIn Profile, www.linkedin.com/pub/megan-moir/2b/955/528, accessed October 15, 2012.
378 Gia Kourlas, "Ballet Dancer Marian Butler Talks About Rodeo," TimeOut New York, October 15, 2012.
379 Marian Butler, email to the author, January 2013.
380 Ashley Jones, Pamphlet, Distinguished Alumni Luncheon, 2012.
381 Carlene Mackereth, "Catherine Frels Nominated for Best Actress Award," January 24, 2012, http://www.wusa9.com/.
382 *Lancer*, September 1993.
383 *Orenda*, 1999.
384 William Strauss and Neil Howe. *The Fourth Turning: An American Prophecy—What the Cycles of History Tell Us About America's Next Rendezvous with Destiny*. Broadway Books, 1997, p. 236.
385 James McSwain, author interview, December 12, 2012.
386 Ibid.
387 David Barron, *Houston Chronicle*, November 14, 2012.
388 Jeff Jenkins, *Houston Chronicle*, July 8, 2004.
389 Brandon LaFell, author telephone interview, January 2013.
390 Jeff Jenkins, "Lamar looks back on incredible run," *Houston Chronicle*, December 24, 2012.
391 Ibid.
392 Hayley McGregory, Biography, http://arluckpromotions.com/athlete-management/detail/hayley-mcgregory, accessed January 2013.
393 Joe Savery, author interview, January 24, 2013.
394 Meet Chelsey. Chelsey Green Website, http://www.chelseygreen.com/meet-chelsey, accessed February 2013.
395 Ann Southwell, author interview, January 24, 2013.
396 Ricardo Garza, author interview, January 17, 2013.
397 Ida Amstead, author interview, January 19, 2013.
398 *Lancer*, Vol. 22, No. 4.
399 Jerome Solomon, *Houston Chronicle*, December 23, 2013.

# SELECTED BIBLIOGRAPHY

## BOOKS

Begeman, June A. *Stepping Back in Time: A History of West University Place*. Houston: D. Armstrong Company, 1999.
Brokaw, Tom. *Boom! Talking About the Sixties: What Happened, How It Shaped Today, Lessons for Tomorrow*. New York: Random House Publishing, 2007.
Chapman, Betty Trapp. *Historic Houston: An Illustrated History and Resource Guide*. San Antonio: Lammert Publishing, 1997.
Daniel, Clifton, ed. *Chronicle of America*. Mount Kisco, New York: Ecam Publishing, 1993.
Davis, Wallace. *Corduroy Road: The Story of Glenn H. McCarthy*. Houston: The Anson Jones Press, 1951.
Fenberg, Steven. *Unprecedented Power: Jesse Jones, Capitalism, and the Common Good*. College Station: Texas A&M University Press, 2011.
Fox, Steven. *Houston, Architectural Guide*. Second Edition. Houston: Herring Press, 1999.
Fuermann, George. *Houston: Land of the Big Rich*. Garden City, New York: Doubleday & Company, 1951.
Fuermann, George. *Houston: The Feast Years*. Houston: Premier Printing Company, 1962.
Green, Tom. *Bright Boys, 1938–1958: Two Decades That Changed Everything*. Natick, Massachusetts: A. K. Peters, 2012.
Gregory, Lloyd J. *Looking 'em Over: Tales of a Texas Sports Writer*. Austin: The Steck Company, 1968.
Hurley, Marvin. *Decisive Years for Houston*. Houston: Houston Chamber of Commerce, 1966.
Johnston, Marguerite. *Houston: The Unknown City, 1836–1946*. College Station: Texas A&M University Press, 1991.
Kellar, William. *Make Haste Slowly: Moderates, Conservatives, and School Desegregation in Houston*. College Station: Texas A&M University Press, 1999.
McComb, David. *Houston: A History*. Austin: University of Texas Press, 1981.
Mod, Anna. *Images of America: Building Modern Houston*. Charleston, South Carolina: Arcadia Publishing, 2011.
Morris, Celia. *Finding Celia's Place*. College Station: Texas A&M University Press, 2000.
Nicholson, Patrick J. *In Time: An Anecdotal History of the First Fifty Years of the University of Houston*. Houston: Gulf Publishing Company, 1977.
Parsons, Jim and David Bush. *Houston Deco: Modernistic Architecture of the Texas Coast*. Albany, Texas: Bright Sky Press, 2008.
Ray, Edgar W. *The Grand Huckster: Houston's Judge Roy Hofheinz*. Memphis, Tennessee: Memphis State University Press, 1980.
Santangelo, Susan H. *Kinkaid and Houston: 75 Years*. Houston: Gulf Publishing, 1981.
Siegel, Stanley. *Houston: A Chronicle of the Super City on Buffalo Bayou*. Aurora, Illinois: Windsor Publishing, 1983.

## PERIODICALS

*Architectural Forum*
*Architectural Record*
*Austin Statesman*
*LIFE* Magazine
*Houston Chronicle*
*Houston Post*
*Houston History Magazine*
*Houston Lifestyles & Homes*
*Houston Magazine*
*Houston Review*
*The River Oaks Magazine*
*Sports Illustrated*
*Texas Monthly*
*The Austin Business Journal*
*The Dallas Morning News*
*The Houston Press* (1911–1964)
*The New York Times*
*Time* Magazine

## PUBLICATIONS

"Lamar High School Fiftieth Anniversary, 1937–1987," Privately Printed History
Lamar High School Distinguished Alumni Luncheon Pamphlets
Lamar High School Distinguished Alumni Videos, 2000–2012
Lamar Students, 1937–1953 (unpublished)
*Orenda*, Lamar High School Yearbook
"Reach for the Stars: Honoring Ruth Denney," Lamar High School Alumni Association Video
*The Corral*, Stephen F. Austin High School Yearbook
*The Lamar Lancer*, Lamar High School Newspaper

## Selected Bibliography

**TELEPHONE INTERVIEWS**

George Barnstone
Hamilton Beazley
Jim Bernhard
Deanna Galyean Brown
S. E. "Bud" Buttrill
Liz Chadderdon
Daniel Clinton
John Cramer
Sherry Evans
Robert Foxworth
Lee Hogan
Brandon LaFell
Dr. Roland Lenarduzzi
Roland Lenarduzzi
Marilyn Lummis
Ann Mahan
Carlin Glynn Masterson
Trula Meglasson
GeeGee Kamrath Mygdal
Alice Ott
Andy Rembert
Dr. Lamar Roemer
Peter Roussel
Joe Savery
Brandon Smith
Gracie Tune
Tommy Tune
Miriam Young
Pam Young
Carol Williams

**PERSONAL INTERVIEWS**

Ida Amstead
Lauren Anderson
Clem Barrere
Ned Battista
Conrad Bering
Jim Bernhard
Charles Boyd
Jimmy Brill
Nancy Brock
Micky Carmichael
Florine Carr
Anne Costlow
Paula Cox
Colonel Joseph David
Diane Foreman
Henry Gadbois
Leila Gadbois
Ricardo Garza
Joan Ryba Gillis
Grace Grierson
Elise Hawkins
Marcile Hollingsworth
Ned S. Holmes
Patty Peckinpaugh Hubbard
Bertha Gray Jamison
Julie Catterton Kempner
Jerry Martinez
Rosalyn Reavis Matusow
Coach Stephen McDonald
Dr. James McSwain
David Munoz
Tom Nolen
Dr. Gary Patterson
J. Doug Pitcock, Jr.
David Purdie
Ray Reiner
Camille Dockery Simpson
Ann Southwell
Nena Conn Dahlstrom Stowers
Barbara Lee Brown Teas
Betty Ruth Robbins Tomfohrde
Penny Tschirhart
Ron Veselka
Tom Whitehead
Sandra Nobles Wilson

**EMAIL ESSAYS**

John Adkins
Hamilton Beazley
Sheleigh Beggs
Martha Gipps Bell
Juana Gregory Bernhard
Paul Bernhard
S. E. "Bud" Buttrill
David Julian Cate
Patrick Cate
Ernest Conner
John Cramer
Robert P. Dunnam
Cay Womack Eckland
Derrick Evans
Hugh Gainey
Deidre Gasper
Marian Butler Gibson
Dick Gregg
Mignon Guidry
Joel Harrell
Tom Herren
Judy Hancock Hilsenteger
Julie Hodges
Laurent Hodges
Dene Hofheinz
Anne Thomas Jarriel
Mike Journeay
R. Norris Keeler
Vicki Keltner
Martha Butler Long
Andrew Lynch
DeeDee McMurtry
Allison Mahlstedt
Michael Mahlstedt
Katherine Taylor Mize
Elizabeth Newnam
Zenobia Gee Perry
Alan Pike
Marianne Hayes Pratt
John Pundt
Madge Thornall Roberts
Dr. Lamar Roemer
Brandon Smith
Judy Talkington
Kris Thomas
Carol Turner
Gordon Vaughan
Sally Riggs Winfrey
Lynn Wiseheart
Lynn Zarr

# INDEX

**A**
Abbott, Bud, 65
Abbott, Chris, 163
Adams, Betty (Conrad), 193
Adams, Bud, 95, 105
Adams, Edward, 129
Ahmad, Abdul, 178
Albertson, Bob, 51
Albright, Secretary of State Madeleine, 172
Albritton, Ford, 35, 36
Albritton, George, 35
Alexander, Kelsey, 187
Allen, Judy (Ley), 94, 181, 191
Altneu, Zach, 171
Amidon, David, 132
Amstead, Ida Lazard, 190
Andell, Bethany, 168
Anderson, Andy, 30
Anderson, Glenn, 178
Anderson, Jack, 178
Anderson, Laura, 125
Anderson, Lauren, 122, 165, 166, 174
Anderson, Lolly, 81
Anderson, Mary Ann, 33
Anderson, Ralph, 30, 112, 113
Anderson, Wes, 173
Anton, Dene (Hofheinz), 113, 114, 147
Archer, Congressman Bill, 148
Ard, Tim, 178
Astaire, Fred, 102, 103
Augsburger, Johnny, 134
Austin, Stephen F., 14, 77
Autry, Gene, 103
Avelallemant, Alex, 172
Ayesu, Barbie, 171

**B**
Baer, Carolyn, 134
Bailey, Pearl, 128
Baker, Betty, 50
Baker, U.S. Marshal Stu, 172
Ball, Bob, 116
Ball, David, 35
Ball, Ellana, 56
Barner, Celious, 178
Barrere, Clem, Jr., 82, 83
Barrow, Ted, 141
Barrow, Thomas, 45, 141
Barry, Dave, 100
Bartheleme, Joan, 85, 108
Barthelme, Donald, 60, 61
Battista, Ned, 100, 101, 102, 133
Bayless, Jimmy, 47
Beaudion, Jonathan, 178
Beazley, Hamilton, 125
Becker, Pat, 96
Belcher, Dr. Angela, 164
Bell, Kenny, 79
Bellows, W. S., 66
Bennett, Kaye, 138
Benny, Jack, 96
Bentz, Peggy, 43
Bergman, Candace, 97
Bering, Conrad, 35, 36

Berkes, Leslie, 121
Bernard, Juana (Gregory), 152
Bernhard, Jim, 103, 162, 194
Bernhard, Paul G., 162, 163
Bertelsen, Emily, 64
Bertner, Dr. E. W., 71
Bertrand, Jimmy, 80
Bessinger, Jess B., 30
Biggs, Thomas M., 76, 91
Bishop, Joey, 96
Blancas, Homero, 80
Blass, Bill, 56
Blieden, Lawrence, 55, 57
Blue, Vincent, 188
Bogar, Katie, 182
Bonney, John, 178
Booth, Steven, 159
Booth, Tom, 134
Borneman, Raymond, 55
Bowen, Ralph, 52
Boyd, Charles, 47, 50
Boynton, James "Jack", 61
Bracewell, Lyn, 25
Brandenburger, Bubba, 139
Brannon, Jimmy, 85
Bravenec, Ed, 134
Brent, Bob, 80
Brew, Ernest, 146
Bright, Joe, 78
Brill, Jimmy, 39, 191
Brindley, Paul, 80
Briscoe, Birdsall, 12, 14, 17
Briscoe, Governor Dolph, 131
Britt, Harriet (Melendy), 114
Brock, Jim, 186
Brokaw, Tom, 111
Brown, Barbara, 24
Brown, George, 71
Brown, Herman, 71
Brown, Mary Lorena, 107
Brummel, Beau, 104
Brunson, Major George, 24
Bryant, Sylvia, 159
Buchan, Bill, 134
Buchan, Celia, 70, 71, 107
Buchanan, Margaret, 59, 108, 127
Buchanan, Russell, 163
Burke, James Lee, 106
Bush, Governor George W., 119, 121, 132
Bush, President George H. W., 170
Butler, George, 192
Butler, Marian, 174
Butler, Martha, 164, 165
Butler, Penny (Hess), 191
Buttrill, S. E., Jr., 118
Buttrill, Sydney, 118
Byrd, Sergeant Stanley, 36

**C**
Caldwell, Candy, 134
Callahan, Fran, 6, 190, 191
Campbell, Graham, 85
Caniff, Milton, 59
Carmichael, Micky, 46, 192

Carmouche, Derrick, 178
Carr, Coach Sandy, 166, 167
Carr, Florine, 7, 116, 117
Carter, President Jimmy, 155
Carter, William, 89
Casares, Kathy, 193
Case, Dr. Carol, 157, 159
Casey, Congressman Bob, 112
Castillo, Sergio, 178
Cato, Jan, 191
Cato, Lamar Q., 11
Caven, Scott, 119
Cayce, Charles, 134
Chadderdon, Liz, 156, 157
Chambers, Mary, 168
Champion, Frank, 43
Champion, John, 43
Chase, Opal (Glen), 107
Chidsey, Alan, 73
Childress, Carol, 81
Childress, Virgil, 12
Chow, Adrea, 179
Chukwu, Phoenix, 178
Clapp, Mabel, 47
Clark, Mary Jo, 55
Clarke, Ewell, 50
Clayton, Ellen (Wright), 148, 149
Clayton, Will, 44
Clement, Lois, 55
Clements, Gene, 116
Clements, Governor Bill, 119
Clemons, Walter, 51, 59, 60
Cline, Catharine, 94
Cobb, Thomas, 61
Coe, Ann, 40
Colbert, Darrell, Jr., 178
Collete, Robert, 187
Collins, Shari, 24
Connally, Governor John B., 92, 119
Connally, Judge Ben, 142
Connally, Louise, 51, 118
Connick, Harry, Jr., 191
Cooley, Susan, 174
Coolidge, Joel, 143
Coop, Mrs. Eletha (B. F.), 11
Costello, Lou, 65
Costlow, Harold, 129, 130, 139, 146
Covington, Nina, 58, 59
Cowan, Judge Finis T., 143
Cox, Edith, 70
Cramer, Brandy, 168
Cramer, John, 74, 87, 88
Crate, Buck, 32
Criner, Betty Claire, 52
Crosby, Bing, 54
Crutchfield, Bob, 96, 97
Culberson, Congressman John, 148
Curtis, Gregory, 144
Curtis, Tony, 96
Cutbirth, Sonny, 77
Cutrer, Emily (Fourmy), 149

**D**
Dahlstrom Stowers, Nena (Conn), 46
Daily, Dr. Ray K., 8, 9, 44
Dambrino, Marmion, 186
Dang, Bill, 178
Daugherty, John, 128
Davidhizar, Paula, 163
Davis, Morgan J., 112
Davis, Philip, 138
Day, Jonathan, 80, 174
Day, Walter, 168, 172, 191
DeGregori, James, 159
Delaney, Pauline (Mills), 13, 36
Denney, Ruth, 57, 70, 85, 95, 96, 98, 99, 102, 103, 104, 113, 115, 116, 136, 147, 191
Depenbrock, R. J., 19
Dewhurst, Lieutenant Governor David, 119, 192
Diamond, Margaret, 81
Dickey, William, 26
Dickson, J. E., 64
Dillman, David, 74
Dinh, Nhi, 182
Dixon, Brandon, 187
Dixon, Sam H., Jr., 14
Dobbins, Dorothy, 85
Doerner, Karl, III, 141, 142
Doran, Julie, 160, 167
Dougherty, Cara, 169
Dougherty, Pat, 55
Douglas, Carolyn, 64
Dover, Jo Lynn, 138
Dow, George, 35
Draper, E. Linn, 119
Druhet, Daijon, 178
Duggan, Andy, 57
Duggan, Ed, 31, 43
Duggan, F. Lee, 70, 90
Dukes, Bill, 163
Duncan, Charles W., Jr., 50, 51
Duncan, Lee, 178
Dunlop, Wayne, 78
Dunwoody, W. McComb "Mac", 119, 120, 151
Durall, Darius, 178
Durst, Bob, 100, 108
Dworkin, Dr. Jason, 164
Dylan, Bob, 111

**E**
Earthman, Charlie, 156
Eason, Marjorie, 117
Ebersole, Bob, 138
Edwards, Norval, 178
Edwards, Shirley, 40
Ehman, Dakota, 64
Eisenhower, General Dwight, 66
Elledge, Dick, 192
Ellerbee, Linda, 135, 136
Ellisofon, Eliot, 97, 98
Elmer, Travon, 178
Elrod, Horace W., 37
Englert, DeAnn, 190
Erwin, Bill, 134
Evans, Derrick, 162, 163

Evans, Sherry, 7, 146
Evans, Stanton, 134

**F**
Farb, Carolyn, 62
Feldman, Claudia, 64
Fernandez, Dino, 178
Ferrell, Edith, 70
Feynman, Richard, 74
Field, Joan, 85
Fields, James H., 27
Filson, Genevieve, 107, 108
Finger, Joseph, 10, 14
Finn, Alfred C., 10
Finnegan, Betty, 41
Fisk, Aubry, 134
Fisk, Holly, 134
Flores, Xavier, 178
Flores, Yesinia, 193
Fogarty, Charlie, 94
Fonda, Jane, 97
Fondren, Walter, III, 79, 80, 124
Fontaine, Ernest, 109
Fonville, Mrs., 26
Ford, Deon, 178
Foreman, Diane, 111
Fox, Stephen, 11
Fox, William, 46, 139
Foxworth, Robert "Bob", 113, 114, 116
Franzheim, Kenneth, 73
Frels, Catherine, 175
Freud, Crete, 52
Friedman, Jakie, 95
Friery, John, 134
Frizzel, Edward, 100
Fuermann, George, 71, 72
Fuller, Buckminster, 113
Fuller, Louise, 146, 147

**G**
Gadbois, Henri, 30, 61
Gadbois, Leila (McConnell), 61, 62
Gallagher, Bill, 78
Gamble, Joseph Scott, 144
Gammage, Ernie, 134
Garay, Reynaldo, 178
Garland, Judy, 71
Garza, Jorge, 188
Garza, Ricardo, 190
Gasper, Deidra, 156, 162
Gentry, Brad, 89, 90, 91, 121
George, Jeanette (Clift), 57, 124, 125
Gerlach, Ed, 102
Gerlach, Elizabeth, 168
Gibson, Gregory, 178
Gibson, Shaquille, 178
Giles, Susan, 134
Gilmore, Joe, 33
Gittings, Paul, 50
Glauser, Harry, 51
Glosup, Rosamund, 129, 133
Glover, Louis, 11
Godwin, Mike, 148

Goodson, W. R., 86
Gossey, Betty Jo, 40
Gradwohl, Jim, 134
Graham, Dr. Billy, 105
Graham, Larry, 76, 77, 78
Graham, Lefty, 77
Graham, Wayne, 188
Gramm, Senator Philip, 172
Gray, Delvin, 172
Gray, John, 147
Gray, Peter, 92
Greacen, Tom, 134
Green, Chelsey, 189
Green, Kate, 123
Green, Tom, 87
Green, Tyrone, 178, 185
Greenwood, Helen, 70, 108, 113, 116, 118, 125, 139
Gregg, Dick, 35
Gregory, Lloyd, Jr., 32
Gregory, Lloyd, Sr., 32
Grierson, Grace, 64
Griffin, Linda (Gillan), 56
Griffith, Benjamin, 189
Grogan, Jeanette, 40
Grover, Henry Cushing, 131
Grubbs, Ed, 24
Gude, Cynthia, 81
Guidry, Mignon, 163
Guyton, Nancy, 168
Gwin, Jack, 43

**H**
Hagelman, Mrs. W. C., 54
Hagelman, Rudy, 54
Halbouty, Michael T., 15
Hamilton, David, 93
Handy, Gabriella, 187
Haragan, Dr. Donald, 93, 149
Hardin, Ty, 61
Hardy, Tom, 31, 32
Harpold, Lew, 76
Harrell, Alice, 70
Hattwick, Dr. Michael, 91
Hawkins, Elise, 107
Haynes, Charlotte, 168
Haynes, Dr. Charles, 163
Haywood, Mark, 170
Heard, Patsy, 85
Hefley, Duane, 166
Helfenstein, Josef, 101
Henderson, Norma, 61, 108
Hepburn, Katherine, 97
Herbert, Gordon, 121
Herring, Arthur, 88
Herring, Robert, 63
Herron, Jackie, 64
Higginbotham, Blanche, 44
Hill, Holton, 178
Hill, Tommy, 78
Hines, Jess, 134
Hitt, Larry, 35
Hoar, Ann, 172

Hobby, Oveta (Culp), 44
Hodges, Laurent, 90, 91
Hoeffler, Jack, 43
Hofheinz, Fred, 92
Hofheinz, Judge/Mayor Roy, 84, 92, 113
Hofheinz, Roy, Jr., 85, 113
Hogan, Lee, 118
Hogg, Ima, 44
Hogue, Jane, 52
Holcombe, Mayor Oscar, 15
Hollie, Justin, 178
Hollingsworth, Marcile, 70, 74, 88, 107, 116, 117
Hollis, John, 76
Holmes, Carol, 35
Holmes, District Attorney John B., 92, 160
Holmes, Lois, 55
Holmes, Ned S., 115, 119, 120, 191
Holmes, Zach, 187
Hooten, Claude, Jr., 131
Hoover, Mrs. Howard, 26
Hope, Bob, 105
Houghton, Dorothy (Knox), 149
House, Randy, 121, 122
Houston, Sam, 25, 60
Howell, Marilyn, 52
Hudson, Harry, 35
Hudson, Rock, 97
Hughes, Jack, 43
Hughes, Judge Lynn, 93
Hull, Maxine (McDermott), 70
Hull, Ralph, 70
Hungerford, Orison Whipple, 61
Hurley, Gary, 112
Hurley, Marvin, 71, 111
Hyder, Braylon, 178

**I**
Ideson, Julia, 44
Ilfrey, Jack M., 29
Ingebritson, Paige, 168
Irvin, Wade Hampton, 18
Isensee, Bradley, 178
Ittner, Linda, 190

**J**
Jackson, Reverend Jesse, 172
Jenkins, Coach John, 167
Jenkins, Dan, 80
Jenkins, Jeff, 186
Jennings, Gray, 116, 118
Jeppesen, Holger, 34
Johnson, Larry, 134
Johnson, Mahlon, 35
Johnson, Phillip, 53
Johnson, Regan, 178
Johnson, Vice President/President Lyndon, 104, 112, 132
Johnston, Jim, 78
Jones, Aaron, 178
Jones, Ashley, 174
Jones, Frank, 121
Jones, Jesse H., 10, 16
Jordan, Senator Barbara, 144
Journeay, Jan, 134
Journeay, Mike, 129
Junger, Mary, 124

**K**
Kamrath, Karl, 107
Kamrath, Karl, Jr., 80
Kamrath Mygdal, Eugenia "GeeGee", 107, 109
Kane, Larry, 135
Kaye, Danny, 96
Keding, Lee S., 52, 53, 66, 67, 70, 84, 104, 105, 107, 127, 189
Keeland, Burdette, 53, 54
Keeler, R. Norris, 62
Kennedy, President John F., 111, 131, 132, 189
Kennedy, Senator Edward, 131
Kernahan, Avis, 138
Kerr, Caldwell, 171
Kestenberg, Louis, 45
Kidd, Phillip, 78
King, Larry, 157
King, Martin Luther, Jr., 111
King, Robert, 62
King Herring Davis, Joanne (Johnson), 62
Kingston Trio, 125
Kivell, Coach Bert, 78
Klevenhagen, Sheriff Johnny, 172
Knapp, Betty, 39
Knauth, Betty, 97
Knauth, Paul, 126
Kohlhausen, Bill, 80
Kollenberg, Charles, 134
Koomey, Paul, 43
Kostial, Ben, 24

**L**
Ladwig, Laurel, 159
LaFell, Brandon, 184, 185
Laguarta, Julio, 76
Lamar, Justice Lucius Q. C., 27
Lamar, Mirabeau B., 14, 24, 25, 27
Lancaster, Cedric, 178
Lane, Coach Duke, 134
Lanier, Sidney, 57
Lantz, Mr., 133
Lawry, Marjorie, 55
Leavell, Ruth, 70
Leavell, Selden, 44
Lehtinen, Samsa, 169
Lemmon, Jack, 96
Lenarduzzi, Dr. Roland, 6, 15
Lenarduzzi, Eraclito G., 12, 15, 16
Lenarduzzi, Nino, 16
Lenarduzzi, Roland, 6
Levy, Melanie, 46
Lewis, Allen, 192
Lewis, Brittany, 176
Lewis, General Carroll, 45
Lewis, Ira, 178
Lewis, Kathy, 104, 106
Lewis, Samuel Winfield, 62
Leyendecker, Charlie, 77
Lindsey, John, 35
Locher, Preston, 43
Loe, Shari, 143
Loep, Iris, 134, 145
Loescher, George A., 32
Long, Martha (Butler), 164, 165
Longcope, Donald, 32, 64, 78, 79, 121
Longoria, Brigadier General Michael, 149, 150
Longoria, Julianna, 182

Lowder, Norma, 128, 133, 147, 148
Lozano, Maynumbi, 182
Lutey, Lemoine, 139

**M**
MacEntyre, Maureen, 115
Mahan, Ann, 173
Mahlstedt, Allison, 175
Mahlstedt, Michael, 175
Mallette, Weldon, 32
Malowitz, Lee, 178, 185
Marr, Dave, 63
Marschner, Robert, 86
Martel, Joe H., 166
Martin, Dean, 95, 96, 128
Martinez, Brandon, 178
Martinez, Jerry, 178, 185, 186
Martyr, Suzanne, 116
Mashburn, Joe, 53
Masterson, Carlin (Glynn), 99
Masterson, Mary (Stuart), 99
Masterson, Peter, 128
McBride, Jimmy, 77
McCall, Mrs. Sterling, 26
McCarthy, Glen, 24
McCarthy, Glenna, 24
McCarty, Hazelle, 70, 107
McCleary, Dale, 121
McCord, Dr. James, 124
McCoy, Tyneisha, 187
McGhee, Jerry, 121
McGregory, Haley, 187
McIngvale, Jim "Mattress Mac", 194
McKelvy, Sheryl, 81
McMahon, Kimball, 100
McMurtry, Burton, 93
McMurtry, DeeDee (Meck), 93
McMurtry, Larry, 59
McSwain, Dr. James, 94, 179, 180, 181, 183, 184, 190, 191, 194
Meeker, Robert, 178
Meglasson, Trula, 145, 146, 156
Melgar, Alan, 178
Melton, Willas, 129
Mendell, Wendell, 89
Mendenhall, Francie, 128, 147
Meredith, Paula, 40
Mickelson, Hal, 64
Mickelson, Harold E., 32
Milburn, Andrew, 155
Miller, Debbi, 160
Miller, Hubbard, 100
Miller, Mike, 134
Miller, Samuel, 149
Miller, Vassar, 57, 58
Millet, Richard, 159
Mills, Ernest, 92
Mills, H. L., 17, 20
Miner, Edna Ruth, 74, 88
Minor, Zelt, 178
Mitchell, Cory, 178
Mitchell, Kyran, 178
Mize, Billy, 192
Mize, Katherine (Taylor), 108
Moers, Sara, 81
Moir, Megan, 174
Montgomery, William, 74, 75

Moore, Julie, 168
Moore, Mrs. Harvin, 26
Morales, Jesse, 178
Morris, Nell, 130
Morris, Wilbur, 71
Morrison, Al, 134
Morrow, Leslie, 182
Moss, Joe, 55
Moss, Nat, 163
Moss, Sam, 35
Moyes, William J., 23, 25, 26, 31, 32, 35, 45, 46, 51, 57, 63, 69, 84, 85, 88, 131, 194
Muench, Jennifer, 193
Muller, Chad, 185
Munoz, David, 186, 188

**N**
Nash, Alan, 137
Nelson, Doug, 52
Nesmith, Frances, 90
Neuhaus, Max, 101
Newnam, Elizabeth, 127
Niemann, Jeff, 188
Nipper, Jean, 138
Noble, Nancy, 81
Noel, Carol, 139, 144
Nolen, John, 186
Nolen, Tom, 183, 184, 186
Norris, Bobby, 43
Norris, Chuck, 173
Norton, Mickey (Lusk), 191

**O**
Oberholtzer, Dr. Edison E., 20, 44
O'Leary, Ralph, 85
Onyekwelu, Charles, 178
Orakpo, Brian, 174, 184
Overstreet, Tommy, 97, 103

**P**
Paige, Dr. Rod, 180
Parker, Mayor Annise, 188, 189
Parks, Bobby, 78
Parsons, Jim, 12, 13
Pass, Laverne, 37
Patterson, Gary, 134, 193
Patton, General George S., Jr., 27
Paul, Kenneth, 76
Payne, Harry, 11
Pecina, Frank, 178
Peebles, Rob, 73
Peel, Earle, 13
Pennington, Betty, 40
Pepper, Coach Fred, 107
Pepper, Harry, 84
Perez, Noel, 178
Perot, H. Ross, 156
Perry, Governor Rick, 119
Perry, Trebie, 55
Petersen, Mary, 73
Petrucciani, Anthony, 189
Petruzielo, Superintendent Frank, 172
Phillips, Dennis C., 144, 145, 150, 153, 162, 188
Phillips, Kate, 189
Picton, Grace, 37
Pike, Alan, 135

Pitcock, James Doug, Jr., 56, 122
Pitner, Abbey, 168
Poland, Bill, 121, 122, 123
Polk, Torrin, 167
Polydoros, Dorothy, 183
Potter, Cynthia, 122, 151
Potter, Hugh, 20, 39, 44
Powell, Tom, 35
Powers, Stephanie, 97
Prentiss, Paula, 96, 97, 147
Prescott, Charles, 90
Pressley, Jenna, 193
Price, Frank, 78
Prince, Alvis, 151
Pundt, John, 107
Puntch, Donald, 31, 32
Purdie, David, 111
Pushard, Gladys, 129
Putney, Jane, 59

**Q**
Quin, Bishop Clinton S., 15, 44

**R**
Ragusa, Paula, 96
Ramsey, Johnny, 134
Ransom, Nell Joan, 34
Ray, Bobby Jean, 73
Ray, Edgar, 112, 113
Rayburn, Eddie, 76
Reagan, Billy, 143, 158
Reagan, President Ronald, 93, 121, 155
Red, H. Lel, 69, 70
Reed, Zenobia, 187
Reeves, Mike, 100
Reiff, Kim, 182
Reiner, Ray, 158, 159, 160, 184, 192
Rembert, Andy, 115, 134
Rendon, Anthony, 188, 189
Rhodes, Jamie, 148
Rice, Jerilyn, 81
Richards, Governor Ann, 119, 157
Richardson, Nicholas, 178
Ricks, Bobby, 43
Ritchey, Laura, 167, 168
Riviere, Bernard J., 63
Robbins, Matt, 179
Roberts, Barry, 100
Roberts, Julia, 63
Roberts, Madge (Thornall), 60
Robertson, Corbin, Jr., 123, 124
Rockwell, Elizabeth (Dennis), 28
Roemer, Lamar, 121
Rogers, Cravon, 178
Rojas, Jorge, 178
Roosevelt, President Franklin D., 10
Rosborough, Elsa (Roberts), 56, 124, 147
Ross, Gloria, 40
Rosson, Todd, 170
Rostrom, Mary, 81
Roussel, Herbert, 121
Roussel, Peter, 121, 192
Royal, Darrell, 80
Rugel, John, 35
Ruiz, Kathy, 150, 151
Russell, Bertrand, 44

Ryba, Jane, 95
Ryba, Joan, 95
Ryba, Ruth Ann, 40

**S**
Saccomano, Debbie, 138
Saldivar, Ernie, 178, 185
Sandel, Bebe, 131
Sands, Tommy, 96, 97, 147
Sanger, Margaret, 44
Santangelo, Susan, 141
Sappington, Margo, 127
Sauer, Betsy, 120
Savery, Joe, 188
Savinoha, Bill, 163
Sawyer, Dr. W. W., 124
Scarborough, John, 100
School, Jane, 97
Schroeder, Darryl, 134
Schulze, Coach Bob, 79, 80
Scott, Mabel, 107, 129, 136
Sears, Betty, 81
Senofsky, Gregory Michael, 150
Settegast, Warren, 43
Settlemyre, Stoop, 33
Sharp, Frank W., 84
Shaw, E. T., 84, 123
Sheldon, Sydney, 172
Shelton, Gilbert, 109
Shepherd, Bob, 37
Shepherd, Keith, 116
Shriner, Herb, 95
Shubert, Fritz, 186
Simmons, C. S., 26
Simmons, Frank, 26
Simpson, Camille (Dockery), 8
Sinatra, Frank, 54, 113
Skelton, Red, 95, 125
Sklar, Suzanne, 168
Smith, Blake, 178
Smith, Brandon, 133, 147
Smith, Darielle, 178
Smith, Dr. June, 157
Smith, Ellen "Jaclyn", 114, 115
Smith, Governor Preston, 45
Smith, Ivy, 178
Smith, Mickey, 79
Smyth, Beverly, 40
Solomon, Jerome, 185, 195
Southwell, Ann, 190
Speier, Tyler, 178
Spitzenberger, Rudy, 77, 78
Staggs, Drew (Black), 44, 69, 70
Stallings, Carmen, 85
Stansell, Abbot, 186
Stanton, Lee, 178
Staub, John, 11, 12
Stedman, Sally, 73
Steffens, Lincoln, 44
Stephenson, C. B., 78
Sterling, Frank, 19
Stevenson, Ben, 165, 166
Stewart, Donald, 73
Stewart, Hester, 33, 37
Stewart, Joshua, 178
Strake, George, 146

Stripling, Dr. Kay, 117
Strong, Dr. Louise (Connally), 51, 118
Strong, Ted, 74
Stubblefield, Charlie, 158
Stubbs, Richard, 55
Stude, Emilie, 137
Stultz, Petrina, 169
Sullivan, Ed, 104
Sullivan, Maurice J., 12, 13, 14, 17
Sumner, Eric, 174
Susman, Harry, 157, 159
Swanwick, Michael, 60
Swartz, Mary Nell, 40
Sween, Gretchen, 164
Sweet, Joanne, 96
Swenson, Stephen, 118
Symonds, H. Gardiner, 71

**T**
Taylor, George, 121
Tellepsen, Howard, Jr., 121
Tellepsen, Howard, Sr., 84
Tellepsen, Mrs. Howard, 26
Teshner, Jennie, 107, 129
Thomas, Congressman Albert, 112
Thomas, Danny, 105
Thompson, Billy, 31
Thompson, E. Brad, 91
Thompson, Maurice, 37
Thompson, Roy, 78
Thurmond, Senator Strom, 125
Tillman, Vance, 182
Tinsley, Richard, 79
Tomfohrde, Betty Jo, 33, 37
Tomfohrde, Betty Ruth (Robbins), 29
Torres, Norma, 193
Trongone, Edward, 100, 101, 102, 129, 133
Truman, President Harry S., 66
Tudor, Bobby, 192
Tudor, Phoebe, 192
Tune, Tommy, 97, 101, 102, 103, 104, 115, 116, 120, 128
Tuttle, Lisa, 147

**U**
Umbach, Clay, 52
Umlauf, Charles, 107

**V**
Vance, Carol S., 92
Vaughan, Gordon, 156
Vaughn, J. D., 64
Vera, Sandy, 189
Veselka, Ronnie, 159
Vinson, David, 116

**W**
Walker, Clint, 61
Walker, Curtis H., 43
Walker, Shelby, 178
Walling, Candy, 81
Walters, Dick, 128
Warnecke, John Carl, 94
Watts, Dr. Woodrow, 129
Wayne, John, 105, 125
Weinberg, Helen, 130
Wells, Beau, 178
Wells, Craig, 139
Wells, H. G., 88
Wells, Rick, 134
Werlein, Kit, 134
Werlin, Ewing, 18
Werner, Val, 52
West, Charlie, 65
Weston, Tevin, 178, 182
Wheeler, Lon, 130
Whilden, Bobby, 78
Whipple, Wayland, 78
White, David Fenwick, 28, 39
White, Governor Mark, 5, 92, 151, 156, 158, 160, 192
White, Hattie Mae, 142
White, John, 52
Whitehead, Tom, 192
Whitehurst, Carol, 81
Whitehurst, James, 33
Whiteing, Levy, 178
Whitfield, Stephen, 178
Whitley, PeeWee, 79
Whitmire, Kathy, 155
Whitworth, Pat, 24
Wilhelm, Don, 43
Williams, Carol (Kinney), 104
Williams, Claude, 71
Williams, Edward Carson, 127
Williams, George, 100
Williams, James, 178
Williams, Jordon, 178
Williams, Sherry (Woodard), 150, 151
Willis, Michael T., 191
Wilson, Alan, 152, 162, 163
Wilson, Chris, 147
Wilson, Clifton, 32, 35
Wilson, Marc, 178
Wilson, Robert "Bob" Woodrow, 87
Wilson, Sandra (Nobles), 70
Wilson, Vivian, 129
Wisdom, Margaret, 136
Wise, Jennifer, 168
Wodehouse, P. G., 91
Wolbrett, Carlita, 64
Wolf, Emil, Jr., 89
Wolf, Lee, 134
Wolfe, Gene, 60
Wolfe, Mike, 166
Wolfe, Mrs., 139
Wolfeld, Nathan, 13
Wood, General Robert E., 71
Wooden, Derrick, 163
Woods, U.S. Attorney Ron, 172
Worsham, Annie Lee (Mills), 17
Wray, Dick, 61, 106
Wright, Bob, 100
Wright, Dudley, 32
Wright, Edith H., 44
Wright, J. H., 85
Wychoff, Jimmy, 85

**Y**
Young, Betty Sue, 40
Young, Mayorca, 187
Young, Pam, 145, 146
Yu, Thomas, 173

**Z**
Zarr, Lynn, 79
Zartman, Wendell, 173
Zipps, David L., 166

LAMAR HIGH SCH
STAT

Bottom row: Trainer Gene Antill, Ripley Ezra "Rippy" Woodard, Walter Bloxsom, Bobby Powell, Jimmy Sm
Middle row: Mike Schuhmacher, Walter Fondren, Mickey Smith, Don Wilson, David Coulter, Clarence McI
Top row: Coach Bob Schulze, Coach Harold Tate, Jim Johnston, Bill Norman, Hart Peebles, Dick Goff, Davi
Duncan Simmons, Bud Wall, Eddie Shipe, Wilbur Morris, Terry McKee, Coach Fred Pepper, Bobby Stillwell,
Back row: Managers Tex Morgan, Herry Passmore, and David Lee.